Praise for *News Quality in the Digital Age*

The book offers a wide range of methodological approaches to the study of news quality being delivered through various communication channels. With chapters ranging from computation science to a more political theory-oriented perspective, this project offers a lot of ways to introduce students to the vital issue of assessing the quality of news that is being produced these days for public consumption.

Steven Farnsworth, *University of Mary Washington*

NEWS QUALITY IN THE DIGITAL AGE

This book brings together a diverse, international array of contributors to explore the topics of news "quality" in the online age and the relationships between news organizations and enormously influential digital platforms such as Facebook, Google, and Twitter. Covering topics ranging from internet incivility, crowdsourcing, and YouTube politics to regulations, algorithms, and AI, this book draws the key distinction between the news that facilitates democracy and news that undermines it. For students and scholars as well as journalists, policymakers, and media commentators, this important work engages a wide range of methodological and theoretical perspectives to define the key concept of "quality" in the news media.

Regina G. Lawrence is Research Director of the Agora Journalism Center at the University of Oregon, and editor of the journal *Political Communication*. Dr. Lawrence's books include *When the Press Fails: Political Power and the News Media from Iraq to Katrina* (University of Chicago Press, 2007, with W. Lance Bennett and Steven Livingston), *Hillary Clinton's Race for the White House: Gender Politics and the Media on the Campaign Trail* (Lynne Rienner Publishers, 2009, with Melody Rose); and *The Politics of Force: Media and the Construction of Police Brutality* (University of California Press, 2000).

Philip M. Napoli is the James R. Shepley Professor of Public Policy in the Sanford School of Public Policy at Duke University, where he is also the Senior Associate Dean for Faculty and Research and the Director of the DeWitt Wallace Center for Media & Democracy. He is the author/editor of seven books, including, most recently, *Social Media and the Public Interest: Media Regulation in the Disinformation Age* (Columbia University Press, 2019).

MEDIA_{and}POWER

David L. Paletz, Series Editor
www.routledge.com/Media-and-Power/book-series/MP

Media and Power is a series that publishes work uniting media studies with studies of power. This innovative and original series features books that challenge, even transcend, conventional disciplinary boundaries, construing both media and power in the broadest possible terms. At the same time, books in the series are designed to fit into several different types of college courses in political science, public policy, communication, journalism, media, history, film, sociology, anthropology, and cultural studies. Intended for the scholarly, text, and trade markets, the series should attract authors and inspire and provoke readers.

Published Books

The Political Voices of Generation Z
Laurie L. Rice and Kenneth W. Moffett

Fixing American Politics
Solutions for the Media Age
Edited by Roderick P. Hart

Spectacle and Diversity
Transnational Media and Global Culture
Lee Artz

News Quality in the Digital Age
Edited by Regina G. Lawrence and Philip M. Napoli

NEWS QUALITY IN THE DIGITAL AGE

*Edited by Regina G. Lawrence and
Philip M. Napoli*

NEW YORK AND LONDON

Designed cover image: © Shutterstock/metamorworks

First published 2023
by Routledge
605 Third Avenue, New York, NY 10158

and by Routledge
4 Park Square, Milton Park, Abingdon, Oxon, OX14 4RN

Routledge is an imprint of the Taylor & Francis Group, an informa business

© 2023 selection and editorial matter, Regina G. Lawrence and Philip M. Napoli
individual chapters, the contributors

The right of Regina G. Lawrence and Philip M. Napoli to be identified as the authors
of the editorial material, and of the authors for their individual chapters, has been asserted
in accordance with sections 77 and 78 of the Copyright, Designs and Patents Act 1988.

All rights reserved. No part of this book may be reprinted or reproduced or utilised
in any form or by any electronic, mechanical, or other means, now known or
hereafter invented, including photocopying and recording, or in any information
storage or retrieval system, without permission in writing from the publishers.

Trademark notice: Product or corporate names may be trademarks or registered trademarks,
and are used only for identification and explanation without intent to infringe.

Library of Congress Cataloging-in-Publication Data
Names: Lawrence, Regina G., 1961– editor. | Napoli, Philip M., editor.
Title: News quality in the digital age / edited by Regina G. Lawrence and Philip M. Napoli.
Description: New York : Routledge, 2023. |
Series: Media and power | Includes bibliographical references and index. |
Identifiers: LCCN 2022038545 (print) | LCCN 2022038546 (ebook) |
ISBN 9781032191782 (hardback) | ISBN 9781032191775 (paperback) |
ISBN 9781003257998 (ebook)
Subjects: LCSH: Online journalism–Objectivity. |
Online journalism–Political aspects. | Social media and journalism.
Classification: LCC PN4784.O62 N495 2023 (print) |
LCC PN4784.O62 (ebook) | DDC 070.4–dcundefined
LC record available at https://lccn.loc.gov/2022038545
LC ebook record available at https://lccn.loc.gov/2022038546

ISBN: 978-1-032-19178-2 (hbk)
ISBN: 978-1-032-19177-5 (pbk)
ISBN: 978-1-003-25799-8 (ebk)

DOI: 10.4324/9781003257998

Typeset in Bembo
by Newgen Publishing UK

To my kids, who are the future.
—*RGL*

To Anne and Donovan, who are all I need in this world.
—*PMN*

CONTENTS

List of Figures	*xi*
List of Tables	*xii*
List of Contributors	*xiii*
Acknowledgments	*xviii*

PART I
Foundations   **1**

1   Introduction   3
Regina G. Lawrence and Philip M. Napoli

2   Communication technology and threats to democracy:
We the people are (also) the problem   13
Johanna Dunaway and Nicholas Ray

PART II
Measurement Approaches to News Quality   **31**

3   Social media metrics and news quality   33
Jieun Shin

4   Is that news for me? Defining news-ness by platform
and topic   49
Emily K. Vraga and Stephanie Edgerly

x Contents

5 User comments as news quality: Examining incivility in comments on perceptions of news quality — 67
Shuning Lu, Hai Liang and Gina M. Masullo

6 Beyond the "trust" survey: Measuring media attitudes through observation — 84
Zacc Ritter and Jesse Holcomb

PART III
Algorithmic Systems and News Quality — 95

7 All the news that's fit to tweet: Sociotechnical local news distribution from the *New York Times* to Twitter — 97
Jack Bandy and Nicholas Diakopoulos

8 Out of control? Using interactive testing to understand user agency in news recommendation systems — 117
Judith Moeller, Felicia Loecherbach, Johanna Möller and Natali Helberger

9 Gaming AI: Algorithmic journalism in Nigeria — 134
Emeka Umejei

10 Editorial values for news recommenders: Translating principles to engineering — 151
Jonathan Stray

PART IV
News Quality, Government, and Media Policy — 167

11 How Australia's competition regulator is supporting news, but not quality — 169
Chrisanthi Giotis, Sacha Molitorisz and Derek Wilding

12 Government interventions into news quality — 187
Philip M. Napoli and Asa Royal

13 Conclusion — 202
Regina G. Lawrence and Philip M. Napoli

Index — *208*

FIGURES

4.1	News cues on AP website (left) and Twitter (right).	55
4.2	Main effects of platform and issue on ratings of news-ness.	56
4.3	Elements important to news-ness on the website (left) and Twitter feed (right).	57
4.4	The elements important to news-ness across issues.	61
5.1	Comment thread following "site announcement for vice presidential debate" (proportion: 20 percent, position: primacy).	74
5.2	Predicting news quality perceptions (post-test only).	78
5.3	Predicting news quality perceptions (change-score approach).	79
7.1	Diagram of curated flows studied in this work.	102
7.2	Monthly production of local, U.S., and world news at the *New York Times*.	105
7.3	Proportional monthly production of local, U.S., and world news at the *New York Times*.	107
7.4	Editorial curation of local, U.S., and world news on the *New York Times* main Twitter account (@nytimes).	108
7.5	Raw engagement with local, U.S., and world news from the @nytimes Twitter account.	109
7.6	Proportional engagement with local, U.S., and world news from the @nytimes Twitter account.	111
8.1	Perceived control (7-point-scale) in the different experimental groups.	126
8.2	Interaction of measurement, control, and satisfaction.	129

TABLES

5.1	Predicting news quality perceptions using multilevel modeling	76
6.1	Structure of literature review	85
6.2	Results of experiment	90
7.1	Events potentially influencing local news production/curation at the *New York Times*	104
11.1	Quality indicators – content attributes table	180

CONTRIBUTORS

Jack Bandy is a Ph.D. candidate in the Computational Journalism Lab, in Northwestern's Technology and Social Behavior program. His research explores algorithmic platforms like Twitter, Apple News, and TikTok, and how the algorithms behind these platforms impact the stories and information we encounter every day.

Nicholas Diakopoulos is an Associate Professor in Communication Studies and Computer Science (by courtesy) at Northwestern University where he is Director of the Computational Journalism Lab (CJL) and Director of Graduate Studies for the Technology and Social Behavior (TSB) Ph.D. program. He is the author of the award-winning book *Automating the News: How Algorithms are Rewriting the Media* from Harvard University Press.

Johanna Dunaway is an Associate Professor of Communication at Texas A&M University. Her work appears in journals such as the *Journal of Politics*, *Public Opinion Quarterly*, *Journal of Communication*, *Political Communication*, *Political Research Quarterly*, *Political Behavior*, *Journalism Studies*, and *Social Science Quarterly*. She is also co-author on the ninth edition of *Mass Media and American Politics*.

Stephanie Edgerly is an Associate Professor and Director of Research at the Medill School at Northwestern University. Edgerly is currently working on a series of research projects identifying the factors that shape judgments about "fake news" and the various strategies people employ for verifying news claims. She is also involved in a multi-year study examining the political and news socialization of adolescents and young adults.

xiv Contributors

Chrisanthi Giotis is a postdoctoral Research Fellow in the School of Communication at the University of Technology, Sydney (UTS). She is examining what constitutes best practice journalism at the local-global interface, with a particular focus on reporting on refugee issues. She teaches in both the journalism and social and political sciences programs at the Faculty of Arts and Social Sciences, UTS.

Natali Helberger is Distinguished University Professor of Law and Digital Technology with a special focus on AI at the University of Amsterdam, an elected member of the Royal Netherlands Academy of Arts and Sciences (KNAW), and the KNAW Social Science Council. Together with Claes de Vreese, Helberger founded the AI, Media & Democracy Lab and the Research Priority Area on Information, Communication, and the Data Society at the University of Amsterdam.

Jesse Holcomb is an Assistant Professor of Journalism and Communication at Calvin University in Grand Rapids, Michigan. Since 2018, Holcomb has served as lead data analyst for the INN Index survey of nonprofit newsrooms, as well as principal advisor to the Knight-Gallup Trust, Media and Democracy research program.

Regina G. Lawrence is Research Director of the Agora Journalism Center at the University of Oregon, and editor of the journal *Political Communication.* Dr. Lawrence's books include *When the Press Fails: Political Power and the News Media from Iraq to Katrina* (University of Chicago Press, 2007, with W. Lance Bennett and Steven Livingston), *Hillary Clinton's Race for the White House: Gender Politics and the Media on the Campaign Trail* (Lynne Rienner Publishers, 2009, with Melody Rose), and *The Politics of Force: Media and the Construction of Police Brutality* (University of California Press, 2000).

Hai Liang is an Associate Professor in the School of Journalism and Communication, the Chinese University of Hong Kong (CUHK). He has published numerous articles in top journals such as *Journal of Communication, Communication Research, Human Communication Research, Journal of Computer-Mediated Communication, New Media & Society,* among others. He is the recipient of CUHK's Young Researcher Award 2018.

Felicia Loecherbach is a Ph.D. Candidate in the Department of Communication Science at the University of Amsterdam. She is studying the diversity of issues and perspectives in (online) news and how it is affected by recommender algorithms and selective exposure. Her research is part of the project "Inside the filter bubble: A framework for deep semantic analysis of mobile news consumption traces" funded by a JEDS grant from NWO.

Contributors **xv**

Shuning Lu is an Assistant Professor at North Dakota State University. Currently, she is pursuing three lines of research. The first line of her work aims to understand the social and psychological mechanisms of news engagement behavior, such as sharing and commenting. The second seeks to unpack the role of online incivility, particularly uncivil news comments, in engendering political outcomes. The third looks at how digital media technologies reshape the civic landscape in China.

Gina M. Masullo is an Associate Professor in the School of Journalism and Associate Director of the Center for Media Engagement in the Moody College of Communication at University of Texas Austin. She is the author of *Online Incivility and Public Debate: Nasty Talk* and *The New Town Hall: Why We Engage Personally with Politicians*. Currently, she is working on a connective democracy initiative, funded by the John S. and James L. Knight Foundation.

Johanna E. Möller is a Postdoctoral Research Fellow at the Technical University of Dresden and interested in socio-technical advances in communication and media studies as well as questions related to privacy as media practices and privacy agency. She is principal investigator of the interdisciplinary research project, Networked Privacy Disruptions, uniting scholars from communication and media studies, IT, and sociology.

Judith Moeller is an Associate Professor of Political Communication at the Department of Communication Science at the University of Amsterdam and an Adjunct Associate Professor at the Department of Sociology and Political Science at the University of Trondheim. She is affiliated with the Amsterdam School of Communication Research (ASCoR), the Center for Politics and Communication (CPC), and the Information, Communication, & the Data Society Initiative (ICDS).

Sacha Molitorisz is a Lecturer at the Centre for Media Transition at the University of Technology, Sydney. Since joining the CMT in January 2018 as a Postdoctoral Research Fellow, his research and teaching areas include media ethics, digital privacy, and public interest journalism. His 2020 book *Net Privacy: How we can be Free in an Age of Surveillance* was published in Australia by New South Books and in Canada by McGill-Queen's University Publishing.

Philip M. Napoli is the James R. Shepley Professor of Public Policy in the Sanford School of Public Policy at Duke University, where he is also the Senior Associate Dean for Faculty and Research and the Director of the DeWitt Wallace Center for Media & Democracy. He is the author/editor of seven books, including, most recently, *Social Media and the Public Interest: Media Regulation in the Disinformation Age* (Columbia University Press, 2019).

xvi Contributors

Nicholas Ray is a second-year Ph.D. student in the Department of Political Science at Texas A&M University. He received his B.A. from the University of South Carolina in 2020. His research interests include understanding the political consequences of the internet and artificial intelligence, both in comparative and American politics.

Zacc Ritter is a Senior Researcher at Gallup. His work employs qualitative, quantitative, and experimental methodologies to examine news consumption habits, attitudes toward the media, misinformation, and the dynamics of unarmed insurrectionary movements. He is also the project director of the Global Flourishing Study, a five-year longitudinal study measuring human flourishing of over 200,000 individuals across 22 countries.

Asa Royal is a Research Associate in the DeWitt Wallace Center for Media & Democracy at Duke University. His research focuses on media institutions, digital platform policy, and misinformation. Recent work has focused on topics such as a cross-national analysis of policies mediating the relationship between digital platforms and news organizations; and an analysis of how well new hyperlocal news networks are meeting community information needs.

Jieun Shin is an Assistant Professor of Telecommunication at the University of Florida. She teaches and conducts research in digital media with a focus on social interaction, information flow, and networks, and is particularly interested in how people create, share, and process information at the individual level and the resulting outcomes at the collective level. Her research has appeared in journals such as the *Journal of Communication*, *New Media & Society*, and *Mass Communication & Society*.

Jonathan Stray is a Research Fellow at Partnership on AI, with a particular interest in recommender systems and how their operation affects human well-being. He also teaches the double masters in computer science and journalism at Columbia Journalism School. He led the development of Workbench, a visual programming system for data journalism, and built Overview, an open-source document set analysis system for investigative journalists. He has written for the *New York Times*, *Foreign Policy*, *ProPublica*, *MIT Tech Review*, and *Wired*.

Emeka Umejei is the author of *Chinese Media in Africa: Perception, Performance and Paradox*. He is one of the authors of the *Nigerian Media Landscape*, responsible for the segments on digital technology, innovation, traditional forms of communication, and the conclusion. He has published his academic research in international academic journals such as *Africa-East-Asian Affairs*, *Chinese Journal of Communication*, and *African Journalism Studies*.

Emily K. Vraga is an Associate Professor in the Hubbard School of Journalism and Mass Communication at the University of Minnesota, where she holds the Don and Carole Larson Professorship in Health Communication. Her research focuses on how individuals respond to news and information about contentious health, scientific, and political issues in digital environments. She prioritizes using diverse and novel methodologies to better match an evolving hybrid media environment.

Derek Wilding is Co-Director of the Centre for Media Transition at the University of Technology, Sydney. Derek came to UTS from an industry-based position as Executive Director of the Australian Press Council. He worked closely on the Council's responses to the Independent Media Inquiry and the Convergence Review and on the adaptation of the Council's structure and governance to embrace smaller, digital-only publishers.

ACKNOWLEDGMENTS

Edited collections are, by their very nature, team efforts, and so we begin by thanking all of the contributors to this volume, who have been on this long journey with us from workshop presentations to draft chapters to revisions and, ultimately, this volume.

But the genesis of this project rests with Michael Miller and his colleagues Penelope Weber and Jason Rhody at the Social Science Research Council. They deserve tremendous thanks for crafting the original idea for the SSRC workshop, News Quality in the Platform Era, that served as the springboard for this volume; for recruiting the two of us to be involved; and for handling all of the logistics around the workshop's call for proposals, submission reviews, and, ultimately the (thanks to covid) online workshop that brought all of the contributors together to share their work and receive in-depth feedback. At this point, we've all had more than our fill of online convenings, but this one stands out from the rest as having been particularly productive and engaging.

Special thanks also to Jennifer Knerr at Routledge, for her enthusiasm for this project, and especially for her patience, as we juggled this project along with far too many administrative responsibilities at our respective universities.

Thanks also to Michelle Nicolosi, newly-minted Ph.D. from the University of Oregon, and Kim Krzwy, of Duke's DeWitt Wallace Center for Media & Democracy, for their help formatting and copyediting the manuscript. Their help was vital in getting us to the finish line.

Regina Lawrence
Phil Napoli

PART I
Foundations

1

INTRODUCTION

Regina G. Lawrence and Philip M. Napoli

On January 6, 2021, supporters of outgoing president Donald Trump descended on the U.S. Capitol in an ill-fated effort to stop the certification of Trump's successor, Joe Biden, as president. The rioters who overwhelmed police, smashed windows, and swarmed into the Capitol Building, and the many thousands cheering them on from just outside the building, were echoing false information spread vociferously via Twitter, Facebook, and other social media (and also via conservative media outlets like FOX News) that the election had been "stolen." And the most prominent spreader of that disinformation was the outgoing president himself, who urged his many Twitter followers to "be there. Will be wild!" In a highly unusual move, Twitter and Facebook suspended Trump's accounts that evening; as of this writing he has only recently been reinstated by an increasingly erratic Elon Musk (Twitter's new owner). But the suspension seemed to many observers a case of too little, too late, since Trump had been stoking the fast-growing "stolen" election narrative for weeks (via accounts that at one point were gaining an average of 100 new followers every 10 seconds)—and Facebook in particular did little to stop it (Barry & Frankel, 2021).

The possibility that narratives spread on social media could lead to violence has played out in deadlier ways in recent years. In Myanmar, for example, where Facebook has become a main mode of news and information sharing, a United Nations report on the 2017 genocide against that country's Muslim Rohingya minority uncovered "a carefully crafted hate campaign" that "exacerbate[d] a climate in which hate speech thrives and in which individuals and groups may be more receptive to calls of incitement to violence" (United Nations Human Rights Council, 2018). Though the campaign played out over various kinds of media, Facebook was a key vector: the report found over 150 public social media accounts, pages and groups, all with between 10,000 and 1 million followers, "that have regularly spread messages amounting to hate speech against Muslims

DOI: 10.4324/9781003257998-2

in general or Rohingya in particular"—often posting daily, even hourly. Political elites, including the country's president, were prominent posters of these kinds of messages. Facebook executives later admitted that the company had failed to prevent its platform from being used to "foment division and incite offline violence" in the country (Stevenson, 2018).

Among other problems, these examples highlight the growing phenomenon of politicians and governments along with foreign agitators turning to social media to spread disinformation and vitriol. This problem of organized disruption that political scientists W. Lance Bennett and Steven Livingston describe as the "disinformation order" (Bennett & Livingston, 2018) also captured public attention in 2016, when Russian operatives aligned with Vladimir Putin posted millions of false, misleading, and divisive posts on Facebook, Twitter, Instagram, and YouTube leading up to the U.S. presidential election, aimed at undermining Democratic candidate Hillary Clinton and boosting Republican candidate Trump (Timberg & Romm, 2018). Two years later, the victory of Jair Bolsonaro in Brazil's presidential election "proved a watershed moment for digital election interference" in that country. According to one report, "Unidentified actors mounted cyberattacks against journalists, government entities, and politically engaged users…Supporters of Bolsonaro and his far-right 'Brazil over Everything, God above Everyone' coalition spread homophobic rumors, misleading news, and doctored images on YouTube and WhatsApp." These kinds of digital interference in elections were documented in 26 out of 30 countries that held elections or referenda that year (Freedom House, 2019, p. 7). In a chilling coda, Brazil's newly elected president then immediately hired the communications consultants who led the disinformation campaign that helped him gain office (Freedom House, 2019, p. 4).

But governments are of course not the only spreaders of disinformation online. The widespread and insidious effects of social media disinformation spread by a variety of actors have manifested globally surrounding the COVID-19 pandemic. This tide of disinformation has come to be known as an "infodemic" (Islam et al., 2020; Simon & Camargo, 2021). As with the 2016 and 2020 elections controversies, other types of media—notably some cable news programming (Bursztyn et al, 2020; Simonov et al., 2020)—are also implicated in the spread of COVID disinformation. But social media have played a special role, particularly since some social media personalities have much wider reach and influence than any public health authority. One report identified twelve individuals particularly responsible for widespread social media disinformation about COVID-19, along with 425 anti-vaccine accounts that were being followed by over 59 million others (Center for Countering Digital Hate, 2021). Perhaps not surprisingly, early research suggests that people who rely on social media were particularly likely to hold misperceptions about the disease and how to combat it (Bridgman et al., 2020; Jamieson & Albarracin, 2020), and to forgo vaccination (Allington et al., 2021). In July of 2021, the U.S. Surgeon General released an advisory "urging all Americans to help slow the spread of health misinformation during the COVID-19 pandemic and beyond" and labeling that misinformation "a serious threat to public health." Slowing the spread of health misinformation, the Surgeon General argued, "is a moral and civic imperative that will require a whole-of-society effort" (Murthy, 2021, p. 2). (In August of 2021, Facebook reported it had banned 3,000 accounts it deemed were spreading COVID-19 misinformation [Bell, 2021]).

A great deal of funding and research are now flowing toward the problem of how to stem the epidemic of online disinformation. Facebook, Google, the United Nations, and a number of other private and governmental organizations have invested millions of dollars to fund research to study the scope of mis- and disinformation and how their effects might be mitigated, and more than a few universities have established research centers devoted to the same questions. As of this writing, Congress is considering legislation to increase platforms' liability for allowing disinformation to spread and to find constitutionally acceptable ways to introduce more friction into social media content-sharing. Revelations by former Facebook employee Frances Haugen, who leaked damning documents and ultimately testified before the Senate Commerce Committee (Allyn, 2021), added urgency to those efforts.

But another critical question has received comparatively less attention: How can society increase the flow and the influence of disinformation's opposite: high-quality online news and information?

Of course, answering that question involves grappling with other questions, such as how "high-quality" news should be defined, how platforms might be designed to encourage it, and how platform users might be encouraged to pay attention to it and share it with their networks. As a practical matter, news consumers—along with platform designers, company executives, and government regulators—determine "quality" as they go about their daily work. But overall, while research is rapidly proliferating on the features of digital platforms that contribute to the spread of disinformation, less attention has been paid to how digital platforms shape flows of higher-quality information, along with citizens' perceptions of news quality. And, of course, the notion of "quality" is, by its very nature, quite subjective, and therefore quite challenging for platforms, policymakers, and news organizations to put into practice in ways that don't provoke scrutiny and resistance.

News and information are increasingly distributed via mobile devices featuring algorithmically driven news feeds created and managed by major digital platforms. In addition, information flows are increasingly influenced by individuals without professional training, from dedicated bloggers monetizing content for niche audiences, to impromptu citizen journalists livestreaming events, to social media feeds featuring all varieties of voices. Mixed within is an ever-expanding cohort of websites that present themselves as traditional news organizations, but which skirt journalistic norms, producing content ranging from opinion-posing-as-fact to outright disinformation like that described above. Today, the gatekeeping role formerly played by traditional news editors is increasingly appropriated by non-professionals and by technology: the search and recommendation algorithms that suggest content to ever greater proportions of news consumers. This diverse, fragmented, and sometimes chaotic media environment gives rise to questions not just about mis- and disinformation, but the broader question of how reliable and trustworthy online information in general is—something that seems to concern many citizens. In the U.S., for example, Consumer Reports published a survey that found that 58 percent of respondents were "not confident that they are getting objective and unbiased search results when using an online platform to shop or search for information" (Subcommittee, 2020, p. 12).

This book comes out of a workshop sponsored by the Social Science Research Council, which brought together a number of researchers from across disciplines including journalism, communication studies, political science, public opinion, data and computer sciences, media policy, media ethics, artificial intelligence, and other fields. The initial charge was for each contributor to bring their own expertise to the question, "How do we define and measure quality news in the platform era?" Contributors were asked to consider that question in the context of the explosive growth in a wide variety of technologies and changing practices by which news is now produced, transmitted, consumed, shared, and modified. The research collected in this volume is the outgrowth of work presented and discussed at a virtual workshop in the summer of 2020.

Each chapter in this book focuses on some aspect of the relationship between digital platforms and news quality. The chapters examine a variety of platforms, and though they draw from a number of literatures and employ many different methodologies, their connective thread is the question of how the rise of platforms shapes possibilities for citizens to become better informed. Covering topics from online incivility, crowdsourcing, and political content to regulations, algorithms, and the role of artificial intelligence in creating daily news, this book considers ways to define and measure news quality and how to distinguish the news that facilitates the democratic process from the news that undermines it. These questions are particularly important at this particular historic moment, when policymakers in many countries are rethinking the relationship between news organizations and digital platforms, and when concerns about "junk news" and disinformation on topics such as election security and global public health are so prominent on the public agenda.

Defining key terms: Platforms, quality, and news

Although the term "platform" is widely used these days, it is useful to pause to consider what that term means, and what it may obscure. "Platform" has been used in a variety of ways in the fields of economics, business and marketing, and information systems (Sun et al., 2015), but for our purposes, a digital platform can be thought of as "a programmable infrastructure upon which other software can be built and run" (Gillespie, 2017; see also Gillespie, 2010). In a more comprehensive and complex view, a digital platform can be thought of as "a sociotechnical assemblage encompassing the technical elements (of software and hardware) and associated organisational processes and standards" (de Reuver et al., 2018, p. 126). "Platforms," in other words, are not just technologies. They are also defined by the organizations that design and operate them. The digital platforms of particular interest in this book are those that have been widely put to use for news and information sharing.

But as media scholar Tarleton Gillespie argues, the term "platform" carries subtle connotations that can actually distort our understanding of how these technologies operate. The common connotation is that a "platform" is a digital service that provides "an opportunity from which to speak, socialize, and participate." But the "platform" metaphor obscures the fact that "these services are not flat," as the metaphor of a railway platform, for example, suggests. Instead,

> Their central service is to organize, structure, and channel information, according both to arrangements established by the platform (news feed algorithms, featured partner arrangements, front pages, categories) and arrangements built by the user, though structured or measured by the platform (friend or follower networks, trending lists). Platforms are not flat, open spaces where people speak or exchange, they are intricate and multi-layered landscapes, with complex features above and dense warrens below.
>
> (Gillespie, 2017)

Thus, digital platforms are power structures—structures that are largely owned and operated by a small handful of highly profitable technology companies who use proprietary algorithms for determining how people encounter information when they search for news-related topics (Moore & Tambini, 2018; Pasquale, 2015).[1] A growing body of research is exploring how the technological "affordances" of digital platforms—that is, what digital platforms enable us to do—may contribute not only to helping human beings connect, create, and become informed in new ways, but also may contribute to dysfunctional information flows. Referencing a widely cited MIT study that demonstrated how false rumors spread more readily online than factual stories (Vosoughi et al., 2018), one observer noted that, "platforms have a built-in commercial incentive to engage users with 'low-value' content that holds viewers' attention — and not the often-costly news reporting that bolsters civic participation and holds local officials to account" (Karr, 2022). Indeed, as media scholar José van Dyck and colleagues (2018) describe them, platforms are positioned as crucial informational intermediaries, but their ability to often evade the responsibilities we might expect such powerful entities to exercise exhibits an important tension between private power and public values, and between traditional distinctions between technology companies and media companies.

The other key terms contained in the title of this book are less easy to define. In fact, defining "quality" and defining "news" have become increasingly complicated with changes in the media environment.

Measuring the quality of news is challenging because of the unique relationship between journalism and democratic society: Presumably, good-quality journalism is that which helps the public play its role as an informed citizenry in representative democracy (Picard, 2000, pp. 97–99). But exactly what citizens need in order to play that role is not always clear. Moreover, news quality can be addressed from at least three perspectives: In terms of measurable elements of its content, rooted in notions of what constitutes a healthy information flow for individual citizens and for society (Lacy & Rosenstiel, 2015, pp. 11–14); in terms of an audience "demand" perspective on what news consumers want from news (Lacy & Rosenstiel, 2015, pp. 15–20), or in terms of information infrastructure constituted by an array of media outlets and other entities that collectively enable (or constrain) public knowledge and civic engagement (Napoli et al., 2017). The "quality" of news is therefore "a dynamic, contingent, and contested construct" (Bachmann et al., 2021, p. 1).

In terms of the first perspective, although many scholars and analysts agree on certain key indices of quality news content, including accuracy, factuality, relevance, and whether information is produced through original reporting and investigation, the chapters in this volume reveal that there is still work to be done in honing our conceptualization and measurement of news quality. And as various chapters in this volume will also suggest, determining news quality is not limited to its actual content. Public perception also matters. If news that researchers unanimously agreed was of high quality was seen as low quality by consumers, that would raise questions about who scholarly measures of quality are *for*. Put differently, abstract definitions are essential to empirically documenting what kinds of information are available to the public, but they are of little practical importance if the public uses entirely different criteria to decide what to pay attention to (see Meijer & Bijleveld, 2016). Crucially, we have not arrived at a practical understanding of how *perceptions* of news quality are shaped by and within contemporary digital information flows—a gap some of the chapters in this volume seek to close. Meanwhile, as various chapters explore, audience demand may powerfully shape what gets produced for digital media and shared via social media, and not necessarily in ways that align with democratic notions of high quality news.

Finally, several of the chapters in this book grapple with the question of which online content counts as "*news.*" In an increasingly complex media environment, "news" can no longer simply be defined as something that only certain kinds of traditional media outlets produce, since many digital native and non-journalistic organizations also contribute to public understanding of issues and events, and because news and news-like content now flows across so many channels and platforms. Our hope is that by the end of this volume, the reader will be able to think critically and perhaps raise new questions about which content found in

Introduction **9**

today's complex media mix should count as "news," and how its value to the individual citizen and to democratic society should be assessed.

Chapter overview

The second introductory chapter to this volume, by political scientists Johanna Dunaway and Nicholas Ray, reviews the growing literature on how digital platforms shape people's access and exposure to news and information. Ray and Dunaway invite us to broaden our scope beyond the structural features of today's digital media environment, such as the fragmentation and proliferation of media, make it easier for people to be exposed to problematic information. Cognitive dynamics also shape how receptive people will be to attending to and accepting information encountered online, while the technical features of digital information may further constrain attention. These features shape not only how likely we are to encounter low-quality news, but also how much time we are likely to spend with it and how likely we are to endorse it.

Part II of the book focuses on the challenging questions of how to define news and measure news quality. In Chapter 3, communication scholar Jieun Shin examines the potential mismatch between the social media metrics platform companies so highly value and the provision of high-quality news. Ultimately, she argues, today's dominant attention marketplace—social media—is not well-designed to preserve high-quality journalism because it is structured to reward content popularity over quality. In Chapter 4, communication scholars Emily Vraga and Stephanie Edgerly explore that question from a citizen/user perspective with an experiment measuring how people decide whether an online story is indeed "news"—what they call "perceptions of news-ness." In Chapter 5, communication scholars Shuning Lu, Hia Liang, and Gina Masullo experimentally explore how comments sections attached to online news stories can shape peoples' perceptions of the quality of that news—particularly when comments are uncivil. Chapter 6, by Zacc Ritter and Jesse Holcomb, also uses experimental methods to examine how people rate the quality of online news stories.

Part III turns to the relationship between news quality and algorithms—the mathematical formulas by which platforms like Facebook and Twitter decide what users will see. How are algorithms shaping peoples' exposure to quality news and information? Jack Bandy and Nicholas Diakopoulos show in Chapter 7 how the algorithmic systems employed by news organizations (in this case, the New York Times) and social media (in this case, Twitter) can undermine a key dimension of quality news—news that has a local orientation. In Chapter 8, Judith Moeller, Felicia Löecherbach, Johanna Möller, and Natali Helberger focus on users' ability to shape algorithms, examining whether the (limited) powers to control what platforms offer to users translate into an actual sense of citizen efficacy to control their personalized news environment. In Chapter 9, Emeka Umejei zooms in on the daily work of journalists—in this case, those working at the first AI-enhanced news outlet in Nigeria and sub-Saharan Africa—to understand how they "write for AI" and how the reality of AI-driven news is shaping their understanding of journalism. Finally, in Chapter 10, AI specialist Jonathan Stray argues for better collaboration between journalists and technologists to improve news recommendation systems. Perhaps by working together, he argues, journalists and technologists could develop metrics, data sets, feedback methods, and evaluative processes for building better functioning recommendation systems that would serve important journalistic and democratic values.

Part IV, the final section of the book, turns to the role of public policy. In Chapter 11, Australian scholars Chrisanthi Giotis, Sacha Molitorisz, and Derek Wilding detail that country's unprecedented efforts to establish a compulsory arbitration process to determine how much Google and Facebook must pay for the news content they distribute. The effects of this policy, which attempted to address the bargaining power imbalance between large digital platforms and the news organizations that are increasingly reliant on those platforms to reach audiences (Nielsen & Ganter, 2022), remain a point of contention and dispute. These dynamics in Australia are being closely watched, as they may hold either affirmative answers or a cautionary tale to the problem of how to sustain local journalism in a platform-dependent media environment. In 2022, a bill with similar aims called the Journalism Competition and Preservation Act was introduced in the U.S. Congress. Finally, in Chapter 12, Philip M. Napoli and Asa Royal explore the political dynamics surrounding policymaking and policy analysis related to the idea of news quality. As they illustrate through a comparative analysis of policy deliberations in the U.S., the U.K., and Australia, the contentious politics surrounding news quality tend to lead policymakers to shift away from the concept as a guiding principle, in favor of less politically charged terms such as public interest journalism.

Note

1 As of September 2020, the combined valuation of Amazon, Apple, Facebook, Google was over $5 trillion—more than a third of the value of the S&P 100: https://judiciary. house.gov/uploadedfiles/competition_in_digital_markets.pdf

References

Allington, D., McAndrew, S., Moxham-Hall, V.L., & Duffy, B. (2021). Media usage predicts intention to be vaccinated against SARS-CoV-2 in the US and the UK. *Vaccine* 39(18): 2595–2603.https://doi.org/10.1016/j.vaccine.2021.02.054

Allyn, B. (2021, October 25). Here are 4 key points from the Facebook whistleblower's testimony on Capitol Hill. *NPR*, www.npr.org/2021/10/05/1043377310/facebook-whistleblower-frances-haugen-congress

Bachmann, P., Eisenegger, M. & Ingenhoff, D. (2021). Defining and measuring news media quality: Comparing the content perspective and the audience perspective. *International Journal of Press/Politics* 27(1): 9–37 doi.org/10.1177/1940161221999666

Barry, D. & Frenkel, S. (2021, January 7). 'Be there. Will be wild!': Trump all but circled the date. *The New York Times*. www.nytimes.com/2021/01/06/us/politics/capitol-mob-trump-supporters.html

Bell, K. (2021, August 18). Facebook has banned 3,000 accounts for COVID-19 and vaccine misinformation. *Engadget*. www.engadget.com/facebook-removed-3000-accounts-covid-vaccine-misinformation-184254103.html

Bennett, W.L. & Livingston, S. (2018) The disinformation order: Disruptive communication and the decline of democratic institutions. *European Journal of Communication 33*(2): 122–139. https://doi.org/10.1177/0267323118760317

Bridgman, A., Merkley, E., Loewen, P.J., Owen, T., Ruths, D., Teichmann, L. & Zhilin, O. (2020) The causes and consequences of COVID-19 misperceptions: Understanding the role of news and social media. *Misinformation Review* 1(3) https://doi.org/10.37016/mr-2020-028

Bursztyn, L., Rao, A., Roth, C. P., & Yanagizawa-Drott, D. H. (2020). Misinformation during a pandemic (No. w27417). Becker Friedman Institute for Research in Economics, https://repec.bfi.uchicago.edu/RePEc/pdfs/BFI_WP_202044_revised.pdf Working paper

Center for Countering Digital Hate (2021). The disinformation dozen: Why platforms must act on twelve leading online anti-vaxxers. https://252f2edd-1c8b-49f5-9bb2-cb57bb47e4ba.filesusr.com/ugd/f4d9b9_b7cedc0553604720b7137f8663366ee5.pdf

de Reuver, M., Sorenson, C., & Basole, R.C. (2018). The digital platform: A research agenda. *Journal of Information Technology 33*(2):124–135. https://doi.org/10.1057/s41265-016-0033-3

Freedom House. (2019). Freedom on the Net 2019. https://freedomhouse.org/sites/default/files/2019-11/11042019_Report_FH_FOTN_2019_final_Public_Download.pdf

Gillespie, T. (2010). The politics of "platforms." *New Media & Society* 12(3): 347–364. https://doi.org/10.1177/1461444809342738

Gillespie, T. (2017, August 24). The platform metaphor, revisited. *Culture Digitally*. https://culturedigitally.org/2017/08/platform-metaphor/

Graves, L. (2021). Lessons from an extraordinary year: Four heuristics for studying mediated misinformation in 2020 and beyond. In H. Tumber & S. Waisbord, (Eds.), *The Routledge companion to media disinformation and populism* (pp. 188–197). Routledge.

Islam, M. S., Sarkar, T., Khan, S. H., Kamal, A. H. M., Hasan, S. M., Kabir, A., Yeasmin, D., Islam, M. A., Chowdhury, K. I. A., Anwar, K. S., Chughtai, A. A., & Seale, H. (2020). COVID-19-related infodemic and its impact on public health: A global social media analysis. *The American Journal of Tropical Medicine and Hygiene 103*(4): 1621–1629. https://doi.org/10.4269/ajtmh.20-0812

Jamieson, K. H., & Albarracin, D. (2020). The relation between media consumption and misinformation at the outset of the SARS-CoV-2 pandemic in the US. *The Harvard Kennedy School Misinformation Review 1*(2) https://doi.org/10.37016/mr-2020-012

Karr, T. (2022, March 18). The future of local news innovation is noncommercial. *Columbia Journalism Review*. www.cjr.org/business_of_news/the-future-of-local-news-noncommercial.php

Lacy, S. & Rosenstiel, T. (2015). Defining and measuring quality journalism. Rutgers School of Communication and Information. http://mpii.rutgers.edu/wp-content/uploads/sites/129/2015/04/Defining-and-Measuring-Quality-Journalism.pdf

Meijer, C. M., & Bijleveld, H. P. (2016). Valuable journalism: Measuring news quality from a user's perspective. *Digital Journalism, 17*(7), 827–839.

Moore, M., & Tambini, D. (2018). *Digital dominance: The power of Google, Amazon, Facebook, and Apple.* Oxford University Press.

Murthy, V. (2021). *Confronting Health Misinformation: The U.S. Surgeon General's Advisory on Building a Healthy Information Environment.* www.hhs.gov/sites/default/files/surgeon-general-misinformation-advisory.pdf

Napoli, P.M., Dunham, I., Mahone, J. (2017). *Assessing news media infrastructure: A state-level analysis.* News Measures Research Project. https://futureoflocalnews.org/portfolio-item/assessing-news-media-infrastructure-a-state-level-analysis/

Nielsen, R. K., & Ganter, S. A. (2022). *The power of platforms.* Oxford University Press.

Pasquale, F. (2015). *The black box society: The secret algorithms that control money and information.* Harvard University Press.

Picard, R.G. (2000). Measuring quality by journalistic activity. In R. G. Picard (Ed.), *Measuring media content, quality, and diversity: Approaches and issues in content research* (pp. 97–104). Turku School of Economics and Business Administration.

Simon, F.M. & Camargo, C. Q. (2021). Autopsy of a metaphor: The origins, use and blind spots of the "infodemic." *New Media & Society.* https://doi.org/10.1177/1461444821 1031908

Simonov, A., Sacher, S. K., Dubé, J. P. H., & Biswas, S. (2020). The persuasive effect of Fox News: Non-compliance with social distancing during the COVID-19 pandemic (No. w27237). National Bureau of Economic Research. www.nber.org/system/files/wor king_papers/w27237/w27237.pdf Working paper

Stevenson, A. (2018, November 6). Facebook admits it was used to incite violence in Myanmar. *The New York Times.* www.nytimes.com/2018/11/06/technology/myanmar-facebook.html

Subcommittee on Antitrust, Commercial and Administrative Law (2020). https://judiciary. house.gov/uploadedfiles/competition_in_digital_markets.pdf

Sun, R., Gregor, S. & Keating, B. (2015). Information technology platforms: Definition and research directions [Conference presentation]. Australasian Conference on Information Systems. https://doi.org/10.48550/arXiv.1606.01445

Timberg, C. & Romm, T. (2018, December 17). New report on Russian disinformation, prepared for the Senate, shows the operation's scale and sweep. *The Washington Post.* www.washingtonpost.com/technology/2018/12/16/new-report-russian-disinformat ion-prepared-senate-shows-operations-scale-sweep/

United Nations Human Rights Council. (2018.) Report of the detailed findings of the independent international fact-finding mission on Myanmar. https://undocs.org/en/ A/HRC/39/CRP.2

van Dijck, J., Poell, T., & de Waal, M. (2018). *The platform society: Public values in a connective world.* Oxford University Press.

Vosoughi, S., Roy, D. & Aral, S. (2018). The spread of true and false news online. *Science 359*(6380): 1146–1151. www.science.org/doi/10.1126/science.aap9559

2

COMMUNICATION TECHNOLOGY AND THREATS TO DEMOCRACY

We the people are (also) the problem

Johanna Dunaway and Nicholas Ray

American democracy faces serious challenges. Partisan polarization is at historic highs, policymaking is in gridlock, and neither policymakers nor citizens can agree with out-partisans on a shared set of facts. Nearly 30 percent of Republican voters do not believe the current president, Democrat Joe Biden, was legitimately elected to office. One of the few sentiments opposing partisans share is that American democracy is in peril (Vinopal, 2021). At the same time, the digital media environment is serving as a scapegoat for these problems. Even though billions of users spend significant amounts of time on social media, people are increasingly likely to report that they don't trust the information they encounter there. People love to hate social media, and politicians, the punditry, and many researchers blame these trends on various aspects of the changing media environment (Pariser, 2011; Sunstein, 2017).[1]

While there might be some truth to those assessments, they are incomplete. Placing blame almost entirely at the feet of the media environment underappreciates other important factors that are contributing to these trends. One problem is that related research focuses primarily on things that drive exposure—exposure to partisan media, exposure to misinformation. Because of their impact on media choice and selective exposure, researchers tend to focus primarily on the infrastructures, affordances, and features of the media environment that affect the market of content offerings in the information climate (e.g., Feldman et al., 2014; Van Aelst et al., 2017). While uncovering how media structures impact peoples' exposure to information and messages is critical, it tells only part of the story. In ways that go beyond their impact on exposure, individual-level cognitive biases and the rapidly proliferating menu of platforms and content structures also influence how information is processed once exposure occurs (e.g., Dunaway et al., 2018; Brugnoli et al., 2019; Dunaway & Soroka, 2021; Nelson & Lei, 2018). Moreover, as we

DOI: 10.4324/9781003257998-3

explain below, the nature and impact of that influence is conditional on whether exposure is motivated (driven by priors) instead of incidental (encountered in the course of other media activity) (Prior, 2007; Stroud, 2011). In addition, there are media system-level drivers—unchanged from earlier eras of information technology—that are also behind these trends.

The central conclusion of this chapter is that to better understand the challenges the digital media environment poses for news and democracy, currently distinct approaches that emphasize either structural or cognitive elements need to be synthesized, and with system-level factors in mind. Elaborating on the market-structural factors that drive exposure without due consideration for how context operates in tandem with individual-level differences to shape processing does little to shed light on political behavior and outcomes. We are not arguing that digital and social media do not play a role in exacerbating these trends, but we stress the need for a full account of the various contributing factors and the conditions under which these threats to democracy will continue to intensify. Drawing from both structural and cognitive explanations underscores that *exposure* to information does not necessitate its *processing*, *acceptance*, or *endorsement*. Rather, beliefs and predispositions drive information consumption and processing as much as they are shaped by them. Without incorporating structural, cognitive, and system-level explanations, attempts to understand and meet challenges for news and democracy will be fruitless.

Defining the threats

As Lawrence and Napoli highlight in the Introduction to this volume, information plays a critical role in most conceptions of a well-functioning democracy. That's one reason the contemporary media environment is at the center of scholarly efforts to understand rising polarization and the rampant dissemination and acceptance of misinformation. It follows that a major objective of this volume is to ask whether and how research can help us identify paths forward for combating these threats. We certainly think it can, but only if the broader research endeavor recognizes the multi-faceted nature of their underlying causes. Most research trying to understand our polarized, misinformed citizenry centers around changing media structures. In this chapter, we challenge what we see as a lopsided focus in this body of work, which places a disproportionate emphasis on structural explanations rather than cognitive and affective processes.

To be clear, structural changes to the media environment are important drivers of these phenomena. The highly fragmented state of today's media certainly allows for exposure to partisan sources of news and political information, and the peer-to-peer sharing affordances of social media networks enable widespread sharing and exposure of misinformation. But we underscore the importance of individual-level and system-level factors—such as cognitive biases and the commercial nature of our media system—both of which are also contributing to the

Communication technology and threats to democracy **15**

crisis. Even if the implementation of policy remedies is only feasible at the media platform, outlet, or market levels, they should be developed with individual- and system-level drivers in mind.

Evidence for structural arguments is evaluated in the next section, followed by a review of the theories explaining the rise of polarization and misinformation through cognitive and affective processes. The following section advocates for a reconciliation between the two approaches in consideration, and the penultimate section emphasizes that this needs to be done with system level influences in mind. We conclude with a discussion of areas for future research.

Structural explanations

Two main characteristics of the digital media environment form the foundation of the leading structural theories of the current democratic, informational crisis. The first is its expanded level of media choice or high rate of media fragmentation. When we say the contemporary media environment is high choice, or highly fragmented, we refer to the expansion of channels, websites, and programming made available with the arrival of cable and the internet (Stroud, 2011; Arceneaux & Johnson, 2013). Though many readers may not remember the days when most households had access to only about five channels on television, five was peak choice for years. Following the arrival of cable, channel offerings expanded rapidly (Prior, 2007). Between the years of 1985 and 2008, the average number of channels grew six-fold to nearly 130 channels per household. By 2013, the average number of channels per household was 189 (Webster, 2014; Guess, 2014).

Later, the arrival of the internet only hastened the expansion of choice and points of access for consuming media content. Not only did consumers have countless channels and programs from which to choose, they could suddenly do so on their computers, too. Broadly, the expansion of content offerings was great for consumers/audiences because it provided something for everyone (Prior, 2007). However, the flexibility and choice afforded by a fragmented media environment also had its downsides—one being its potential for encouraging media selectivity and ideological segregation (Stroud 2011). Researchers quickly recognized the potential for encouraging polarization. One prominent theory, for example, posits a causal relationship between polarization and the development of "partisan echo chambers" and "partisan enclaves," alleging that selective exposure produces informal silos that discourage incidental exposure to alternative or oppositional perspectives (Stroud, 2011; Sunstein, 2017). And if the high-choice setting and the threat of selectivity were not enough, online consumers of news can find themselves isolated too, segregated by algorithmic filtering based on prior online behavior and predictive models of partisanship (Pariser, 2011). These "filter bubbles" and "echo chambers" are worrisome because they reduce the likelihood of exposure to alternative views and sources of information. That is problematic in the eyes of many observers because according to democratic theory, exposure to oppositional perspectives should be associated with tolerance and support for compromise (Pariser, 2011; Sunstein, 2017).

Social media platforms are also characterized by structural features associated with polarization (Settle, 2018) and exposure to misinformation (Lazer et al., 2018). In addition to offering high (but limited) levels of choice and filtered exposure, their peer-to-peer networking structures and sharing capabilities allow for the possibility of routine exposure to misinformation and polarizing political content (Sunstein, 2017). Extant research demonstrates how rapidly and frequently inaccurate information spreads online and through social media networks (Boxell et al., 2017; Lazer et al., 2018).

Misinformation and polarization can also exacerbate one another. Strong partisan identities and polarization often facilitate selective exposure, which occurs when people to seek out information sources in line with their existing views (Jerit & Zhao, 2020). Here the high-choice media structure promotes misinformation exposure by encouraging regular engagement with in-party media via selectivity, algorithmic filtering, or homogeneous social networks (Sunstein, 2017). These can assist in the spreading and acceptance of misinformation because perceived credibility is ostensibly higher within homogeneous networks and among in-partisans.

However, research on the effects of the high-choice media environment and algorithmic filtering tell a more complicated story. Evidence for online ideological segregation through partisan enclaves, network homophily, and low exposure diversity is inconclusive (e.g., Weeks et al., 2017; Bruns, 2019), as is evidence about its effects (Flaxman et al., 2016; Peterson et al., 2018). Even though the structural arrangements of social networking sites promote exposure to agreeable political views more often than oppositional views, exposure to information from opposition-party friendly sources occurs regularly. Up to half of user exposure involves cross-cutting material (Bakshy et al., 2015). Some research finds that social media use—via network ties and endorsements—increases exposure diversity rather than reducing it (Goel et al., 2010; Messing & Westwood, 2014). Research examining web traffic data reveals a very high proportion of the internet audience is highly concentrated on mainstream sites (Hindman, 2018; Flaxman et al., 2016).

Even historical and demographic patterns challenge the notion of a causal relationship between recent changes to the media environment and polarization. Polarization started its climb in the mid-20th century, temporally preceding even the arrival of cable and the internet (Prior, 2013), not to mention social media. Further, the demographic groups using digital media least and spending the least amount of time online are most polarized (Boxell et al., 2017).

Extant research also challenges the premise that exposure to oppositional views necessarily encourages moderation and support for compromise (Kunda, 1990). In fact, when partisans are exposed to perspectives challenging their own, the effect is to strengthen existing predispositions as opposed to moderating them (Arceneaux & Vander Wielen, 2013; Bail et al., 2019). This may explain one reason why there is little evidence of attitudinal or behavioral effects even when echo chambers are found (Peterson et al., 2018).

Discerning their impact on political attitudes and behavior is also difficult because the structures of social media platforms were developed with social—and not necessarily political—considerations in mind. This complicates researchers' ability to find direct causal linkages between social media use and polarization (Messing & Westwood, 2014; Settle, 2018). Thus, even though research can establish that the opportunity for exposure and attention to polarizing information in the contemporary media environment is high, its true impact on attitudes and behavior is still unknown (Bail et al., 2019).

The emergence of digital media introduced many disruptive structural changes, some with the potential to encourage polarization or lead to the development of misperceptions (Sunstein, 2017; Weeks, 2018). Thus, structural accounts are understandable. Yet scholars have unearthed a significant amount of evidence to refute the notion that these structures are the primary drivers of an increasingly polarized and misinformed public (e.g., Prior, 2007; Webster & Ksiazek, 2012; Arceneaux & Johnson, 2013). The view that expanding media choice and rising polarization have incentivized media selectivity and fact avoidance, and therefore have increased audiences' vulnerability to misinformation is certainly warranted, but we contend—and other research suggests—these structural changes only provide a partial explanation for these problems.

Processing explanations

In contrast to structural accounts, processing-based explanations for a polarized and misinformed public portray the structural features of the media environment as more handmaiden than driver of misperceptions. Specifically, they point to the importance of cognitive biases and polarization in terms of how they affect the processing of information upon exposure (Flynn et al., 2017; Weeks & Garrett, 2014).

Motivated reasoning theories, for example, posit that both the collection and consumption of information is motivated by certain goals. Accuracy goals are aimed at coming to an informed decision, while directional goals seek support for attitude-consistent conclusions. Directional goals are guided by partisanship in the processing of political information (Druckman et al., 2013; Lodge & Taber, 2013). For this reason, the development of misperceptions is often attributed to directional motivated reasoning (Jerit & Zhao, 2020). Structural theories emphasize that directional motivated reasoning can guide how people *seek* information to yield attitude-consistent conclusions; cognitive explanations emphasize its influence on how people *process* information to yield attitude-consistent conclusions.

We focus here on how motivated reasoning affects processing. One way is through partisanship as a social identity. According to social identity theory explanations of partisanship, party identification is an affective and psychological attachment. As such, partisans interpret information in ways to support a benign view of the partisan in-group (Lelkes, 2018). The development of inaccurate beliefs is, from this perspective, often a response to identity threat. This explains why people interpret economic information in ways that are consistent with defense of their partisan identities, regardless of its accuracy (Schaffner & Roche, 2016). It's also why partisans endorse conspiracies consistent with their political views (Miller et al., 2016). Identity protection even extends to motivated reasoning about information aimed at correcting or retracting misinformation. Partisans are reluctant to dismiss misinformation even in the face of corrections, if that misinformation is consistent with their political predispositions (Kunda, 1990; Arceneaux & Vander Wielen, 2013; Bail et al., 2018).

However, when it comes to exposure to misinformation or disinformation, it is important to recall that under motivated reasoning, directional motivated reasoning goals should condition the effect. If directional motivated reasoning is occurring, congenial or attitude-consistent misinformation should be accepted, and disagreeable misinformation resisted. In other words, exposure to counter-attitudinal misinformation is not likely to exert persuasive influence because it is inconsistent with in-group arguments and consistent with those of the out-group. In fact, some research suggests it should have a backlash effect where exposure to counter-attitudinal information prompts counter-arguments as part of a defensive strategy, ultimately increasing in-group identity salience (Kunda, 1990; Arceneaux & Vander Wielen, 2013; Bail et al., 2018). If anything, pre-existing attitudes should emerge stronger after such exposure and identity-threatening misinformation should be dismissed or rejected. Political identity conditions the acceptance of misinformation more than mere exposure to misinformation (Thorson, 2016; Nyhan & Reifler, 2010).

Recent lines of work on affective polarization and partisan sorting (e.g., Iyengar et al., 2012; Iyengar & Westwood, 2015; Mason, 2015; 2016) also highlight the importance of cognitive processing. This work illustrates how cognitive biases and existing predispositions shape responses to encounters with political information. Affective polarization—defined by Druckman and Levendusky (2019, p. 119) as "the tendency of Democrats and Republicans to dislike and distrust one another," is on the rise in America (Iyengar et al., 2012; Iyengar & Krupenkin, 2018; Mason & Wronski, 2018). At the same time, the public is becoming more sorted along partisan and ideological lines. Partisan-ideological sorting describes a process by which political identities are becoming more consistent and better organized. As sorting occurs, party identification gets further entwined with other social and cultural identities, strengthening the partisan identity and affect (Mason, 2015; 2016). These patterns are reflected in higher levels of in-group favoritism and out-group dislike (Huddy et al., 2015; Iyengar & Krupenkin, 2018; Mason & Wronski, 2018).

A polarized and sorted political context should only exacerbate the influence of cognitive biases when people are exposed to political information. Sorted and affectively polarized citizens are those especially likely to seek out and process information as highly motivated reasoners. Whether they ignore or process misinformation will depend on its direction and relationship with existing beliefs

(Lewandowsky et al., 2005; Gaines et al., 2007; Nyhan & Reifler, 2010). Research on misinformation supports this view. Misinformation is commonly used to support existing opinions and beliefs (Reedy et al., 2014). When misinformation is consistent with political identity, it is more likely to be accepted or endorsed in support of in-party evaluations (e.g., Flynn et al., 2017; Weeks & Garrett, 2014; Marsh & Yang, 2018; Garrett et al., 2016; Gaines et al., 2007; Schaffner & Roche, 2016).

Research on expressive responding examines whether agreeing with political misperceptions reflects partisan cheerleading rather than sincere beliefs (Bullock et al., 2015; Khanna & Sood, 2018; Schaffner & Luks, 2018). Evidence for this argument is still inconclusive (Berinsky, 2018; Jerit & Zhao, 2020). Similarly, related work on the measurement of misperceptions (Cor & Sood, 2016; Jerit & Zhao, 2020) asserts that misperceptions expressed in survey responses reflect inconsistencies associated with top-of-the-head responses, rather than true misperceptions, consistent with early work on response instability (Zaller & Feldman, 1992). This work questions whether misperceptions reflect beliefs about facts or fact-bending to fit existing beliefs.

Either way, these perspectives illustrate how the challenges of rising polarization and misinformation are borne from more than just structural changes occurring in the media environment. Structural changes might allow for more exposure to partisan information and misinformation, but exposure does not necessarily equate with attention, and the impact of information exposure is conditional on whether and how it is attended to and processed (Zaller, 1992; Dunaway & Searles, 2022). Even as the media landscape and information technologies have continued to evolve, they've done so in ways that influence more than just market offerings or content choice. Information is now delivered in different volumes through many different platforms or venues throughout the day (Molyneux, 2018). Even if the content to which various users are exposed is not entirely different, its presentation is. Whether through differences among platforms or differences between televisions, desktop machines, and mobile devices, the structure of the information as presented to us has most certainly changed, and it has done so in ways that are likely to affect how we process it (Dunaway & Searles, 2022). This suggests that any complete explanation for the problems of polarization and misinformation must consider how cognitive biases and individual differences shape information seeking and processing. The need for a richer theory, one that incorporates the constraint on attention wrought by devices, platforms, and other structural facets with research on cognitive and affective processing, is detailed in the next section.

Combining the two: Structured processing

The same cognitive biases leading us to avoid effortful processing induced by exposure to counter-attitudinal information also deter us from effortful processing induced by affordances and features of new communication technologies

(Dunaway & Searles, 2022). For example, mobile news consumers spend far less time reading news stories (Dunaway et al., 2018), even when exposed to them several times a day (Molyneux, 2018). They also tend to be less cognitively and emotionally engaged (Dunaway & Soroka, 2021). Do the fleeting attention spans of mobile users make them more or less susceptible to effects of misinformation or polarizing content?

Research on attentiveness to digital, social, and mobile news suggests attention scarcity in the digital media environment might limit the impact of exposure to information (Dunaway et al., 2018; Hindman, 2018). Facebook and other social media referrals drive traffic to news websites, but many referred users only stay for fractions of a second (Hindman, 2018; Kamerer, 2020). However, it is worth noting that most platforms use "dwell time" as a quality signal; high bounce rates and quick user returns to social media platforms indicate poor content, which is then down-ranked (Yoshida et al., 2020). Such platform features will aim to prioritize content that will capture and keep attention.

Much information sharing and re-sharing via peer-to-peer social networks also occurs without much attention to content. Senders take cues from headlines and make inferences from social and endorsements in lieu of attending to actual content (Pennycook et al., 2020; but see Beam et al., 2016). Thus, while widespread sharing of information might be indicative of engagement, it can often reflect mere expression based on such cues, and therefore it is not necessarily indicative of anything more than brief exposure (Pennycook et al., 2020). While we have far less evidence on behavior and reactions among recipients of shares and re-shares, the limited evidence we do have suggests we cannot assume informational cues will work similarly on social media as with traditional media (Messing & Westwood, 2014).

What effects should we expect if exposure is fleeting on digital, social, and mobile media? Messages must capture attention if they are to affect attitudes or behavior. We are only just beginning to understand the limits of the typical digital media attention-span. Moreover, platform-specific content formats such as news feeds also affect exposure and processing. News feeds, for example, restrict choice and selectivity, thereby increasing the likelihood of incidental exposure through algorithmic filtering and network effects. Several studies suggest that restricted choice through news feed structures increase rates of incidental exposure and facilitates learning (Bode, 2016) and agenda-setting effects from media (Feezell, 2018).

News feeds can also blend and display social and political information in ways that shape cognitive and affective responses to encourage polarization. At present, there is mixed evidence on the question of whether the social aspects of social media make us polarized. While social endorsements on social media sites can override partisan source cues in ways that are ostensibly depolarizing (Messing & Westwood, 2014), Settle's (2018) work suggests the blending of social and political information on Facebook is a driver of polarization. The structural effects of news feeds provide a clear example of how changes to communication technology can affect information processing and opinion formation, in combination with cognitive processes.

Structured processing in context

While so many things have changed to affect how we encounter and process messages in today's information environment, the economic, profit-based nature of our media system has stayed largely the same. Though the metrics for measuring audience interest and attention have changed significantly, the underlying economic model has not—media companies earn revenue by attracting and capturing audience attention (Napoli, 2011; Webster, 2014). As such, perceptions about what will capture audience attention exert influence over the information we encounter. Such perceptions are influenced by metrics based on previous audience behaviors, as well as inferences made from those behaviors and what is known about our common cognitive biases.

Facebook's recent struggles make for a good case in point. Since 2016, the social media giant has been in and out of trouble with lawmakers and the public for its problems with misinformation. Most recently, the company earned negative publicity for tweaking its algorithm for determining who sees what in ways that created troubling—even if unintended—social and political consequences. The tweak was a solution for what the company viewed as an "engagement problem"—they were losing users for the first time, and the engagement metrics were showing it. The objective of the tweak was to adjust the algorithm to allow for more "meaningful social interactions" by changing the way content—posts, reactions, shares, and re-shares—were scored for engagement. Put simply, the new algorithm prioritized material that earned higher levels of engagement (i.e., comments and responses going beyond the usual likes). In practice, the effect was to amplify the most divisive content such as misinformation, heated exchanges, and violent content (Hagey & Horwitz, 2021).

According to an internal Facebook report and investigative reporting by the *Wall Street Journal*, the new algorithm's heavy weighting of re-shared material in its News Feed made heated voices and exchanges louder. By prioritizing views of high-engagement content, it also had the effect of incentivizing media, political actors, and individual users to produce even more of this kind of content. European political parties, for example, reportedly shifted their policy positions in more extreme directions to resonate more on the platform. Similarly, party leaders relied increasingly on negative and inflammatory rhetoric to maintain high engagement on the site (Hagey & Horwitz, 2021). CEO Mark Zuckerberg and other Facebook executives were criticized heavily for failing to act in response when confronted with this information, expressing concern about what changing it back would mean for engagement numbers. But this should be no surprise. Because Facebook's revenue model is based on sustained engagement on the site, they have an economic incentive to structure content in ways that sustain time on site, as well as likes and shares (Hagey & Horwitz, 2021).

Facebook's recent struggles make for a timely example, but they exemplify an age-old problem: the temptation media companies face when forced to choose whether to prioritize content with earning potential or content with societal value. All too often, profit considerations win out, but such choices are not specific to any one company or CEO. These choices are dictated by perceptions of audience tastes. If more audiences tune in or stay on the page in response to negative, sensational, or inflammatory content, the temptation to prioritize it is difficult to resist absent other incentives to do so. For similar reasons, research documents an inverse relationship between the profit motives of media outlets and informativeness in news reporting (Hamilton, 2004). Entertainment and crime news stories typically attract and retain more audiences than in-depth reporting on public policy-related news. The same incentives are also apparent in studies of media reporting on political advertising during campaigns. When news media started covering negative attack ads at much higher rates than neutral and positive ads, campaigns aired more attack ads in response. Because media coverage amplifies the messages in campaign ads (Ridout & Smith, 2008), the free airtime the negative ads earned created the incentive to produce them more (Geer, 2012).

Scores of studies document humans' psychological tendency to pay more attention to negative information than neutral or positive information; research also shows this pattern of attention allocation applies to how we consume news and political information (Soroka, 2014). The cognitive bias for negative and inflammatory content is one reason why "if it bleeds, it leads" on local television news. It is likely for the same reasons that polarizing and inflammatory content is prioritized on Facebook. In other words, such decisions are likely attributable to the fact that they are incentivized by the predominantly for-profit nature of our media system, audience tastes, and the metrics we use to track those tastes more than anything else. While the evidence to suggest this is true for the Facebook case is only anecdotal, decades of research on traditional media show that news values born from the need to attract and retain audiences often produce lowest common denominator-type content (McManus, 1994). Whether we get infotainment, hard news, objective, or slanted news is largely determined by perceptions about what audiences want (Hamilton, 2004; Gentzkow & Shapiro, 2010). Market demand is powerful, and audience preferences are known to shape media content.

Discussion and conclusion

Researchers and democratic observers are intensely concerned about polarization and misinformation (e.g., DiFonzo et al., 2016; Flynn et al., 2017; Thorson et al., 2018). Both play a role in the widespread formation of misperceptions and inaccurate beliefs, and both loom as threats to democracy. The contemporary

Communication technology and threats to democracy **23**

digital media environment is a natural place to look for causal explanations, but research suggests there is more to the story.

While the structural components of digital media orchestrate opportunities for avoiding facts and encountering misinformation, peoples' beliefs and predispositions motivate what information is sought and how it is processed. Put differently, beliefs and predispositions influence the processing and consumption of information to a greater degree than they are altered by them. In the U.S. context, currently characterized by growing affective polarization and elite polarization, the effects of motivated reasoning and political identities should only increase their influence over how people seek and process information. If partisanship is rigid enough to shape how we *evaluate* information to which we are exposed, the likelihood that oppositional misinformation will have persuasive effects is likely minimal (Bennett & Iyengar, 2008; Iyengar, 2017).

Yet, whether there are important behavioral effects from such exposure remains an open question. Far less work focuses on how exposure shapes actual behavior relative to studies of exposure itself. Even though extant work suggests that the direct effects of factual misinformation might be minimal—or at the very least conditional, despite high rates of mass exposure—our ability to make this kind of conclusion depends on several questions that are yet unresolved by the literature. One possibility is that high rates of motivated exposure to political information may result in an increase in information that is processed and accepted but with little effect on currently held attitudes and beliefs. Similarly, rates of incidental exposure may be high, especially on some platforms, but not sufficiently high to encourage those with little interest to engage in processing to produce acceptance or behavioral change. These are answers to important questions we do not yet know.

We should also consider what cultural, political, and institutional processes are strengthening political identities and increasing affective polarization, and we need to question whether and how the continual strategic misuse of political information by elites is going to exacerbate those trends and their effects. To do this successfully, we need to go beyond questions about who will be exposed to what and to move toward understanding how misinformation is processed across individuals, platforms, and contexts, and to what effect.

We must also consider how different platforms and devices will impact likelihood, duration, and nature of exposure. Today, political information is shared, displayed, blended, and presented in many forms, affecting attention and processing in consequential ways. At the same time, we need to reconcile how cognitive biases shape content on the front end, by creating the market demand for it, and what this means for the strategic communication incentives for media companies and political elites. Many new affordances and features characterize the contemporary digital media environment. They have a clear impact on citizens' willingness and ability to process information upon exposure (Molyneux, 2018; Dunaway et al., 2018; Settle, 2018; Dunaway & Soroka, 2021). Yet our limited digital attention spans mean that digital media companies and other generators of content will continue to seek means by which to attract and retain our attention.

People worry about partisan news and other partisan sources of information on social media, but the system incentivizes media to amplify negative and sensational content because many of our cognitive biases create a market demand for it. While digital and social media may vastly expand our opportunities for exposure to negative, polarizing, or inaccurate content, it is important to remember that the audience appetites incentivizing its use existed well before the dawn of digital and social media. When it comes to understanding the various drivers of polarization and misinformation, we the people are also part of the problem.

Note

1 Various parts of this chapter draw on arguments made in Dunaway (2021) and Dunaway & Settle (2021).

References

Ahler, D. J., & Sood, G. (2018). The parties in our heads: Misperceptions about party composition and their consequences. *The Journal of Politics, 80*(3), 964–981. https://dx.doi.org/10.1086/697253

Allcott, H., Gentzkow, M., & Chuan Y. (2019). Trends in the diffusion of misinformation on social media. *Research & Politics, 6*(2). https://doi.org/10.1177/2053168019848554

Althaus, S. L., & Tewksbury, D. (2000). Patterns of Internet and traditional news media use in a networked community. *Political Communication, 17*(1), 21–45. https://doi.org/10.1080/105846000198495

Arceneaux, K., & Johnson, M., (2013). *Changing minds or changing channels?: Partisan news in an age of choice.* University of Chicago Press.

Arceneaux, K., & Vander Wielen, R. J. (2013). The effects of need for cognition and need for affect on partisan evaluations. *Political Psychology, 34*(1), 23–42. https://doi.org/10.1111/j.1467-9221.2012.00925.x

Badawy, A., Ferrara, E., & Lerman, K. (2018, August 28–31). Analyzing the digital traces of political manipulation: The 2016 Russian interference Twitter campaign. In *2018 IEEE/ACM International Conference on Advances in Social Networks Analysis and Mining (ASONAM)* (pp. 258–265). IEEE. https://doi.org/10.1109/ASONAM44025.2018

Bail, C. A., Argyle, L. P., Brown, T. W., Bumpus, J. P., Chen, H., Hunzaker, M. B. F., Lee, J., Mann, M., Merhout, F., & Volfovsky, A. (2018). Exposure to opposing views on social media can increase political polarization. *Proceedings of the National Academy of Sciences, 115*(37), 9216–9221. https://doi.org/10.1073/pnas.1804840115

Bakshy, E., Messing, S., & Adamic, L. A. (2015). Exposure to ideologically diverse news and opinion on Facebook. *Science, 348*(6239), 1130–1132. https://doi.org/10.1126/science.aaa1160

Beam, J. A., Hutchens, M. J., & Hmielowski, J. D.. (2016). Clicking vs. sharing: The relationship between online news behaviors and political knowledge. *Computers in Human Behavior, 59*, 215–220. https://doi.org/10.1016/j.chb.2016.02.013

Bennett, W. L., & Iyengar, S. (2008). A new era of minimal effects? The changing foundations of political communication. *Journal of Communication, 58*(4), 707–731. https://doi.org/10.1111/j.1460-2466.2008.00410.x

Berinsky A. J. (2018). Telling the truth about believing the lies? Evidence for the limited prevalence of expressive survey responding. *Journal of Politics, 80*(1), 211–224. https://doi.org/10.1086/694258

Bode, L. (2016). Political news in the news feed: Learning politics from social media. *Mass Communication and Society, 19*(1), 24–48. https://doi.org/10.1080/15205436.2015.1045149

Bode, L., & Vraga, E. K. (2015). In related news, that was wrong: The correction of misinformation through related stories functionality in social media. *Journal of Communication, 65*(4), 619–638. https://doi.org/10.1111/jcom.12166

Boxell, L., Gentzkow, M., & Shapiro, J. M. (2017). Greater Internet use is not associated with faster growth of political polarization amongst demographic groups. *PNAS, 114*(40), 10612–10617. https://doi.org/10.1073/pnas.1706588114

Brugnoli, E., Cinelli, M., Zollo, F., Quattrociocchi, W., & Scala, A. (2019). Lexical convergence and collective identities on Facebook. arXiv preprint arXiv:1903.11452. https://doi.org/10.48550/arXiv.1903.11452

Bruns, A. (2019). *Are filter bubbles real?* John Wiley & Sons.

Bullock, J. G., Gerber, A. S., Hill, S. J. and Huber, G. A. (2015). Partisan bias in factual beliefs about politics. *Quarterly Journal of Political Science, 10*(4), 519–78. http://dx.doi.org/10.1561/100.00014074

Carpini, M. X. D., & Keeter, S. (1996). *What Americans know about politics and why it matters.* Yale University Press.

Converse, P. E. (1964). The nature of belief systems in mass publics. In D. E. Apter (Ed.),. *Ideology and discontent* (pp. 206–261). Free Press of Glencoe.

Cor, M. K., & Sood, G. (2016). Guessing and forgetting: A latent class model for measuring learning. *Political Analysis, 24*(2), 226–242. https://doi.org/10.1093/pan/mpw010

DiFonzo, N., Beckstead, J. W., Stupak, N., & Walders, K. (2016). Validity judgment of rumors heard multiple times: The shape of the truth effect. *Social Influence, 11*(1), 22–39. https://doi.org/10.1080/15534510.2015.1137224

Druckman, J. N., & Levendusky, M. S. (2019). What do we measure when we measure affective polarization?. *Public Opinion Quarterly, 83*(1), 114–122. https://doi.org/10.1093/poq/nfz003

Druckman, J. N., Peterson, E., & Slothus, R. (2013). How elite partisan polarization affects public opinion formation. *American Political Science Review, 107*(1), 57–79. doi:10.1017/S0003055412000500

Dunaway, J. (2021). Polarisation and misinformation. In H. Tumber & S. Waisbord (Eds.), *The Routledge companion to media disinformation and populism* (pp. 131–141). Routledge. https://doi.org/10.4324/9781003004431

Dunaway, J. L., & Searles, K. N. (2022) *News attention in a mobile era.* Under contract with Oxford University Press.

Dunaway, J. L., & Settle, J. E. (2021). Opinion formation and polarization in the news feed era: Effects from digital, social, and mobile media. In D. Osborne and C. Sibley (Eds.), *The Cambridge handbook of political psychology,* Cambridge University Press. https://doi.org/10.1017/9781108779104.035

Dunaway, J. L., & Soroka, S. N. (2021). Smartphone-size screens constrain cognitive access to video news stories. *Information, Communication, & Society, 24*(1) 69–84. https://doi.org/10.1080/1369118X.2019.1631367

Dunaway, J. L., Searles, K., Sui, M., & Paul, N. (2018). News attention in a mobile era. *Journal of Computer-Mediated Communication, 23*(2) 107–124. https://doi.org/10.1093/jcmc/zmy004

Feezell, J. T. (2018). Agenda setting through social media: The importance of incidental news exposure and social filtering in the digital era. *Political Research Quarterly, 71*(2), 482–494. https://doi.org/10.1177/1065912917744895

Feldman, L., Myers, T. A., Hmielowski, J. D., & Leiserowitz, A. (2014). The mutual reinforcement of media selectivity and effects: Testing the reinforcing spirals framework in the context of global warming. *Journal of Communication, 64*(4), 590–611. https://doi.org/10.1111/jcom.12108

Flaxman, S., Goel, S., & Rao, J. M. (2016). Filter bubbles, echo chambers, and online news consumption. *Public Opinion Quarterly, 80*(S1), 298–320. https://doi.org/10.1093/poq/nfw006

Flynn, D. J., Nyhan, B., & Reifler, J. (2017). The nature and origins of misperceptions: Understanding false and unsupported beliefs about politics. *Political Psychology, 38*(S1), 127–150. https://doi.org/10.1111/pops.12394

Gaines, B. J., Kuklinski, J. H., Quirk, P. J., Peyton, B., & Verkuilen, J. (2007). Same facts, different interpretations: Partisan motivation and opinion on Iraq. *The Journal of Politics, 69*(4), 957–974. http://dx.doi.org/10.1111/j.1468-2508.2007.00601.x

Garrett, R. K., Weeks, B. E., & Neo, R. L. (2016). Driving a wedge between evidence and beliefs: How online ideological news exposure promotes political misperceptions. *Journal of Computer-Mediated Communication, 21*(5), 331–348. https://doi.org/10.1111/jcc4.12164

Geer, J. G. (2012). The news media and the rise of negativity in presidential campaigns. *PS: Political Science & Politics, 45*(3), 422–427. https://doi.org/10.1017/S1049096512000492

Gentzkow, M., & Shapiro, J. M. (2010). What drives media slant? Evidence from US daily newspapers. *Econometrica, 78*(1), 35–71. https://doi.org/10.3982/ECTA7195

Geuss, M. (2014, May 6). On average, Americans get 189 cable TV channels and only watch 17. *Ars Technica.* https://arstechnica.com/information-technology/2014/05/on-average-americans-get-189-cable-tv-channels-and-only-watch-17/

Gil de Zúñiga, H., Weeks, B., & Ardèvol-Abreu, A. (2017). Effects of the news-finds-me perception in communication: Social media use implications for news seeking and learning about politics. *Journal of Computer-Mediated Communication, 22*(3), 105–123. https://doi.org/10.1111/jcc4.12185

Goel, S., Mason, W., & Watts, D. J. (2010). Real and perceived attitude agreement in social networks. *Journal of Personality and Social Psychology, 99*(4), 611–621. https://doi.org/10.1037/a0020697

Grabe, M. E., Lang, A., Zhou, S., & Bolls, P. D. (2000). Cognitive access to negatively arousing news: An experimental investigation of the knowledge gap. *Communication Research, 27*(1), 3–26. https://doi.org/10.1177/009365000027001001

Hagey, K., & Horwitz, J. (2021, September 15). Facebook tried to make its platform a healthier place. It got angrier instead. *The Wall Street Journal,* www.wsj.com/articles/facebook-algorithm-change-zuckerberg-11631654215?mod=article_inline

Hamilton, J. T. (2004). *All the news that's fit to sell: How the market transforms information into news.* Princeton University Press.

Hindman, M., (2018). *The Internet trap: How the digital economy builds monopolies and undermines democracy.* Princeton University Press.

Huddy, L., Mason, L., & Aarøe, L. (2015). Expressive partisanship: Campaign involvement, political emotion, and partisan identity. *American Political Science Review*, *109*(1), 1–17. https://doi.org/10.1017/S0003055414000604

Iyengar, S. (2017). A typology of media effects. In K. Kenski & K. H. Jamieson (Eds.), *The Oxford handbook of political communication* (pp. 59–68). Oxford University Press.

Iyengar, S., & Krupenkin, M. (2018). The strengthening of partisan affect. *Political Psychology*, *39*(S1), 201–218. https://doi.org/10.1111/pops.12487

Iyengar, S., & Westwood, S. J. (2015). Fear and loathing across party lines: New evidence on group polarization. *American Journal of Political Science*, *59*(3), 690–707. https://doi.org/10.1111/ajps.12152

Iyengar, S., Sood, G., & Lelkes, Y. (2012). Affect, not ideology a social identity perspective on polarization. *Public Opinion Quarterly*, *76*(3), 405–431. https://doi.org/10.1093/poq/nfs038

Iyengar, S., Lelkes, Y., Levendusky, M., Malhotra, N., & Westwood, S. J. (2019). The origins and consequences of affective polarization in the United States. *Annual Review of Political Science*, *22*, 129–146. https://doi.org/10.1146/annurev-polisci-051117-073034

Jerit, J., & Barabas, J. (2012). Partisan perceptual bias and the information environment. *The Journal of Politics*, *74*(3), 672–684. https://doi.org/10.1017/S0022381612000187

Jerit, J., & Zhao, Y. (2020). Political misinformation. *Annual Review of Political Science*, *23*, 77–94. https://doi.org/10.1146/annurev-polisci-050718-032814

Kamerer, D. (2020). Reconsidering bounce rate in web analytics. *Journal of Digital & Social Media Marketing*, *8*(1), 58–67.

Khanna, K., & Sood, G. (2018). Motivated responding in studies of factual learning. *Political Behavior*, *40*(1), 79–101. https://doi.org/10.1007/s11109-017-9395-7

Kim, Y. M., Hsu, J., Neiman, D., Kou, C., Bankston, L., Kim, S. Y., Heinrich, R., Baragwanath, R., & Raskutti, G. (2018). The stealth media? Groups and targets behind divisive issue campaigns on Facebook. *Political Communication*, *35*(4), 515–541. https://doi.org/10.1080/10584609.2018.1476425

Kuklinski, J. H., Quirk, P. J., Jerit, J., Schwieder, D., & Rich, R. F. (2000). Misinformation and the currency of democratic citizenship. *Journal of Politics*, *62*(3), 790–816. https://doi.org/10.1111/0022-3816.00033

Kunda, Z. (1990). The case for motivated reasoning. *Psychological Bulletin*, *108*(3), 480–498. https://doi.org/10.1037/0033-2909.108.3.480

Lazer, D. M., Baum, M. A., Benkler, Y., Berinsky, A. J., Greenhill, K. M., Menczer, F., Metzger, M. J., Nyhan, B., Pennycook, G., Rothschild, D., & Schudson, M. (2018). The science of fake news. *Science*, *359*(6380), 1094–1096. https://doi.org/10.1126/science.aao2998

Lelkes, Y. (2018). Affective polarization and ideological sorting: A reciprocal, albeit weak, relationship. *The Forum*, *16*(1), 67–79. https://doi.org/10.1515/for-2018-0005

Lewandowsky, S., Ecker, U. K., & Cook, J. (2017). Beyond misinformation: Understanding and coping with the "post-truth" era. *Journal of Applied Research in Memory and Cognition*, *6*(4), 353–369. https://doi.org/10.1016/j.jarmac.2017.07.008

Lewandowsky, S., Stritzke, W. G. K., Oberauer, K., & Morales, M. (2005). Memory for Fact, Fiction, and Misinformation: The Iraq War 2003. *Psychological Science*, *16*(3), 190–195. https://doi.org/10.1111/j.0956-7976.2005.00802.x

Lodge, M. & Taber, C. S. (2013). *The rationalizing voter*. Cambridge University Press.

Lopez, J., & Hillygus, D. S. (2018). Why so serious?: Survey trolls and misinformation. http://dx.doi.org/10.2139/ssrn.3131087

Lupia, A., McCubbins, M. D., & Arthur, L. (1998). *The democratic dilemma: Can citizens learn what they need to know?* Cambridge University Press.

Marsh, E. J., & Yang, B. W. (2018). Believing things that are not true: A cognitive science perspective on misinformation. In B. G. Southwell, E. A. Thorson & L. Sheble (Eds.), *Misinformation and mass audiences* (pp. 15–34). University of Texas Press. https://doi.org/10.7560/314555-003

Mason, L. (2015). "I disrespectfully agree": The differential effects of partisan sorting on social and issue polarization. *American Journal of Political Science, 59*(1), 128–145. https://doi.org/10.1111/ajps.12089

Mason, L. (2016). A cross-cutting calm: How social sorting drives affective polarization. *Public Opinion Quarterly, 80*(S1), 351–377. https://doi.org/10.1093/poq/nfw001

Mason, L., & Wronski, J. (2018). One tribe to bind them all: How our social group attachments strengthen partisanship. *Political Psychology, 39*(S1), 257–277. https://doi.org/10.1111/pops.12485

McManus, J. H. (1994). *Market-driven journalism: Let the citizen beware?* Sage Publications.

Messing, S., & Westwood, S. J. (2014). Selective exposure in the age of social media: Endorsements trump partisan source affiliation when selecting news online. *Communication Research, 41*(8), 1042–1063. https://doi.org/10.1177/0093650212466406

Miller, J. M., Saunders, K. L., & Farhart, C. E. (2016). Conspiracy endorsement as motivated reasoning: The moderating roles of political knowledge and trust. *American Journal of Political Science, 60*(4), 824–844. https://doi.org/10.1111/ajps.12234

Molyneux, L. (2018). Mobile news consumption: A habit of snacking. *Digital Journalism, 6*(5), 634–650. https://doi.org/10.1080/21670811.2017.1334567

Napoli, P. M. (2011). *Audience evolution: New technologies and the transformation of media audiences.* Columbia University Press.

Nelson, J. L., & Lei, R. F. (2018). The effect of digital platforms on news audience behavior. *Digital Journalism, 6*(5), 619–633. https://doi.org/10.1080/21670811.2017.1394202

Nyhan, B., and Reifler, J. (2010). When corrections fail: The persistence of political misperceptions. *Political Behavior, 32*(2), 303–330. https://doi.org/10.1007/s11109-010-9112-2

Pariser, E. (2011). *The filter bubble: How the new personalized web is changing what we read and how we think.* Penguin.

Pennycook, G., McPhetres, J., Zhang, Y., Lu, J., & Rand, D. (2020). Fighting COVID-19 misinformation on social media: Experimental evidence for a scalable accuracy nudge intervention. *Psychological Science, 31*(7), 770–780. https://doi.org/10.1177/0956797620939054

Peterson, E., Goel, S. & Iyengar, S. (2018). Echo chambers and partisan polarization: Evidence from the 2016 presidential campaign. [Unpublished manuscript.] https://5harad.com/papers/selecfive-exposure.pdf

Prior, M. (2007). *Post-broadcast democracy: How media choice increases inequality in political involvement and polarizes elections.* Cambridge University Press.

Prior, M. (2013). Media and political polarization. *Annual Review of Political Science, 16*, 101–127. Doi: 10.1146/annurev-polisci-100711-135242

Redlawsk, D. P. (2002). Hot cognition or cool consideration? Testing the effects of motivated reasoning on political decision making. *Journal of Politics, 64*(4), 1021–1044. https://doi.org/10.1111/1468-2508.00161

Reedy, J., Wells, C., & Gastil, J. (2014). How voters become misinformed: An investigation of the emergence and consequences of false factual beliefs. *Social Science Quarterly, 95*(5), 1399–1418. https://doi.org/10.1111/ssqu.12102

Reeves, B., Lang, A., Kim, E. Y., & Tatar, D. (1999). The effects of screen size and message content on attention and arousal. *Media Psychology, 1*(1), 49–67. https://doi.org/10.1207/s1532785xmep0101_4

Ribeiro, F. N., Saha, K., Babaei, M., Henrique, L., Messias, J., Benevenuto, F., … & Redmiles, E. M. (2019, January). On microtargeting socially divisive ads: A case study of Russia-linked ad campaigns on Facebook. In *Proceedings of the Conference on Fairness, Accountability, and Transparency* (pp. 140–149). https://doi.org/10.1145/3287560.3287580

Ridout, T. N., & Smith, G. R. (2008). Free advertising: How the media amplify campaign messages. *Political Research Quarterly, 61*(4), 598–608. https://doi.org/10.1177/1065912908314202

Schaffner, B. F., & Luks, S. (2018). Misinformation or expressive responding? What an inauguration crowd can tell us about the source of political misinformation in surveys. *Public Opinion Quarterly, 82*(1), 135–147. https://doi.org/10.1093/poq/nfx042

Schaffner, B. F., & Roche, C. (2016). Misinformation and motivated reasoning: Responses to economic news in a politicized environment. *Public Opinion Quarterly, 81*(1), 86–110. https://doi.org/10.1093/poq/nfw043

Settle, J. E. (2018). *Frenemies: How social media polarizes America.* Cambridge University Press.

Simonsen, K. B., & Bonikowski, B. (2022). Moralizing immigration: Political framing, moral conviction, and polarization in the United States and Denmark. *Comparative Political Studies, 55*(8), 1–34. https://doi.org/10.1177/00104140211060284

Soroka, S. N. (2014). *Negativity in democratic politics: Causes and consequences.* Cambridge University Press.

Stroud, N. J. (2011). *Niche news: The politics of news choice.* Oxford University Press.

Stroud, N. J. (2017). Selective exposure theories. In K. Kenski & K. H. Jamieson (Eds.), *The Oxford handbook of political communication.* Oxford University Press. https://doi.org/10.1093/oxfordhb/9780199793471.013.009_update_001

Sunstein, C. R. (2017). *Republic: Divided democracy in the age of social media.* Princeton University Press.

Swire, B., Berinsky, A. J., Lewandowsky, S., & Ecker, U. K. (2017). Processing political misinformation: Comprehending the Trump phenomenon. *Royal Society Open Science, 4*(3). https://doi.org/10.1098/rsos.160802

Taber, C. (2003). Information processing and public opinion. In D. O. Sears, L. Huddy & R. Jervis (Eds.), *The Oxford handbook of political psychology* (pp. 433–476). Oxford University Press.

Tewksbury, D., & Althaus, S. L. (2000). Differences in knowledge acquisition among readers of the paper and online versions of a national newspaper. *Journalism & Mass Communication Quarterly, 77*(3), 457–479. https://doi.org/10.1177/107769900007700301

Thorson E. (2016). Belief echoes: The persistent effects of corrected misinformation. *Political Communication, 33*(3), 460–80. https://doi.org/10.1080/10584609.2015.1102187

Thorson, E. A., Shelbe, L., & Southwell, B. G. (2018). An agenda for misinformation research. In B. G. Southwell, E. A. Thorson, & L. Sheble (Eds.), *Misinformation and mass audiences* (pp. 289–293). University of Texas Press.

Van Aelst, P., Strömbäck, J., Aalberg, T., Esser, F., De Vreese, C., Matthes, J., … & Stanyer, J. (2017). Political communication in a high-choice media environment: a challenge for democracy? *Annals of the International Communication Association, 41*(1), 3–27. https://doi.org/10.1080/23808985.2017.1288551

Vinopal, C. (2021, July 2). 2 out of 3 American believe U.S. democracy is under threat. PBS NewsHour. www.pbs.org/newshour/politics/2-out-of-3-americans-believe-u-s-democracy-is-under-threat

Vosoughi, S., Roy, D., & Aral, S. (2018). The spread of true and false news online. *Science, 359*(6380), 1146–1151. https://doi.org/10.1126/science.aap9559

Waisbord, S. (2018). The elective affinity between post-truth communication and populist politics. *Communication Research and Practice, 4*(1), 17–34. https://doi.org/10.1080/22041451.2018.1428928

Webster, J. G. (2014). *The marketplace of attention: How audiences take shape in a digital age.* MIT Press.

Webster, J. G., & Ksiazek, T. B. (2012). The dynamics of audience fragmentation: Public attention in an age of digital media. *Journal of Communication, 62*(1), 39–56. https://doi.org/10.1111/j.1460-2466.2011.01616.x

Weeks, B. E. (2018). Media and political misperceptions. In B. G. Southwell, E. A. Thorson & L. Sheble (Eds.), *Misinformation and mass audiences* (pp. 140–156). University of Texas Press. https://doi.org/10.7560/314555

Weeks, B. E., & Garrett, R. K. (2014). Electoral consequences of political rumors: Motivated reasoning, candidate rumors, and vote choice during the 2008 U.S. presidential election. *International Journal of Public Opinion Research, 26*(4), 401–422. https://doi.org/10.1093/ijpor/edu005

Weeks, B. E., Lane, D. S., Kim, D. H., Lee, S. S., and Kwak, N. (2017). Incidental exposure, selective exposure, and political information sharing: Integrating online exposure patterns and expression on social media. *Journal of Computer-Mediated Communication, 22*(6), 363–379. https://doi.org/10.1111/jcc4.12199

Yoshida, A., Higurashi, T., Maruishi, M., Tateiwa, N., Hata, N., Tanaka, A., … & Fujisawa, K. (2020). New performance index "attractiveness factor" for evaluating websites via obtaining transition of users' interests. *Data Science and Engineering, 5*(1), 48–64. https://doi.org/10.1007/s41019-019-00112-1

Zaller, J. R. (1992). *The nature and origins of mass opinion.* Cambridge University Press.

Zaller, J., & Feldman, S. (1992). A simple theory of the survey response: Answering questions versus revealing preferences. *American Journal of Political Science, 36*(3), 579–616. https://doi.org/10.2307/2111583

PART II

Measurement Approaches to News Quality

3

SOCIAL MEDIA METRICS AND NEWS QUALITY

Jieun Shin

Social media have become a major pathway to news in the past decade. According to a Pew Research Center survey (Shearer & Mitchell, 2021), one in four adults in the United States say that they often get news via social media platforms, such as Facebook, YouTube, and Twitter. Social media surpassed print newspapers as a source of news in 2017. For example, approximately 40 percent of Twitter users indicate that the main reason they use the platform is to follow news (Shin, 2020). This trend of news consumption via social media is likely to grow in the future because younger generations tend to rely on social media sites for news (Kalogeropoulous, 2019; Nielsen et al., 2020).

Social media are a popular news venue, in part because they offer a variety of ways to engage with news. People can create their own media repertoire by actively following a set of news media accounts. They can also passively encounter news through friends' sharing behaviors and the recommendation algorithms of the platform (Fletcher & Nielsen, 2018). Indirect news exposure is so prevalent that people widely assume that news will eventually find them through social networks, if it is important enough (Gil de Zúñiga et al., 2017). Social media users can also express their opinions about news content and check the social responses of others via platform features, such as shares, comments, and likes. Thus, today social media serve as a one-stop shop where one can enjoy news streaming in from different brands, curated by both the consumer and other users.

As the role of social media grows for the dissemination of news, audience metrics generated by these social media sites are becoming increasingly important (Dwyer & Martin, 2017). On the one hand, they provide information about audience feedback—specifically, what people find to be worth their attention and sharing (Carlson, 2020). Such reactions can be instructive in terms of which stories will be well received. On the other hand, audience data reveal meta-information

DOI: 10.4324/9781003257998-5

about the underlying quality of news stories and the status of the media outlets (Dwyer & Martin, 2017). The number of followers, shares, and likes can serve as heuristic cues for news consumers, and subsequently affect perceptions of credibility regarding the message and the source (Waddell, 2018). In this sense, social media metrics function as an alternative measure that gauges the relative performance and authority of the news media, similar to the circulations and viewership numbers previously used by newspapers and TV programs (Napoli, 2011).

Social media metrics are a conundrum for the media, and for journalists who care about providing high-quality news. Although the numbers generated by social media users can provide legitimate feedback from the audience, there are also concerns that over-reliance on these metrics can lead to market-driven journalism, ultimately posing a threat to provision of high-quality news (Hanusch & Tandoc, 2019). Social media metrics are multifaceted, representing the many different reasons that social media users consume news. News users may be driven by entertainment values, social bonding, political expression, and information needs. Sometimes, social metrics are a result of automatic psychological responses and an artifact of a self-breeding mechanism whereby popularity begets further popularity (Ciampaglia et al., 2018; Salganik et al., 2006). Metrics can also be manipulated through algorithms that promote certain content over others (Webster, 2014). Nonetheless, because these numbers provide competitive advantages to news organizations, many news outlets are incentivized to prioritize content that caters to the appetite of social media users, rather than high-quality news.

The following sections discuss the multifaceted nature of social media metrics, and ways to understand the complex relationships between social media logic and news quality, drawing on the literature from the fields of journalism, economics, and psychology. Prior to this discussion, I first define high-quality news from a normative journalistic view and consider whether such a concept is measurable. Then, I will explain how the current social media space is not designed to promote high-quality news, but rather to maximize user interest and engagement.

News quality

The quality of news is difficult to measure because there are no agreed-upon standards that satisfy everyone's definition of high quality. The term *quality* generally refers to any attribute, service, or performance that is highly valued within a group or a community (Gambetta, 2009; Podolny, 2010). Defining quality is thus context-dependent, field-specific, and subject to individual preferences and tastes. It is important to note, however, that compared to other cultural products such as music and paintings, journalistic content is unique because it has a strong civic and democratic component. The idea of the press as the "fourth estate" stems from the expectation that high-quality journalism promotes democratic ideals by playing the role of a watchdog, providing a public forum, and serving as a reliable information provider (McNair, 2009; Nielsen, 2019). Therefore, when discussing news quality, normative aspects cannot be overemphasized.

Media scholars and journalists have extensively discussed what constitutes good journalism—some of which includes accuracy, comprehensiveness, transparency, objectivity, originality, diversity, and relevance (Bachmann et al., 2022; Fürst, 2020; Lacy & Rosenstiel, 2015; Prochazka et al., 2018). Of these, certain news qualities are easier to identify than others. According to the economists' typology, there are three types of commodities based on the level of difficulty in estimating the quality of the product or service: search goods, experience goods, and credence goods (Darby & Kami, 1973; Nelson, 1970). Search goods are those whose quality can be estimated reliably by inspecting product information before consumption. Examples of search goods include furniture, laptops, and other durables. Experience goods refers to products or services whose quality can only be determined upon consumption. Movies, music, and food are some examples. However, credence goods are commodities whose qualities cannot be determined, even immediately after experiencing the service or product. For example, the quality of legal services, education, and insurance products can only be determined in the long term, or via the judgement of skilled experts.

Drawing on this classification, media scholars have categorized news either as experience goods or credence goods, depending on what qualities are under consideration (McManus, 1995; Nielsen, 2019). For example, the comprehensiveness of a news story and the presentation style of news can be evaluated by a consumer immediately upon experiencing the news. Similarly, it is relatively easy to determine the degree of transparency (e.g., whether the story is disclosing the source) in a news story. According to these dimensions, *news* falls into the category of experience goods. However, some components of quality cannot be evaluated immediately upon the consumption of news. For example, it is not always easy to assess whether a news story is accurate. Oftentimes, verification requires a dedicated team to fact-check the truth of a statement. Similarly, the extent to which a news story is original can be only determined by comparing it with other news stories. This implies that determining high news quality is not an easy task and requires costly investments in terms of human labor and media literacy skills.

When it comes to real-world applications of evaluating news quality, there are generally two approaches. The first approach employs a minimal threshold for news quality, focusing on detecting false content that is explicitly harmful to a democracy or public health. This view is aligned with the broad concept of false information, such as fake news, misinformation, and disinformation. Most professional fact-checking organizations, such as Snopes and Factcheck.org, investigate the veracity of popular rumors circulating on social media, statements made by politicians, and news stories. Similarly, social media platforms focus on ferreting out outright false content from the rest of the site by partnering with third-party fact-checkers and developing machine learning techniques to scale the process. With this low-threshold quality approach, "news" does not receive any special distinction and is treated similarly to other types of information, using the same standards.

The second approach raises the bar to a higher standard by incorporating the journalistic values and professional norms into the evaluation of news quality. For decades, various journalism awards have undertaken this role. For example, as some of the most prestigious awards in journalism, the Pulitzer Prizes have been awarded each year since 1971 to news organizations that produce high-quality stories and employ best practices in the field (Jenkins & Volz, 2018; Lanosga, 2015). Quality judgements for the Pulitzer Prizes are made by juries, comprised of expert news editors, writers, and academics. The *New York Times* is known for winning the most Pulitzer Prizes, which positions it at the top of professional journalistic institutions (Usher, 2014). In addition, there are other prestigious awards such as the Peabody Awards and the Dupont Awards, that recognize excellence of broadcast journalism (Murray, 1999).

However, these journalism awards are usually limited to a handful of the mainstream news organizations because their goal is to boost the reputation of high-quality news producers and encourage best practices, rather than penalize bad actors. In the past few years, several projects have been launched to fill this gap by providing quality assessments for a comprehensive list of news outlets. For example, NewsGuard was founded in 2018 and currently rates over 7,000 news websites from around the world on a scale from 0 (lowest quality) to 100 (highest quality). Scores are determined by a team of full-time journalists and based on nine categories, including correction policy, accurate and factual content, transparency about ownership, use of credible information sources, separation between opinions and news, clear disclosure of advertising, revealing conflicts of interest, provision of names of content creators, and avoidance of deceptive headlines. Although not in the form of numeric indicators, other projects such as NewsQ and The Trust Project similarly provide a tool that assesses the extent to which a news website follows the best journalistic practices (e.g., explaining ownerships and funding sources of news sites). However, it should be noted that these projects assess the overall credibility of the news outlet, not the quality of news content. This limitation comes from the difficulty to track and evaluate individual articles flooding into the Internet.

Relationship between news quality and social media popularity

A small but growing body of literature has empirically examined the prevalence and success of low-quality news on social media, and the endangerment of quality journalism in the digital platform era. Typically, this line of research has adopted the minimal definition of quality in news (i.e., veracity) and investigated how false news and rumors are received on social media in comparison to true news and rumor corrections. For example, one large-scale study (Vosoughi et al., 2018) found that false news reached more people and spread faster on Twitter than true news. In this study, news was defined as any claim on social media that was verified by fact-checking organizations, including political rumors. The authors argued that the novelty effect of false news could explain its faster and wider spread compared with true news. Another study similarly found that social media posts containing an URL from a misinformation website were shared at a higher rate than posts containing URLs to high-quality information sites (Singh et al., 2020).

Beyond false news, a few other studies (Shin & Ognyanova, 2022) have looked at how journalistic quality is related to the level of social media engagement. One study (Shin & Ognyanova, 2022) examined the extent to which news outlets' reputation and credibility related to various types of social media engagements using a representative sample of Twitter users. They found that news organizations with more prestigious awards had more followers and higher levels of engagement than others. However, when holding this brand reputation constant, source credibility did not matter much for social media popularity. That is, that there were no significant differences between high-quality news sources and low-quality news sources in terms of how much attention and retweets they received from users. Moreover, the study found that during some periods of time, news posts from low-quality news outlets generated more engagement (i.e., retweets) than content from high-quality news outlets. In particular, the discrepancy between source quality and social media engagement was found to be larger among conservative users than liberal users.

Although these metrics are not a perfect measure of news quality alone, especially given that they are measured at the news outlet level rather than the content level, they still serve as a useful benchmark to track the performance of quality journalism in social media. The findings of the studies available to date portend ominous signs for the future of journalism. In the past decade, anecdotal evidence and the sentiment shared among journalists have been pessimistic about social media dynamics, consistent with recent empirical findings. Hamilton Nolan (2020), the public editor of the *Washington Post*, expressed a concern that social media has turned legitimate newspapers into entities that compete with hyperpartisan commentators, putting them all in the same bucket. Media scholar Philip Napoli (2019) also observed that "our media ecosystem is now evolving in such a direction that the gap between normative theory and empirical reality is no longer just a gap but something much greater and more dangerous" (p. 131). All in all, the current social media environment and logic cast the future of journalism into an unfavorable light.

What, then, can explain the limited role of quality in the audience reception of news on social media? How does an abundance of low-quality news influence the news industry, and how can the observed decoupling between quality and news engagement on social media be mitigated, if at all? The questions are considered in the section below.

Drivers of social media engagement

The "marketplace of ideas" metaphor is often used in debates about how social media should be treated, and whether an intervention is necessary (Napoli, 2019; Webster, 2014). The marketplace concept contends that truth and high-quality ideas will rise to the top through competition, according to the laws of supply and demand. In this model, audience members are assumed to behave rationally and independently by weighing the quality of information and consuming what is best for them and the public. However, the idea of social media users as rational, interested, and accuracy-oriented news consumers does not reflect reality.

First, news consumption on social media is not necessarily influenced by users' judgement of news quality. The behavior of people on social media is, to a great extent, socially motivated. Thus, information quality may not be a key determinant of engagement for social media users. For instance, the partisan selective exposure and selective sharing literature (Shin, 2020; Stroud, 2017) suggests that an individual's partisan identity plays a critical role in message exposure and sharing. Because content sharing is visible to the followers of a user and publicly available to others, those with a strong political identity may share posts that are favorable to their own group, with little consideration of news quality. In addition, social media users may follow or share content for entertainment value rather than informational value. Many previous studies (Ng & Zhao, 2020; Tenenboim & Cohen, 2015) have shown that people respond to novel, sensational, and alarming news content, thereby increasing its visibility.

Second, audience metrics—a measure of news consumption—can also be an artifact of algorithmic output, which is irrespective of underlying quality. Today, the attention of social media users is increasingly shaped by a platform's algorithms such as ranking and recommendations. For example, more than 70 percent of YouTube views are driven by YouTube's recommendation algorithm (Solsman, 2018). Also, the rank positions of content through a search algorithm are a strong predictor of visibility and click-through rates. Studies have shown that higher-ranked content is more likely to be clicked and engaged with, even when lower-ranked content is more relevant to the user's search (Epstein & Robertson, 2015; Unkel & Haas, 2017).

These gatekeeping and agenda-setting roles were traditionally tasked to news editors, who determined newsworthiness. However, news curation is now increasingly determined by blackbox-like algorithms involving hundreds of parameters (Bandy & Diakopoulos, 2020; Thorson, 2020). Some of these parameters correspond to quality signals. Facebook (2021) argues that its news feed algorithm promotes original, authoritative, and accurate news content, for instance by incorporating the misinformation warning labels provided by third-party fact-checkers. However, the recommendation algorithms prioritize popularity over quality since they are fundamentally designed to maximize user engagement (Smith & Linden, 2017). One study (DeVito, 2017) examined how in Facebook's own press releases and other documents discussing its News Feed feature, content quality was much less frequently mentioned than content popularity such as comments, likes, clicks, and shares. Another study found that Amazon's algorithms recommend anti-vaccine books to target users based on popularity, consumption of other users with similar interests, and items previously liked (Shin & Valente, 2020).

Power of popularity cues

The rewards of being popular on social media are immense, and are consistent with a "rich get richer" phenomenon. The famous music lab experiment conducted by Salganik and colleagues (2006) illustrates this point well. The authors created an artificial "music market" in which participants could listen to and download unknown songs under various conditions. When participants arrived sequentially and could see how other previous participants downloaded and rated the songs, their own choices and ratings were strongly influenced by the judgement of others. The process is similar to the "band-wagon" effect and the "preferential attachment" phenomenon. Many have argued that this social mechanism can widen the success gap between popular and unpopular songs, giving a cumulative advantage to earlier popular items (DiPrete & Eirich, 2006; Zhu & Lerman, 2016).

Popularity or public attention on social media can be both tangible and intangible assets for organizations and actors. Saxton and Guo (2014), for instance, developed the notion of "social media capital" as a new genre of resources provided by social media sites. Social media capital is a directly observable resource that can be monitored through metrics such as the number of followers, shares, and likes. Such publicly available evaluations of users' experiences and opinions have important consequences for "the formation of organizational reputation, understood as the prominence of an organization in the public's mind and collective perceptions" (Etter et al,. 2019, p. 3). Once accumulated, social media capital can further be leveraged to achieve other resources and outcomes, both financial or non-financial, such as reputation (Saxton & Guo, 2020).

Likewise, social media capital is an important tangible and intangible resource for news organizations. Many news organizations rely on digital advertising to support their journalism (Pew, 2021). Currently, the digital advertising market is dominated by Google and Facebook, who earn 60 percent of all U.S. digital advertising revenue (Dang, 2019). Only a small fraction goes to the news media, according to the number of clicks and views by social media users. In particular, social media metrics attract advertisers because they are "visible, accessible and seemingly such transparent markers of popularity and engagement" (Baym, 2013). Although this stream of revenue is not nearly enough for professional news organizations to alleviate current economic challenges and produce expensive news coverage (Myllylahti, 2018), this flow of money may provide motivation to content farmers to produce cheap clickbait content (Munger, 2020).

More importantly, social media capital can provide symbolic resources, such as reputation and legitimacy, that are critical for journalistic institutions (Baym, 2013; Shin & Ognyanova, 2022). Although news organizations comprise the same field, individual media outlets compete over status. In this sense, social media can be a powerful status-generating machine that sorts accounts hierarchically, based on the numbers of followers and retweets. These numbers are indicative of the ability of an individual news outlet to command the public's attention and influence the public agenda (Himelboim & Golan, 2019). Having a higher status also provides actors and organizations with various practical advantages, leading to their "rich get richer" phenomenon. For example, prestigious news organizations can hire talented journalists, collaborate with other powerful actors (e.g., columnists), and interview high-profile figures (e.g., the President) more easily than less prestigious news organizations.

At the micro-level, more popular content can give the impression of better quality and legitimate content. Despite the lack of a strong relationship between popularity and actual underlying content quality, when it is difficult to observe quality directly, people rely on available cues to infer it. The dual process framework, a well-established theory of human cognition, suggests that cognition and behavior can be categorized by two mental processing types (Chaiken, 1987; Evans & Stanovich, 2013; Kahneman, 2003). One type involves intuitive, effortless, and heuristic processing. The other type involves deliberate, effortful, and analytic processing. The two types are commonly referred to as *Type 1* and *Type 2*. Previous studies have shown that people resort to heuristic cues in making decisions and forming attitudes, especially in situations characterized by information overload and high uncertainty (Go et al., 2014; Metzger & Flanagin, 2015; Sundar et al., 2007).

Social media are filled with information shortcuts that users use to form quality judgements (Munger, 2020). Indeed, previous studies examining the attitudes and behaviors of social media users have found that the endorsement of news stories by other users has a powerful effect on the perception of news quality (Chung, 2017; Luo et al., 2020). For example, Chung (2017) showed that the effects of social media metrics are particularly strong when the credibility of the news media is low. This suggests that when social media users confront news outlets with whom they are not familiar, they are more likely to use other people's reactions to news (e.g., the number of retweets) as a proxy of news quality and to be influenced by such information. This example demonstrates exactly how social media capital can lend an air of legitimacy to clickbait sites and hyper-partisan news sites (Munger, 2020)

Consequences of the current social media ecosystem

Above, I have summarized two conditions that help predict the future of journalism by focusing on social media, a major conduit to current news and a special type of attention market. That is, first, social media algorithms and metrics are not designed to favor high-quality journalistic content. The current metrics (followers, shares, likes) can be expressions of different motivations, including one's partisan identity and entertainment, or an artifact of algorithms that are unrelated to journalistic quality. Second, nonetheless, attention and engagement garnered from social media serve as important resources for news organizations. They not only implicate advertising dollars, but also give a competitive advantage to popular news outlets, elevating their status in the field of journalism. People tend to consume what seems to be popular, and at times to infer quality from audience metrics.

The reward system set up by social media, as well as the impact of metrics, point in the direction of a "market failure." A market failure describes "situations where public goods, such as news and information are given inadequate support, having detrimental effects on society" (Pickard, 2019, p. 155). Although this concern has long been raised, social media seems to have worsened the condition by providing an extreme version of market-driven journalism. High-quality news (e.g., investigative reporting and in-depth analysis) is expensive and labor intensive to produce. By contrast, low-quality news, such as fake news, is cheap to produce and easy to spread. Unlike genuine journalism, which is bounded by facts, fake news has no limits as to what it can imagine. Content can be created on a whim and is inherently more interesting—key ingredients for viral spread. In other words, in the current digital media environment, low-quality news can easily outperform high-quality news in terms of ROI (return on investment).

The unfair competitive advantage enjoyed by low-quality news has the potential to slowly drive out high-quality news media. Economists call this phenomenon the "lemons problem" (Akerlof, 1970), which refers to decreasing overall quality of products or services, thus lemons, in a market. Eventually, the negative consequences of a lemons market fall on consumers who are not able to get high-quality goods easily. In particular, in the context of the news market, low-quality news (e.g., misinformation) has negative externalities that go beyond its effect on the individuals who directly consume it, such as regrettable election results based on false information, as well as decreased trust in news media institutions.

A recent study (Tandoc Jr. et al., 2021) showed that experiencing fake news, whether intentionally or unintentionally, can decrease a user's trust in the news media as a whole. Moreover, decreased news quality is already evident in some mainstream news media, whereby editors prioritize eye-catching news headlines and soft news over original news and hard news. Studies have shown that, for newsrooms, the tabloidization of news is linked to economic pressure and an obsession with performance on social media (Fürst, 2020; Lamot, 2022; Lischka & Garz, 2021). This type of news pollution may occur so gradually that people may not notice the damage in the process. A decreased quality of news in the mainstream media may be even more serious than the serious problem of fake news and misinformation.

Proposed solutions for preventing a lemons market

To mitigate the problem, many ideas have been called upon for consideration. These potential solutions can be grouped into those that are internal to social media space, and those that reflect a fundamental change in the economic system faced by journalism.

First, scholars have argued for the importance of public interest-minded algorithms that promote societal good (Diakopoulos, 2015; Napoli, 2019). As mentioned above, several projects currently provide indicators of news quality (e.g., NewsGuard) in an attempt to channel public attention toward the high-quality content that matters in a functioning democratic society. The key goal of these projects is to feed algorithms with quality-related signals so that the platforms recommend and give visibility to high-quality news. Although this sounds like an easy technological solution, social media algorithms are primarily concerned with maximizing user interest and profits, rather than public interests; thus, an intense struggle remains between those who try to put pressure on platform operation and the tech firms that resist this outside pressure.

Related to strengthening the civic role of algorithms, some have argued that social media should experiment with a tool that gives users an option to directly evaluate quality in terms of accuracy or overall news quality, rather than relying on popularity features such as retweets and likes (Pennycook & Rand, 2019; Shin & Ognyanova, 2022). Crowd-based quality control measures have the potential to be scalable and reliable, if users are nudged in the right direction. A few previous studies have provided evidence that trust ratings of news articles from crowds are reasonably consistent and correlated with those of experts, such as fact-checkers (Bachmann et al., 2022; Pennycook & Rand, 2019). Other studies have shown that simply nudging people to think about accuracy before sharing news on social media improves choices about what to share (Andi & Akesson, 2020; Pennycook et al., 2020).

In January 2021, as part of this endeavor, Twitter launched a pilot program called "Birdwatch" that enables average users to flag tweets as misleading and add notes to the questionable tweets (Allen et al., 2021). Although the program narrowly focuses on misinformation and harmful content, insights gained could be applied to building a healthier digital news ecosystem. Incorporating audience feedback into news-making, albeit in aggregated form, does not inherently lead to market-driven journalism, and may facilitate public representation and be a partial remedy to the problem of media elitism in the United States.

However, it should be recognized that certain caveats and conditions would render user feedback on quality more or less reliable. As a whole, social media users are not representative of the general public, and many social media accounts are bots (Elvestad & Phillips, 2018). Social media users tend to be younger, better educated, and more liberal than non-users (Mellon & Prosser, 2017). Therefore, to ensure diversity and representativeness, the system would require information about each user who participates in the quality ratings including demographic information (e.g., pre-registration). In addition, ratings from non-partisan third-party organizations (e.g., The Trust Project), or a consortium that consists of experts, could complement a citizen rating model. Although no rating or social feature is likely to be immune from biases, it would be worth trying a self-correcting mechanism to mitigate the current popularity-based contest.

The third approach to sustaining quality journalism could be through long-term subsidies for the public news media, provided through governments, foundations, or tech companies. Due to its nature as a public good, quality news is under-provisioned (Cagé, 2016; Napoli, 2019). Even though people acknowledge the civic benefits of the press, few people want to pay for quality news. Instead, they gravitate toward free options available on social media and the Internet (Chyi & Ng, 2020). Like other public goods, such as public education and the postal service, the market alone is insufficient to fund the distribution of quality news. The case in point is the disappearance of local news, a pillar of local communities and democracy, giving a rise to "news deserts" in the U.S. According to a recent report (Abernathy, 2020), more than a quarter of the U.S. newspapers have closed since 2004, with most of those being local newspapers.

For this reason, Victor Pickard and others have strongly advocated for a stable stream of government funding for journalism (Pickard, 2019). Indeed, the United States has a far smaller sector of government-funded public media compared to other democratic countries, such as the United Kingdom, Norway, and Sweden (Pickard & Neff, 2021). Others (Benson, 2018) have considered foundation-funded journalism as a viable option. Over the last decade, there has been a trend for private foundations to financially support investigative reporting and public service-oriented news (Ferrucci & Nelson, 2019; Konieczna, 2018). Also, support from tech companies such as Google and Facebook have been suggested as a solution to the problem of underfunding in journalism, despite the fact that these companies have played a central role in dismantling the traditional advertising model for news (Ingram, 2018).

Each solution has its own potential disadvantages and conflicts of interest. Although there is no consensus on how to solve the problems that journalism faces today, it is widely agreed that journalism is too vulnerable and yet too essential to be left to market whims. Social media, the dominant type of marketplace of attention, is not designed to preserve journalism and surface quality news. Social media, once touted as a free and open-networked public sphere, has become a numbers game that rewards content popularity over quality (Watts & Rothschild, 2017). This concern calls for an intervention, be it through algorithm redesign, quality nudging, or subsidies for quality journalism. To be sure, it is a highly complex, interdependent, and unstable problem, and thus requires an interdisciplinary approach to find solutions.

References

Abernathy, P. M. (2020). *News deserts and ghost newspapers: Will local news survive?* University of North Carolina Press.

Akerlof, G. A. (1970). The market for "lemons": Quality uncertainty and the market mechanism. *Quarterly Journal of Economics, 84*(3), 488–500.

Allen, J., Arechar, A. A., Pennycook, G., & Rand, D. G. (2021). Scaling up fact-checking using the wisdom of crowds. *Science Advances, 7*(36). https://doi.org/10.1126/sciadv.abf4393

Andı, S., & Akesson, J. (2020). Nudging away false news: Evidence from a social norms experiment. *Digital Journalism, 9*(1), 106–125. https://doi.org/10.1080/21670811.2020.1847674

Bachmann, P., Eisenegger, M., & Ingenhoff, D. (2022). Defining and measuring news media quality: Comparing the content perspective and the audience perspective. *The International Journal of Press/Politics, 27*(1) 9–37 https://doi.org/10.1177/1940161221999666

Bandy, J., & Diakopoulos, N. (2020, May). Auditing news curation systems: A case study examining algorithmic and editorial logic in apple news. In *Proceedings of the International AAAI Conference on Web and Social Media, 14*, 36–47. https://ojs.aaai.org/index.php/ICWSM/article/view/7277

Baym, N. K. (2013). Data not seen: The uses and shortcomings of social media metrics. *First Monday, 18*(10). https://doi.org/10.5210/fm.v18i10.4873

Benson, R. (2018). Can foundations solve the journalism crisis? *Journalism, 19*(8), 1059–1077. https://doi.org/10.1177/1464884917724612

Cagé, J. (2016). *Saving the media.* Harvard University Press.

Carlson, M. (2020). *Measurable journalism: Digital platforms, news metrics and the quantified audience.* Routledge.

Chaiken, S. (1987). The heuristic model of persuasion. In M. P. Zanna, J. M. Olson, C. P. Herman (Eds.), *Social influence: The Ontario Symposium* (Vol. 5, pp. 3–39). Psychology Press.

Chyi, H. I., & Ng, Y. M. M. (2020). Still unwilling to pay: An empirical analysis of 50 US newspapers' digital subscription results. *Digital Journalism, 8*(4), 526–547. https://doi.org/10.1080/21670811.2020.1732831

Chung, M. (2017). Not just numbers: The role of social media metrics in online news evaluations. *Computers in Human Behavior, 75*, 949–957. https://doi.org/10.1016/j.chb.2017.06.022

Ciampaglia, G. L., Nematzadeh, A., Menczer, F., & Flammini, A. (2018). How algorithmic popularity bias hinders or promotes quality. *Scientific Reports, 8*(1), 1–7. https://doi.org/10.1038/s41598-018-34203-2

Dang, S. (2019). Google, Facebook have tight grip on growing U.S. online ad market: Report. *Reuters.* www.reuters.com/article/us-alphabet-facebook-advertising/google-facebook-have-tight-grip-on-growing-u-s-online-ad-market-report-idUSKCN1T61IV

Darby, M. R., & Karni, E. (1973). Free competition and the optimal amount of fraud. *The Journal of Law and Economics, 16*(1), 67–88. https://doi.org/10.1086/466756

DeVito, M. A. (2017). From editors to algorithms: A values-based approach to understanding story selection in the Facebook news feed. *Digital Journalism, 5*(6), 753–773. https://doi.org/10.1080/21670811.2016.1178592

Diakopoulos, N. (2015). Algorithmic accountability: Journalistic investigation of computational power structures. *Digital Journalism, 3*(3), 398–415.

Diakopoulos, N. (2019). *Automating the news.* Harvard University Press.

DiPrete, T. A., & Eirich, G. M. (2006). Cumulative advantage as a mechanism for inequality: A review of theoretical and empirical developments. *Annual Review of Sociology, 32*, 271–297. https://doi.org/10.1146/annurev.soc.32.061604.123127

Dwyer, T., & Martin, F. (2017). Sharing news online: Social media news analytics and their implications for media pluralism policies. *Digital Journalism, 5*(8), 1080–1100. https://doi.org/10.1080/21670811.2017.1338527

Elvestad, E., & Phillips, A. (2018). *Misunderstanding news audiences: Seven myths of the social media era.* Routledge.

Epstein, R., & Robertson, R. E. (2015). The search engine manipulation effect (SEME) and its possible impact on the outcomes of elections. *Proceedings of the National Academy of Sciences, 112*(33), E4512–E4521. https://doi.org/10.1073/pnas.1419828112

Etter, M., Ravasi, D., & Colleoni, E. (2019). Social media and the formation of organizational reputation. *Academy of Management Review, 44*(1), 28–52 https://doi.org/10.5465/amr.2014.0280

Evans, J. S. B., & Stanovich, K. E. (2013). Dual-process theories of higher cognition: Advancing the debate. *Perspectives on Psychological Science, 8*(3), 223–241. https://doi.org/10.1177/1745691612460685

Facebook (2021). News content on Facebook. www.facebook.com/business/help/224099772719228

Ferrucci, P., & Nelson, J. L. (2019). The new advertisers: How foundation funding impacts journalism. *Media and Communication, 7*(4), 45–55. https://doi.org/10.17645/mac.v7i4.2251

Fletcher, R., & Nielsen, R. K. (2018). Are people incidentally exposed to news on social media? A comparative analysis. *New Media & Society, 20*(7), 2450–2468. https://doi.org/10.1177/1461444817724170

Fürst, S. (2020). In the service of good journalism and audience interests? How audience metrics affect news quality. *Media and Communication, 8*(3), 270–280. https://doi.org/10.17645/mac.v8i3.3228

Gambetta, D. (2009). Signaling. In P. Bearman & P. Hedström (Eds.), *The Oxford handbook of analytical sociology* (pp. 168–194). Oxford University Press. https://doi.org/10.1093/oxfordhb/9780199215362.013.8

Gil de Zúñiga, H., Weeks, B., & Ardèvol-Abreu, A. (2017). Effects of the news-finds-me perception in communication: Social media use implications for news seeking and learning about politics. *Journal of Computer-Mediated Communication, 22*(3), 105–123. https://doi.org/10.1111/jcc4.12185

Go, E., Jung, E. H., & Wu, M. (2014). The effects of source cues on online news perception. *Computers in Human Behavior, 38*, 358–367. https://doi.org/10.1016/j.chb.2014.05.044

Guo, C., & Saxton, G. D. (2014). Tweeting social change: How social media are changing nonprofit advocacy. *Nonprofit and Voluntary Sector Quarterly, 43*(1), 57–79. https://doi.org/10.1177/0899764012471585

Haas, A., & Unkel, J. (2017). Ranking versus reputation: perception and effects of search result credibility. *Behaviour & Information Technology, 36*(12), 1285–1298.

Hanusch, F., & Tandoc Jr., E. C. (2019). Comments, analytics, and social media: The impact of audience feedback on journalists' market orientation. *Journalism, 20*(6), 695–713. https://doi.org/10.1177/1464884917720305

Himelboim, I., & Golan, G. J. (2019). A social networks approach to viral advertising: The role of primary, contextual, and low influencers. *Social Media + Society, 5*(3). https://doi.org/10.1177/2056305119847516

Ingram, M. (2018, May 16) The platform patrons: How Facebook and Google became two of the biggest funders of journalism in the world. *Columbia Journalism Review.* www.cjr.org/special_report/google-facebook-journalism.php

Jenkins, J., & Volz, Y. (2018). Players and contestation mechanisms in the journalism field: A historical analysis of journalism awards, 1960s to 2000s. *Journalism Studies, 19*(7), 921–941. https://doi.org/10.1080/1461670X.2016.1249008

Kahneman, D. (2003). A perspective on judgment and choice: Mapping bounded rationality. *American Psychologist, 58*(9), 697. https://doi.org/10.1037/0003-066X.58.9.697

Kalogeropoulos, A. (2019) How younger generations consume news differently. Reuters Institute. https://www.digitalnewsreport.org/survey/2019/how-younger-generations-consume-news-differently/

Konieczna, M. (2018). *Journalism without profit: Making news when the market fails.* Oxford University Press.

Lacy, S., & Rosenstiel, T. (2015). *Defining and measuring quality journalism.* Rutgers School of Communication and Information.

Lamot, K. (2022). What the metrics say. The softening of news on the Facebook pages of mainstream media outlets. *Digital Journalism, 10*(4), 517–536. https://doi.org/10.1080/21670811.2021.1974917

Lanosga, G. (2015). The power of the prize: How an emerging prize culture helped shape journalistic practice and professionalism, 1917–1960. *Journalism, 16*(7), 953–967. https://doi.org/10.1177/1464884914550972

Lischka, J. A., & Garz, M. (2021). Clickbait news and algorithmic curation: A game theory framework of the relation between journalism, users, and platforms. *New Media & Society.* https://doi.org/10.1177/14614448211027174

Luo, M., Hancock, J. T., & Markowitz, D. M. (2020). Credibility perceptions and detection accuracy of fake news headlines on social media: Effects of truth-bias and endorsement cues. *Communication Research.* https://doi.org/10.1177/0093650220921321

McManus, J. (1995). A market-based model of news production. *Communication Theory, 5*(4), 301–338. https://doi.org/10.1111/j.1468-2885.1995.tb00113.x

McNair, B. (2009). Journalism and democracy. In K. Wahl-Jorgensen & T. Hanitzsch (Eds.), *The handbook of journalism studies* (pp. 257–269). Routledge.

Mellon, J., & Prosser, C. (2017). Twitter and Facebook are not representative of the general population: Political attitudes and demographics of British social media users. *Research & Politics, 4*(3). https://doi.org/10.1177/2053168017720008

Metzger, M. J., & Flanagin, A. J. (2015). Psychological approaches to credibility assessment online. In S. S. Sundar (Ed.), *The handbook of the psychology of communication technology,* (pp. 445–466). John Wiley & Sons. https://doi.org/10.1002/9781118426456.ch20

Munger, K. (2020). All the news that's fit to click: The economics of clickbait media. *Political Communication, 37*(3), 376–397. https://doi.org/10.1080/10584609.2019.1687626

Murray, M. D. (Ed.). (1999). *Encyclopedia of television news.* Greenwood Publishing Group.

Myllylahti, M. (2018). An attention economy trap? An empirical investigation into four news companies' Facebook traffic and social media revenue. *Journal of Media Business Studies, 15*(4), 237–253. https://doi.org/10.1080/16522354.2018.1527521

Napoli, P. M. (2011). *Audience evolution: New technologies and the transformation of media audiences.* Columbia University Press.

Napoli, P. M. (2019). *Social media and the public interest.* Columbia University Press.

Nelson, P. (1970, March–April). Information and Consumer Behavior. *Journal of Political Economy, 78*(2), 311–378.

Nielsen, R. K. (2019). Economic contexts of journalism. In n K. Wahl-Jorgensen & T. Hanitzsch (Eds.), *The handbook of journalism studies* (pp. 324–340). Routledge.

Nielsen, R., Fletcher, R., Newman, N., Brennen, S., & Howard, P. (2020). Navigating the 'infodemic': How people in six countries access and rate news and information about coronavirus. https://reutersinstitute.politics.ox.ac.uk/infodemic-how-people-six-countries-access-and-rate-news-and-information-about-coronavirus

Ng, Y. L., & Zhao, X. (2020). The human alarm system for sensational news, online news headlines, and associated generic digital footprints: A uses and gratifications approach. *Communication Research, 47*(2), 251–275. https://doi.org/10.1177/00936 50218793739

Nolan, H. (2020). Washington Post public editor: The powerful have realized they don't need the Post. *Columbia Journalism Review.* www.cjr.org/public_editor/washington-posttesla-trump-power.php

Pennycook, G., & Rand, D. G. (2019). Fighting misinformation on social media using crowdsourced judgments of news source quality. *Proceedings of the National Academy of Sciences, 116*(7), 2521–2526.

Pennycook, G. et al. (2020). Fighting COVID-19 misinformation on social media: Experimental evidence for a scalable accuracy-nudge intervention. *Psychological Science, 31*(7), 770–780. https://doi.org/10.1177/0956797620939054

Pew Research Center (2021). Newspapers fact sheet. https://www.pewresearch.org/jou rnalism/fact-sheet/newspapers/#economics

Pickard, V. (2019). *Democracy without journalism? Confronting the misinformation society.* Oxford University Press.

Pickard, V., & Neff, T. (2021, June 2). Op-ed: Strengthen our democracy by funding public media. *Columbia Journalism Review.* www.cjr.org/opinion/public-funding-media-democracy.php

Podolny, J. M. (2010). *Status signals.* Princeton University Press.

Prochazka, F., Weber, P., & Schweiger, W. (2018). Effects of civility and reasoning in user comments on perceived journalistic quality. *Journalism Studies, 19*(1), 62–78. https://doi.org/10.1080/1461670X.2016.1161497

Salganik, M. J., Dodds, P. S., & Watts, D. J. (2006). Experimental study of inequality and unpredictability in an artificial cultural market. *Science, 311*(5762), 854–856. https://doi.org/10.1126/science.1121066

Saxton, G. D., & Guo, C. (2020). Social media capital: Conceptualizing the nature, acquisition, and expenditure of social media-based organizational resources. *International Journal of Accounting Information Systems, 36*, https://doi.org/10.1016/j.accinf.2019.100443

Shearer, E., & Mitchell, A. (2021). News use across social media platforms in 2020. *Pew Research Center.* www.journalism.org/2021/01/12/news-use-across-social-media-platforms-in-2020

Shin, J. (2020). How do partisans consume news on social media? A comparison of self-reports with digital trace measures among Twitter users. *Social Media and Society, 6*(4). https://doi.org/10.1177/2056305120981039

Shin, J., & Ognyanova, K. (2022). Social media metrics in the digital marketplace of attention: Do journalistic capital matter for social media capital? *Digital Journalism, 10*(4), 579–598. https://doi.org/10.1080/21670811.2022.2031242

Shin, J., & Valente, T. (2020). Algorithms and health misinformation: A case study of vaccine books on Amazon. *Journal of Health Communication, 25*(5), 394–401. https://doi.org/10.1080/10810730.2020.1776423

Singh, L., Bode, L., Budak, C., Kawintiranon, K., Padden, C., & Vraga, E. (2020). Understanding high-and low-quality URL sharing on COVID-19 Twitter streams. *Journal of Computational Social Science, 3*(2), 343–366. https://doi.org/10.1007/s42001-020-00093-6

Smith, B., & Linden, G. (2017). Two decades of recommender systems at Amazon.com. *IEEE Internet Computing, 21*(3), 12–18. https://doi.org/10.1109/MIC.2017.72

Solsman, J. (2018, January 10). YouTube's AI is the puppet master over most of what you watch. *CNET*. www.cnet.com/tech/services-and-software/youtube-ces-2018-neal-mohan/

Stroud, N. J. (2017). Selective exposure theories. In K. Kenski & K. H. Jamieson (Eds.), *The Oxford handbook of political communication*. Oxford University Press.

Sundar, S. S., Knobloch-Westerwick, S., & Hastall, M. R. (2007). News cues: Information scent and cognitive heuristics. *Journal of the American Society for Information Science and Technology, 58*(3), 366–378. https://doi.org/10.1002/asi.20511

Tandoc Jr., E. C., Duffy, A., Jones-Jang, S. M., & Wen Pin, W. G. (2021). Poisoning the information well? The impact of fake news on news media credibility. *Journal of Language and Politics, 20*(5), 783–802. https://doi.org/10.1075/jlp.21029.tan

Tenenboim, O., & Cohen, A. A. (2015). What prompts users to click and comment: A longitudinal study of online news. *Journalism, 16*(2), 198–217. https://doi.org/10.1177/1464884913513996

Thorson, K. (2020). Attracting the news: Algorithms, platforms, and reframing incidental exposure. *Journalism, 21*(8), 1067–1082. https://doi.org/10.1177/1464884920915352

Usher, N. (2014). *Making news at the New York Times*. University of Michigan Press.

Vosoughi, S., Roy, D., & Aral, S. (2018). The spread of true and false news online. *Science, 359*(6380), 1146–1151.

Waddell, T. F. (2018). What does the crowd think? How online comments and popularity metrics affect news credibility and issue importance. *New Media & Society, 20*(8), 3068–3083.

Watts, D., & Rothschild, D. (2017). Rebuilding legitimacy in a post-truth age. https://medium.com/@duncanjwatts/rebuilding-legitimacy-in-a-post-truth-age-2f9af19855a5

Webster, J. G. (2014). *The marketplace of attention: How audiences take shape in a digital age*. MIT Press.

Zhu, L., & Lerman, K. (2016). Attention inequality in social media. arXiv preprint arXiv:1601.07200.

4

IS THAT NEWS FOR ME?

Defining news-ness by platform and topic

Emily K. Vraga and Stephanie Edgerly

Definitions of news are increasingly fraught in today's media environment. A long history has suggested that news holds "special status" in the imagination of the public, heralded for the role it plays in facilitating citizens to be informed and participatory members of democratic societies (Edgerly & Vraga, 2020a; Fiske, 1987; Schudson, 1998). More recent work has questioned whether this special status still applies, or whether the meaning of "news" and how it is recognized is undermined in a media environment where news can be found anywhere—from traditional news platforms (like a news organization website) to co-existing alongside a mishmash of content from a range of sources on social media feeds (Tong et al., 2020). Therefore, understanding *what* audiences perceive to be news and *how* they make these judgments is of paramount importance to scholars in journalism studies, political communication, democratic theory, or media psychology.

The concept of news-ness allows us to perform this interrogation of how audiences think about content quality. Edgerly and Vraga define news-ness as "the extent to which audiences characterize specific media content as news" and have demonstrated that source cues, content tone, and audience political orientations can influence assessments of news-ness (2019a, p. 808). In other words, news-ness represents what audiences perceive news to be and the degree to which any specific piece of content lives up to this internalized definition. Previous research shows that perceptions of high relevance, importance, and timeliness are associated with the concept of news (Sundar, 1999). Similarly, audience assessments of when news is of high quality are based on the content criteria of relevance, contextualization, professionalism, and diversity (Bachmann et al., 2022). As such, broader judgments about the degree to which a piece of media *is* news can be considered an important component of news credibility and quality (Edgerly & Vraga, 2020b).

DOI: 10.4324/9781003257998-6

50 Emily K. Vraga and Stephanie Edgerly

Edgerly and Vraga (2020a) propose a conceptual model of news-ness that urges researchers to consider what features influence audience assessments of news-ness, what news-ness means to audiences, and the implications of considering something as higher or lower in news-ness. This chapter squarely examines the first component of the model—the features of news-ness—to focus on how people make judgments about the news-ness of content depending on the platform on which a post is found (e.g., the Associated Press's website or Twitter). In addition, this chapter investigates the features of the content that people rely upon when making decisions about news-ness, and whether these differ for content seen on Twitter versus the website. We replicate this design for four issues, covering mental health and financial topics, that are important to the public (Horowitz & Graf, 2019; Kennedy & Funk, 2015). Our results suggest the *platform* on which information is found affects audience judgments of news-ness, but that many of the news cues being used to evaluate news-ness remain similar across platforms.

Platform effects

Platform differences in how audiences process information and make evaluations are well documented (Metzger et al., 2010; Newhagen & Nass, 1989). Early research studying online versus print news, for example, found that reading the *New York Times* in print produced different perceptions about the most important problem facing the country (i.e., an agenda setting effect) compared to reading the *New York Times* in web form (Althaus & Tewksbury, 2002). Similarly, Flanagin and Metzger (2000) found that audiences rated five types of news media (web, television, magazines, newspapers, radio) differently in credibility, with newspapers perceived as highest and no other differences among the remaining media types.

These medium-based differences are hardly coincidental. In sizing up the proliferation of media, Eveland, Jr. (2003) suggests that a "mix of attributes" approach is needed to better understand medium-based differences. That is, modern media are defined by their mixture of attributes (e.g., structure, control, interactivity), which provide different news experiences and produce different media effects. For example, audiences may rate print newspapers higher in credibility because audiences associate the medium with traditional storytelling structures, greater control, and low interactivity, as compared to similar content viewed online.

Questions of platform effects become even more important when we consider the different ways that information is presented in online spaces. Consider, for example, encountering the same news story on an organization's website compared to a social media site. Both are common ways of getting news—more Americans report getting news "often" from websites (33 percent) and social media (20 percent) compared to print newspapers (16 percent) (Shearer, 2018)—yet these spaces are distinct. They have a different mix of attributes, or structural design features (DeSanctis & Poole, 1994; Smock et al., 2011) that shape the experience of consuming news. Social media sites, for example, are more open.

Users see posts from a wide variety of users and groups, ranging from friends and family to community organizations, informal groups, and news organizations; from accounts people choose to follow to those they do not, like sponsored content (Thorson & Wells, 2016). As such, a news story can be sandwiched in between posts from friends and other non-news accounts. A different set of dynamics are at play when encountering a news story directly on an organization's website, where there is a consistent flow of content from a single known source, i.e., the news organization.

Ultimately, these platform differences create an environment with specific expectations for consuming news. According to Flanagin and Metzger (2007), one factor for assessing the credibility of a message is where it is located, and specifically, the website genre and design (p. 338). Social media sites are spaces where users commonly encounter news *and* are wary of its quality. Over 80 percent of U.S. adults say that "one-sided news" and "inaccurate news" is a "very big" or "moderately big problem" on social media sites (Shearer & Grieco, 2019). In contrast, news websites are digital representations of traditional newspapers, often mimicking the style and format of their print counterparts (Chadwick, 2013). As such, digital news websites tend to rate higher in credibility than social media websites (Boothby et al., 2021; Johnson & Kaye, 2014; Schmierbach & Oeldorf-Hirsch, 2012).

Thus far, the bulk of the research on platform differences has focused on credibility assessments—which are related to but meaningfully different from assessments of news quality or news-ness (Edgerly & Vraga, 2020a; 2020b). While research exists on how people understand information quality (Kim & Niehm, 2009) and on platform differences in news consumption and effects (e.g., dos Santos et al., 2019; Lee et al., 2022), to our knowledge, these studies have not been united to examine how the characteristics of platforms inform evaluations of news quality. Furthermore, many studies of news quality focus on the presence of specific reporting characteristics (Bachmann et al., 2022), while not considering audience evaluations about the overall genre. For example, a story with a low writing proficiency (e.g., awkward syntax, long quotes, no contextual information) was viewed as lower in news quality compared to a high-proficiency story (Molyneux & Coddington, 2020).

We begin this effort by studying platform effects in the context of news-ness. Edgerly and Vraga (2020a) theorize that where audiences encounter a specific piece of media can influence their ratings of news-ness. To test this argument, we compare a story headline posted to the Associated Press' website versus their Twitter account. Given that source has been a key factor in this previous research (Edgerly & Vraga 2019a; 2020b), we chose the Associated Press (AP) as the single, non-partisan, and well-known source (Gallup/Knight, 2018). We expect that the reputation of Twitter—as an open space for fake news, rumors, entertainment as well as news—will result in a tweet regarding a news story from the AP rating lower in news-ness than the same headline posted to the AP website.

Considering story elements across platforms

Related to platform effects are the specific interface cues that people use when evaluating media content (Go et al., 2014; Flanagin & Metzger, 2007). Whereas platform attributes describe the overall characteristics of a medium or website, platform cues are specific visible elements or tools. The attribute of interactivity, for example, can be seen by the specific cue of a website having a comment button. Admittedly, disentangling the differences between platform attributes and cues can be murky (Evans et al., 2017). For our purposes, we explore which specific elements or cues related to seeing a story on the AP's website versus Twitter are used when making assessments of news-ness.

When encountering information, people try to answer the question "what is going on here?" (Weick et al., 2005). In the case of news-ness, they will be considering the extent to which a specific piece of media is news. There are several *news cues* that aid this sensemaking about news. According to Sundar and colleagues (2007), news cues help people make quick judgments about news by triggering mental shortcuts about its quality, accuracy, and importance. For example, traditional offline news cues include story placement and headline size: A print newspaper story that is "above the fold" signals its heightened importance and newsworthiness (Althaus & Tewksbury, 2002; Boukes et al., 2020).

Many traditional offline news cues still apply to digital news websites. For example, prominence and placement of news stories remain important cues in the digital world (Lee et al., 2014). But digital media can also provide an additional set of cues (Go et al., 2014). Hinsley (2021) identifies eleven news cues including the date published, headline, author, photos/visuals, location URL, and links in the story. By paying attention to these elements, individuals can make quick assessments about whether or the degree to which something is news (Hinsley, 2021; Sundar et al., 2007).

Similarly, news cues help people make sense of information on social media platforms. Dvir-Gvirsman (2019) identified various "areas of interest," or cues, regarding a Facebook post containing a news story (e.g., source, headline, subheading text, picture, comments, reactions/likes). Using eye-tracking technology, she found that people pay the most attention to the story headline and subheading text, with the source of the post garnering the same attention as the comments responding to the post.

We are interested in the specific cues that individuals use when assessing levels of news-ness, and whether these cues differ on the website versus Twitter. In other words, when a person deems a story to be high in news-ness, what specific elements of the story help them in making this judgment, and are they the same across platforms? Based on past research, we expect that the headline, source, photo/visuals, and time published will be helpful in determining the extent to which a news story is considered news (Dvir-Gvirsman, 2019; Go et al., 2014; Hinsley, 2021; Sundar et al., 2007). On one hand, these news cues may be useful across platforms. That is, the same cues are helpful when accessing the news-ness of a story posted to the AP's website and the AP's Twitter feed. On the other hand, we might see platform differences with certain cues being more helpful for certain platforms. It might be that the time published is a more helpful news-ness cue for Twitter than it is for websites. Or it may be that certain platform-specific cues, like a source handle that includes a verification badge on Twitter, or the headline of a story that dominates the webpage for the website, are used more frequently.

Replicating across issues

Past studies of news-ness have only featured a single policy issue. However, the issue addressed in a story—which Edgerly and Vraga (2020a) describe as "what is communicated"—may also influence audiences' assessments of news-ness. For example, "hard" issue topics, such as politics, the economy, or business, are often contrasted with "soft" issues that focus on cultural or entertainment topics (Digital News Report, 2016; Scott & Gobetz, 1992)—with soft news approaches tending to be seen as lower in news-ness than hard news (Edgerly & Vraga, 2019a).

Given our focus on platform effects, we deliberately select four "hard" issues that should rate highly in news-ness overall by exploring issues related to mental health (depression and Alzheimer's) and finance (student loan debt and retirement savings). In doing so, we can assess whether platform differences in people's assessments of news-ness are relatively consistent, or whether platform effects on news-ness are idiosyncratic to a specific hard news issue.

Methods

To better understand how people make assessments about news-ness, we use an experimental design manipulating two factors: on which platform people saw the news post (Twitter post versus AP website), and the topic addressed in the news post. All participants saw a single image of the headline and lede of a news story from the Associated Press on one of four topics. Of the participants, 49.6 percent were randomly assigned to see the headline formatted to appear as if it was shared by the AP's verified account on Twitter, while 50.4 percent viewed the post as it would appear on the AP's website. Other than the necessary formatting differences associated with Twitter versus the website, all content between the two platforms was consistent. Additionally, within each platform, participants randomly saw one headline about a study finding an increase in (1) depression diagnoses, (2) Alzheimer's disease diagnoses, (3) student debt, or (4) a decrease in retirement savings.

Data were collected in July 2020 via the Lucid Theorem platform. Lucid uses a combination of screening questions and quota sampling on the basis of age, race, ethnicity, education, income, party affiliation, and region to construct online panel samples that approximate the U.S. population (Coppock & McClellan, 2019). A total of 786 participants completed the online questionnaire, of which 50.6 percent were female, 74.4 percent were white, 10.6 percent were Latino, and 12.2 percent were black; 49.7 percent of the sample had at least a college degree, with 41.2 percent identifying as Democrats, 18.3 percent as Independent, and 40.4 percent as Republican, and averaged 45 years old (M= 45.40, S.D.=16.78).

Measures

News-ness

Four items were used to measure news-ness. First, we included the single-item used by Edgerly and Vraga (2020b), which asked people how they would best categorize the post they just saw on a five-point scale from "definitely not news" to "definitely news." Participants also rated their agreement on seven-point scales (from strongly disagree to strongly agree), with a series of three statements about whether the post is a "good example" of news, whether it is "what I expect news to be," and "is not very news-like" (reversed). These items were standardized and averaged to create a scale (alpha=.74, M=.00, S.D.=.75). We provide descriptive statistics on each item in the Appendix to help interpret these results; the means for these items all suggest that the posts were seen as relatively high in news-ness, so analyses reflect differences in degrees of news-ness rather than its presence or absence.

Story elements

After answering questions about the news-ness of the post, participants were again shown the same post from either the AP website or Twitter feed and asked to select the area(s) of the article they thought were most important to deciding the degree to which the article is "news." For each platform, a total of seven areas could be selected as important (see Figure 4.1). Three of these areas are constant across platform: the time stamp for when the article was posted, the lede for the story, and the picture associated with the story. Four additional areas on each platform could be selected but did not perfectly align on the website versus Twitter, given differences in platform formatting and attributes. One of these categories is the *source cues* associated with the story. On the website, a single source cue existed: the header for the website, which includes the AP's logo, the label of "AP News," and a search function. On Twitter, three separate source cues were available: the AP news icon, the AP news handle and verification mark, and the link to the AP news website beneath the lede. A second category relates to the headline and author of the story, which were combined into the tweet text (a single area) on the Twitter feed, but could be selected separately (headline and byline) on the AP website. Finally, the AP website contained social media icons (including Twitter) at the

Is that news for me? Defining news-ness by platform and topic 55

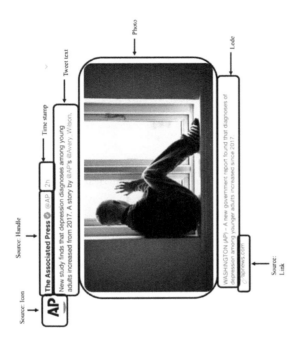

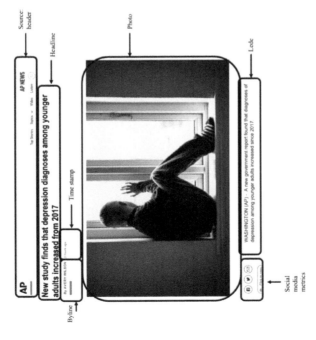

FIGURE 4.1 News cues on AP website (left) and Twitter (right).

bottom of the page that was a separate area participants could select as important. Participants were allowed to select as many areas as they wished. When viewing the content on Twitter, 42.1 percent of participants did not select any areas as important, 35.4 percent selected a single area, 14.9 percent selected two areas, and the remaining 7.7 percent selected three or more areas. When viewing the content on the website, 40.9 percent selected no areas as important, 29.0 percent selected a single area, 19.2 percent selected two areas, and 10.9 percent selected three or more areas.

What affects news-ness?

We start by considering whether participants systematically evaluated the news-ness of the *same* content differently when they encounter it on the Associated Press's website versus Twitter feed—and whether these evaluations further depend on the topic of the news article itself. To answer this question, we use a two-way ANOVA, which allows us to consider the independent effect of platform on news-ness, and whether those platform effects are moderated by issue.

These analyses find that when people see content on the AP's website, they rate it as higher in news-ness as compared to when they see that content as a post appearing on the AP's verified Twitter feed (see Figure 4.2), although this difference is relatively small in magnitude, $F(1, 778) = 3.90, p = .05, \eta_p^2 = .005$. Importantly, the effects of platform on these assessments of news-ness do not depend on the topic of the post, as the interaction between these two factors (platform and topic) is not significant, $F(3, 778) = .89, p = .44, \eta_p^2 = .003$.

These results suggest that not only are news websites seen as more credible than social media sites (Johnson & Kaye, 2014; Boothby et al., 2021), but are also seen as higher in news-ness across a range of hard news issues, building our confidence that these effects are durable, despite being small in size. However, we cannot say whether this advantage in news-ness for the AP's website would hold for "softer"

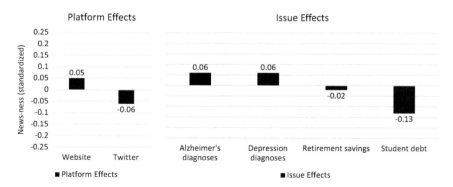

FIGURE 4.2 Main effects of platform and issue on ratings of news-ness.

news topics that involve more entertainment or opinion; it is a question that future research might test.

While not the explicit focus of this study, there is an overall difference in evaluations of news-ness depending on the topic of the post, $F(3, 778)=2.74$, $p=.04$, $\eta_p^2=.010$. The post-hoc analyses suggest that the student debt issue is rated as lowest in news-ness, significantly lower than either the Alzheimer's diagnoses ($p=.01$) or depression diagnoses ($p=.01$) issues, with the retirement savings issue not significantly different from any of the other issues. This suggests that the two mental health issues were seen as higher in news-ness than the two financial issues, especially student debt. Overall, these results suggest that perceptions of news-ness are affected separately by the issue context and the platform on which the story is found.

How people make assessments of news-ness

Having established that people viewed content viewed on the AP's website as higher in news-ness than the same content viewed on Twitter—and that these effects are consistent across issues—we turn to understanding *how* people make these assessments. Specifically, we are interested in the story elements that people turn to when deciding the degree to which something is "news," and whether the elements people report using to make their decisions differ when they view content on Twitter versus the AP's website.

We begin by examining the cues people selected as important to making their decisions about news-ness when viewing the AP's website (see Figure 4.3). We

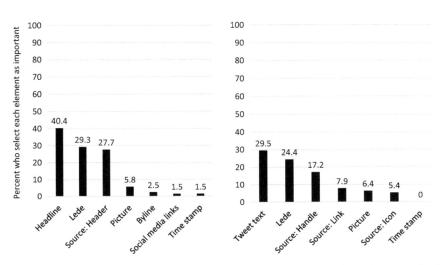

FIGURE 4.3 Elements important to news-ness on the website (left) and Twitter feed (right).

find that the headline was most often selected as important to making decisions about the news-ness of the article, with just over 40 percent rating this element as important to their evaluations of news-ness. The dominance of the headline element on the AP's website for making decisions is unsurprising—it is the most prominent feature on the website, designed to draw attention and provide the most important information regarding the story.

Participants' reliance on the lede and the source of the story are the second and third most important elements—rated as important by just over a quarter of participants—also aligns with existing research. Like the headline, the lede should provide critical information about the story topic (Harcup, 2015), allowing participants to decide whether the content is high in news-ness or something else lower in news-ness, like entertainment or opinion (Edgerly & Vraga, 2019a; 2020a). Similarly, existing research has demonstrated the importance of source cues both for credibility (Hinsley, 2021; Sundar et al., 2007) and news-ness assessments (Edgerly & Vraga, 2020a); this research formally supports that many participants are consciously relying on the lede in making these judgments.

Finally, the picture, byline, social media links, and time stamp were infrequently selected as relevant to this decision. The fact that so few participants rated the time the story was posted (two hours ago) as important to their decision is surprising, given the centrality of "timeliness" to news values (Schultz, 2007). Likewise, despite its prominence and theoretical significance (Dvir-Gvirsman, 2019; Hinsley, 2021), few participants rated the picture as important to their decisions about news-ness. This could be an artifact of our design; in order to keep the pictures similar across issues, they all focus on a single individual and provide little critical information about the story. Thus, participants' reluctance to use the picture for their decisions may be a logical dismissal of an unimportant cue—but such a cue could be utilized if it provides newsworthy information.

Turning to the elements people selected as relevant to making decisions about news-ness when viewing the Twitter feed, many similar elements were selected as important to making news-ness assessments (see Figure 4.3). Specifically, the tweet text (analogous to the headline and byline on the website) and the lede were the two most frequently used elements, with roughly a quarter of participants selected each of these cues. The source handle, which included Twitter's verification mark, occupied the third position, with the other two source cues (the AP icon and the link to the AP's website) being selected much less frequently. The reliance on the handle—rather than the icon or link—may reflect the attributes of social media, wherein content can come from a variety of sources, making checking the source immediately important for each tweet. It could also indicate that the "verified" label in the source handle is used to help make judgments of news-ness, although existing research has cast doubt on its influence on credibility assessments (Edgerly & Vraga, 2019b). Much like the AP's website, few participants selected either the picture associated with the news headline or when the tweet was posted as relevant to their decisions about news-ness.

These initial descriptive statistics reveal several key similarities in how people make assessments about news-ness that appear to transcend whether they see the news story on Twitter versus on a website. But despite these similarities in terms of the *ranking* of which elements are important to deciding news-ness across the website and Twitter, the relative *utility* of each source cue in making judgments about news-ness may differ. Therefore, we now examine differences between the platforms in the actual *percentages* of people who use each element on the website versus Twitter, using a series of chi-square tests. We focus on the three elements that were commonly selected as important on both platforms: (1) the lede of the story, (2) the headline and byline, and (3) the source cues associated with the post, to maintain statistical power.

This comparison is simplest when considering selection of the lede of the story as relevant to evaluations of news-ness, as this element was held completely constant across the two platforms. There is no significant difference between Twitter (24.4 percent) and the website (29.3 percent) in the percentage of people who select the lede as relevant to their decision making about news-ness ($\chi^2=2.44$, $p=.12$) suggesting its value is maintained across platforms.

This comparison is more complicated when we consider source. To account for differences in the attributes between the platforms, we compare the percentage of people who selected *any* source cue on Twitter (icon, handle, or link) versus those who selected the single source cue on the website (the website header). The percentage of people who rely on at least one of the three possible source cues on Twitter (23.3 percent) is not significantly different ($\chi^2=.04$, $p=.84$) from the percentage of people who selected the single source cue of the header on the website (22.7 percent).

The finding that source cues were equally important on Twitter versus the AP's website, despite differences in how they are displayed, presents several interesting possibilities. First, the prominence of the source cues on the AP's website—at the top of the webpage—could drive up their perceived relevance and utility. Second, the percentage of people relying on these cues when viewing the website may be artificially inflated by our experimental design—wherein they are assigned to the AP's webpage rather than navigating there themselves. Of course, a long line of selective exposure research demonstrates that sources are critical for making decisions about the credibility and news-ness, as well as what news to consume (Edgerly & Vraga, 2020b; Meztger et al., 2020; Stroud, 2011); people's selection of the source cue may simply reflect this reliance on sources in making these judgments.

What may in fact be more surprising is the relative *infrequency* with which source cues are used on Twitter. Just over half of Twitter users say they "regularly" get news there (Walker & Matsa, 2021); social and entertainment goals remain highly important for most users (Pelletier et al., 2020). The attributes of social media tend to reinforce these issues; a variety of sources occupy the same screen real estate with little differentiation in formatting or design. Therefore, recognizing and utilizing

60 Emily K. Vraga and Stephanie Edgerly

source cues should be even more important on Twitter and other social media platforms as compared to other spaces for news. Our findings do not support this idea. Of course, this is another place where our experimental design may limit the external validity of our results. Specifically, we tell participants it is a tweet from the AP in the prompt and they rate the elements that are important to them on a second viewing of the tweet, wherein the source should be recalled. They also see a single tweet from the AP, rather than a tweet embedded in a long feed of posts. We might expect that source cues become more important in these complicated mixed-message environments—a question that future research should test.

Finally, we compare those who selected either the headline or the byline on the website versus those who selected the tweet text on Twitter (which contained both the headline and the byline). In this case, we do find that the difference between the two platform was significant ($\chi^2=13.22$, $p<.001$), with more people selecting either of these cues on the website (41.9 percent) as compared to Twitter (29.5 percent). One possible explanation for this difference may be the size and placement of the headline, which (following actual formatting) is much larger and centrally located on the AP's website as compared to Twitter; alternatively, people may be more used to relying on the headline when they are reviewing news articles in digital outlets, compared to the plethora of cues available on social media platforms.

We also return to the question of the relatively high percentage of people who did not select any story elements as relevant to making assessments of news-ness—roughly 40 percent of our sample on both platforms. It could indicate a methodological flaw, if many people did not understand the question or decided against responding. Another explanation is that people who saw the post as relatively lacking in news-ness found *no* elements indicative of news-ness, and thus did not respond. A supplemental analysis provides some evidence for this argument, as people who did not select any areas as relevant rated the post as lower in news-ness ($M=-.09$, $S.E.=.04$) compared to those who selected at least one element ($M=.06$, $S.E.=.03$). Finally, it could be that many people were making a more holistic judgment of news-ness, without consciously linking it to any specific elements within the post. The fact that similar numbers of people did not select any story elements as relevant for both the website and Twitter, despite differences in platform structures and affordances, supports this idea. Future research should continue to investigate new ways to understand how people process information in order to make judgments about its quality. Pairing our unique approach of selecting story elements with qualitative investigations of *how* people use salient cues for evaluating the news-ness of a selected piece of content would be especially valuable.

Do the elements people use differ by issue?

Lastly, we consider whether the elements people select as important to the news-ness of a story seen on the AP's website versus Twitter post differ depending on the

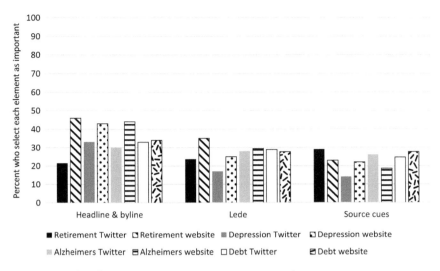

FIGURE 4.4 The elements important to news–ness across issues.

issue context. To test this, we produce the same descriptive statistics to compare the percentage of people who report using the headline/byline, the lede, or the source cues in making news-ness assessments separately for each of the four issues examined. Given the lack of interaction between platform and issue in predicting perceptions of news-ness, we expect that the cues used to determine news-ness should be similar across issues.

The analyses largely support this expectation (see Figure 4.4). Specifically, the cues that people rely upon for making decisions about the news-ness of a post are largely consistent across the four issues, with the possible exception of the student debt issue, which also was rated as significantly lower in news-ness than the other issue studied. Future research should consider whether there are conditions under which the issues intersect with the platform to produce differences in news-ness evaluations.

Conclusions

This study examines how platforms affect people's evaluations of news-ness when the same content is viewed on the AP's news website versus on their Twitter feed. We further explore how people make these decisions by asking people about the news cues they rely on when making their evaluations of news-ness. Our results suggest that content viewed on the AP's website is seen as higher in news-ness than the same content viewed posted by the AP to Twitter, but that the news cues that people turn to when making these evaluations tend to be more similar than not between the two platforms.

The similarities regarding the utility of source cues across the website and Twitter manipulations requires further consideration. In the current media environment, a plethora of sources make distinguishing high-quality from low-quality information especially important. Nowhere is this more true than social media, where tweets from news organizations co-exist alongside updates from friends and family, as well as from people and organizations we've never met (Thorson & Wells, 2016). Different platform cues offer important heuristics about news quality. But if people are making judgments about news-ness in similar ways on social media as they do in traditional news websites—where there is only one source of news—they may be missing opportunities to efficiently and accurately distinguish news from other types of content.

For example, on Twitter, three different source cues were available for participants to select—the icon, the link to the news story on the AP's website, and the Twitter handle, including the verification tag. Combined, however, these three source cues are referenced less than a quarter of the time as relevant to judgments about news-ness—and this was no different than the AP's website. In focus groups, people often report that they rely heavily on source reputation in making evaluations about credibility (Metzger et al., 2010), and experimental research validates that *known* partisan source cues weigh heavily in evaluations of credibility and news-ness (Edgerly & Vraga, 2020b; Knobloch-Westerwick et al., 2015). However, other source cues may be ignored; for example, Twitter's verification tags tend to have little influence on credibility judgments even for unknown sources (Edgerly & Vraga, 2019b). This suggests that platforms may need to do more to help people quickly identify source cues to help them make evaluations of news-ness. Similarly, news literacy education could help audiences recognize which cues are especially important for making judgments about news—and how their relevance may differ across platforms. The number of people who failed to select these news elements may reinforce the need for this kind of news literacy training among the population. Overall, this study highlights the need to know more about the larger socialization processes by which individuals today acquire knowledge about the reputations and uses of different media platforms and the specific cues that aid their sensemaking about news.

Ultimately, this chapter explores *what* people consider to be news and *how* they make such decisions. Understanding this process is especially important as judgments about news-ness carry weight—they are associated with evaluations of credibility and have a unique influence on peoples' willingness to verify information (Edgerly & Vraga, 2020b). So long as news maintains its special status in the imagination of the American public, defining something as high in news-ness likely privileges that content and carries the assumption that it is of higher quality. But this status is by no means sacrosanct, and future research should investigate which indicators of information quality are most closely tied to evaluations of news-ness, and for which populations.

Our findings also point to the nuanced differences and similarities that are used when assessing the news-ness of a story posted on the website versus Twitter page of a relatively neutral, mainstream news organization. For example, research suggests that "loud" cues—especially partisan source cues—may drown out other possibly relevant cues like the platform or topic (Edgerly & Vraga, 2019; 2020b; Sundar et al., 2007). These findings invite more research on this topic. As people encounter news on a wide range of platforms and sources, the question of which specific cues they use in determining "Is this news?" will continue to be important.

References

Althaus, S. L., & Tewksbury, D. (2002). Agenda setting and the "new" news: Patterns of issue importance among readers of the paper and online versions of the *New York Times*. *Communication Research*, *29*(2), 180–207. https://doi.org/10.1177/009365020202 9002004

Bachmann, P., Eisenegger, M., & Ingenhoff, D. (2022). Defining and measuring news media quality: Comparing the content perspective and the audience perspective. *The International Journal of Press/Politics*, *27*(1), 9–37.

Boothby, C., Murray, D., Polovick Waggy, A., Tsou, A., & Sugimoto, C. R. (2021). Credibility of scientific information on social media: Variation by platform, genre and presence of formal credibility cues. *Quantitative Science Studies*, 1–30. https://doi.org/10.1162/qss_a_00151

Boukes, M., Jones, N. P., & Vliegenthart, R. (2020). Newsworthiness and story prominence: How the presence of news factors relates to upfront position and length of news stories. *Journalism*, *23*(1). https://doi.org/10.1177/1464884919899313

Chadwick, A. (2013). *The hybrid media system: Politics and power*. Oxford University Press.

Coppock, A., & McClellan, O. A. (2019). Validating the demographic, political, psychological, and experimental results obtained from a new source of online survey respondents. *Research & Politics*, *6*(1), 2053168018822174. https://doi.org/10.1177/2053168018822174

DeSanctis, G., & Poole, M. S. (1994). Capturing the complexity in advanced technology use: Adaptive structuration theory. *Organization Science*, *5*(2), 121–147. https://doi.org/10.1287/orsc.5.2.121

Digital News Report (2016). Distinctions between hard and soft news. Reuters Institute for the Study of Journalism. www.digitalnewsreport.org/survey/2016/hard-soft-news-2016/

dos Santos Jr, M. A., Lycarião, D., & de Aquino, J. A. (2019). The virtuous cycle of news sharing on Facebook: Effects of platform affordances and journalistic routines on news sharing. *New Media & Society*, *21*(2), 398–418.

Dvir-Gvirsman, S. (2019). I like what I see: Studying the influence of popularity cues on attention allocation and news selection. *Information, Communication & Society*, *22*(2), 286–305. https://doi.org/10.1080/1369118X.2017.1379550

Edgerly, S., & Vraga, E. K. (2019a). News, entertainment, or both? Exploring audience perceptions of media genre in a hybrid media environment. *Journalism*, *20*, 807–826. https://doi.org/10.1177/1464884917730709

Edgerly, S., & Vraga, E. K. (2019b). The blue check of credibility: Does account verification matter when evaluating news on Twitter?. *Cyberpsychology, Behavior, and Social Networking, 22*(4), 283–287. https://doi.org/10.1089/cyber.2018.0475

Edgerly, S., & Vraga, E. K. (2020a). Deciding what's news: News-ness as a concept for the hybrid media environment. *Journalism and Mass Communication Quarterly, 97*, 416–434. https://doi.org/10.1177/1077699020916808

Edgerly, S., & Vraga, E. K. (2020b). That's not news: Audience perceptions of news-ness and why it matters. *Mass Communication and Society, 25*, 730–754. https://doi.org/10.1080/15205436.2020.1729383

Evans, S. K., Pearce, K. E., Vitak, J., & Treem, J. W. (2017). Explicating affordances: A conceptual framework for understanding affordances in communication research. *Journal of Computer-Mediated Communication, 22*(1), 35–52. https://doi.org/10.1111/jcc4.12180

Eveland Jr., W. P. (2003). A "mix of attributes" approach to the study of media effects and new communication technologies. *Journal of Communication, 53*(3), 395–410. https://doi.org/10.1111/j.1460-2466.2003.tb02598.x

Fiske, J. (1987). *Television culture*. Routledge.

Flanagin, A. J., & Metzger, M. J. (2000). Perceptions of Internet information credibility. *Journalism & Mass Communication Quarterly, 77*(3), 515–540. https://doi.org/10.1177/107769900007700304

Flanagin, A. J., & Metzger, M. J. (2007). The role of site features, user attributes, and information verification behaviors on the perceived credibility of web-based information. *New Media & Society, 9*(2), 319–342. https://doi.org/10.1177/1461444807075015

Gallup/Knight. (2018, June 20). Perceived accuracy and bias in the news media. Knight Foundation. https://knightfoundation.org/reports/perceived-accuracy-and-bias-in-the-news-media/

Go, E., Jung, E. H., & Wu, M. (2014). The effects of source cues on online news perception. *Computers in Human Behavior, 38*, 358–367. https://doi.org/10.1016/j.chb.2014.05.044

Harcup, T. (2015). *Journalism: Principles and practice* (3rd edition). Sage.

Hinsley, A. (2021). Cued up: How audience demographics influence reliance on news cues, confirmation bias and confidence in identifying misinformation. *International Symposium on Online Journalism, 11*(1), 89–109.

Horowitz, J. M., & Graf, N. (2019). Most U.S. teens see anxiety and depression as major problems for their peers. Pew Research Center. www.pewresearch.org/social-trends/2019/02/20/most-u-s-teens-see-anxiety-and-depression-as-a-major-problem-among-their-peers/

Kennedy, B., & Funk, C. (2015). Public interest in science and health linked to gender, age, and personality. Pew Research Center. www.pewresearch.org/science/2015/12/11/public-interest-in-science-and-health-linked-to-gender-age-and-personality/

Knobloch-Westerwick, S., Johnson, B. K., & Westerwick, A. (2015). Confirmation bias in online searches: Impacts of selective exposure before an election on political attitude strength and shifts. *Journal of Computer-Mediated Communication, 20*(2), 171–187. https://doi.org/10.1111/jcc4.12105

Johnson, T. J., & Kaye, B. K. (2014). Credibility of social network sites for political information among politically interested Internet users. *Journal of Computer-Mediated Communication, 19*(4), 957–974. https://doi.org/10.1111/jcc4.12084

Kim, H., & Niehm, L. S. (2009). The impact of website quality on information quality, value, and loyalty intentions in apparel retailing. *Journal of Interactive Marketing, 23*(4), 221–233.

Lee, A. M., Lewis, S. C., & Powers, M. (2014). Audience clicks and news placement: A study of time-lagged influence in online journalism. *Communication Research*, *41*(4), 505–530. https://doi.org/10.1177/0093650212467031

Lee, S., Nanz, A., & Heiss, R. (2022). Platform-dependent effects of incidental exposure to political news on political knowledge and political participation. *Computers in Human Behavior*, *127*. www.sciencedirect.com/science/article/pii/S074756322100371X

Metzger, M. J., Flanagin, A. J., & Medders, R. B. (2010). Social and heuristic approaches to credibility evaluation online. *Journal of Communication*, *60*(3), 413–439. https://doi.org/10.1111/j.1460-2466.2010.01488.x

Metzger, M. J., Hartsell, E. H., & Flanagin, A. J. (2020). Cognitive dissonance or credibility? A comparison of two theoretical explanations for selective exposure to partisan news. *Communication Research*, *47*(1), 3–28. https://doi.org/10.1177/0093650215613136

Molyneaux, L., & Coddington, M. (2020). Aggregation, clickbait and their effect on perceptions of journalistic credibility and quality. *Journalism Practice*, *14*(4), 429–446.

Newhagen, J., & Nass, C. (1989). Differential criteria for evaluating credibility of newspapers and TV news. *Journalism Quarterly*, *66*(2), 277–284.

Pelletier, M. J., Krallman, A., Adams, F. G., & Hancock, T. (2020). One size doesn't fit all: A uses and gratifications analysis of social media platforms. *Journal of Research in Interactive Marketing*, *14*(2), 269–284. https://doi.org/10.1108/JRIM-10-2019-0159

Schmierbach, M., & Oeldorf-Hirsch, A. (2012). A little bird told me, so I didn't believe it: Twitter, credibility, and issue perceptions. *Communication Quarterly*, *60*(3), 317–337. https://doi.org/10.1080/01463373.2012.688723

Schudson, M. (1998). *The good citizen: A history of American civic life*. Free Press.

Schultz, I. (2007). The journalistic gut feeling: Journalistic doxa, news habitus and orthodox news values. *Journalism Practice*, *1*(2), 190–207. https://doi.org/10.1080/1751278070 1275507

Scott, D. K., & Gobetz, R. H. (1992). Hard news/soft news content of the national broadcast networks, 1972–1987. *Journalism & Mass Communication Quarterly*, *69*(2), 406–412. https://doi.org/10.1177/107769909206900214

Shearer, E. (2018, Dec 10). Social media outpaces print newspapers in the U.S. as a news source. Pew Research Center. www.pewresearch.org/fact-tank/2018/12/10/social-media-outpaces-print-newspapers-in-the-u-s-as-a-news-source/

Shearer, E., & Grieco, E. (2019, Oct 2). Americans are wary of the role social media sites play in delivering the news. Pew Research Center www.journalism.org/2019/10/02/americans-are-wary-of-the-role-social-media-sites-play-in-delivering-the-news/

Smock, A. D., Ellison, N. B., Lampe, C., & Wohn, D. Y. (2011). Facebook as a toolkit: A uses and gratification approach to unbundling feature use. *Computers in Human Behavior*, *27*(6), 2322–2329. https://doi.org/10.1016/j.chb.2011.07.011

Stroud, N. J. (2011). *Niche news: The politics of news choice*. Oxford University Press.

Sundar, S. S. (1999). Exploring receivers' criteria for perception of print and online news. *Journalism & Mass Communication Quarterly*, *76*(2), 373–386.

Sundar, S. S., Knobloch-Westerwick, S., & Hastall, M. R. (2007). News cues: Information scent and cognitive heuristics. *Journal of the American Society for Information Science and Technology*, *58*(3), 366–378. https://doi.org/10.1002/asi.20511

Thorson, K., & Wells, C. (2016). Curated flows: A framework for mapping media exposure in the digital age. *Communication Theory*, *26*(3), 309–328. https://doi.org/10.1111/comt.12087

Tong, C., Gill, H., Li, J., Valenzuela, S., & Rojas, H. (2020). "Fake news is anything they say!"—Conceptualization and weaponization of fake news among the American public. *Mass Communication and Society*, *23*(5), 755–778. https://doi.org/10.1080/15205 436.2020.1789661

Walker, M., & Matsa, K. E. (2021). News consumption across social media in 2021. Pew Research Center. www.pewresearch.org/journalism/2021/09/20/news-consumption-across-social-media-in-2021/

Weick, K. E., Sutcliffe, K. M., & Obstfeld, D. (2005). Organizing and the process of sensemaking. *Organization Science*, *16*(4), 409–421. https://doi.org/10.1287/orsc.1050.0133

5

USER COMMENTS AS NEWS QUALITY

Examining incivility in comments on perceptions of news quality[1]

Shuning Lu, Hai Liang and Gina M. Masullo

High-quality news has important implications for both journalism and a democratic society. The commercialization and digitalization of the news ecosystem, however, have posed new challenges to quality journalism. One notable aspect is that online news articles are often accompanied by user comments. Those poorly worded and frequently uncivil user comments (Coe et al., 2014) remain one of the most concerning issues for news workers (Grieve, 2014). Uncivil comments posted on news have been shown to lead to media bias (Anderson et al., 2018), dampen credibility judgment (Masullo et al., 2021), and lower news quality perceptions (Prochazka et al., 2018; Weber et al., 2019).

Given the growing role of user comments in signaling news quality, both news organizations and social media companies have devoted themselves to ranking user comments, such as prioritizing certain comments in the thread, to represent a range of views that either indicate their quality or popularity. Most organizations rely on either human-selection or social endorsement cues (e.g., the number of likes, shares, comments) to rank user comments under news stories. Yet, few have explored what impact—if any—the composition of civil versus uncivil comments in a given thread may have on people's perceptions of news quality. Part of the rationale for foregrounding the composition of civil and uncivil comments rather than removing all uncivil content is that recent research suggests that uncivil messages online are not always intrinsically harmful (Rossini, 2020), or perceived as such (Liang & Zhang, 2021). Thus, understanding the effects of (de)prioritizing uncivil comments in comment threads on users' perceptions of news quality becomes pivotal.

In response, this study conducted a mixed-design online experiment in the United States and systematically varied the proportion and position of uncivil content in a comment thread across obtrusive and unobtrusive issues. Drawing

DOI: 10.4324/9781003257998-7

on repetition and serial effects in communication and social psychology, we investigated how the proportion and position of online incivility could impact news quality perceptions among audiences. Further, we explored the effects across issues with which audiences had either low or high amounts of direct personal experience. One underlying assumption is that people may devote varying amounts of attention to issues with or without personal relevance, which in turn shapes the effects of online incivility on their evaluations of news quality.

The present study adds to the extant scholarship on online incivility and news quality in the following aspects. Building on research that examines the effects of incivility as opposed to civility (Anderson et al., 2018; Chen & Lu, 2017), our study takes a step further by exploring how the arrangement of incivility—proportion and position in particular—affects news quality perceptions. While previous research tested the effects of uncivil comments on news quality in Germany (Prochazka et al., 2018; Weber et al., 2019), our study looks at the *Associated Press* (hereafter *AP news),* a well-known news brand in the United States. The study also provides novel evidence on the differences in the effects of online incivility across different issue contexts, which goes beyond existing research that used a single-issue experimental design (Prochazka et al., 2018; Weber et al., 2019). Practically, this study suggests guidance about mitigating the detrimental impacts of uncivil user comments on news quality by carefully arranging comment threads for different types of issues.

Theoretical framework

News quality and user comments

News quality is crucial to understand from the audience perspective, because it is conducive to news consumption. News organizations, by providing quality content, could foster audience loyalty in the long term. Yet, news quality is a contested concept in the existing literature. First, the objects of news quality could be very different, ranging from media systems, media organizations to specific types of news and single news items (see Plasser, 2005; Humprecht & Esser, 2018). Second, the criteria of news quality are also widely debated. Some studies focus on normative dimensions of news quality, such as diversity, impartiality, objectivity, and ethics (McQuail, 2013; Urban & Schweiger, 2014); others focus on the informational dimension, including readability, comprehensibility and accuracy (Graefe et al., 2018; Waddell, 2020). Given both dimensions constitute the key aspects of news quality, this study follows Prochazka and colleagues (2018) and taps into normative and informational aspects of news quality to understand audience evaluations of commented-on news articles.

Accumulating evidence has suggested that in most cases, news audiences cannot evaluate the quality of news sufficiently. In an experimental study, Urban and Schweiger (2014) found that news users could better recognize news quality with regard to relevance, impartiality, and diversity than ethics, objectivity, and comprehensibility. Researchers note news users' difficulty in developing sensible quality judgments based on news articles themselves could be attributed to the unique nature of online information processing (Prochazka et al., 2018; Weber et al., 2019). For instance, news users may rely on less complex components and heuristic cues, such as news brand, bandwagon metrics, and user comments, in judging journalistic quality (Conlin & Roberts, 2016; Waddell, 2020).

Since the inception of Web 2.0, user comments have become an integral part of news websites. About 55 percent of Americans have left a comment online and 77.9 percent have read online comments on news websites at some point (Stroud et al., 2016). Not surprisingly, user comments serve as an important heuristic cue for audience to form news evaluations. For instance, Conlin and Roberts (2016) show that the mere appearance of user comments could decrease news site credibility. Other studies also found that users may infer a news item's quality from the characteristics of user comments, such as authenticity and sentiment (see Waddell, 2020).

Online incivility and news quality

The definition of incivility varies across theoretical traditions, research contexts, and empirical foci. Following the tradition of deliberative theory, one school of thought conceptualizes incivility as a deviation from the classic ideals of public deliberation. Accordingly, incivility refers to the discourse that lacks attributes of deliberation, such as reciprocity, or that disrespect citizens' rights or threaten democracy (Papacharissi, 2004), which Muddiman (2017) calls public-level incivility. The other school draws on politeness theory (Brown & Levinson, 1987) and conceptualizes incivility as violations of interpersonal politeness norms or personal-level incivility (Muddiman, 2017). When studying user comments on news websites, researchers have operationalized personal-level incivility as personal attacks, rude language, profanity, and words in all capital letters (Coe et al., 2014; Chen & Lu, 2017; Prochazka et al., 2018). Following this line of research, we focus on personal-level incivility in this study because it is more prevalent in online comments than other forms of online incivility (Chen, 2017; Coe et al., 2014).

A growing body of literature has explored the effects of online incivility on audience evaluations of adjacent content. One study, for instance, shows that news stories were seen as biased and less credible if uncivil comments were posted on them (Anderson et al., 2018). Relevant to this study, studies have offered some mixed evidence on the impact of uncivil user comments on news quality perceptions. Prochazka and colleagues (2018) demonstrated that incivility in comments dampened users' perceptions of the news quality for both well-known and unknown news brands in Germany, whereas Weber and colleagues (2019) found that incivility decreased news quality perceptions only with an unknown news brand. Such inconsistent findings could be attributed to the lack of explicit measurement of brand awareness for the real news sites, which could confound the findings across unknown and well-known news brands. Another limitation is that both studies only tested the effects with a single issue in Germany. It remains unknown how those findings could be generalized into other types of issues and a different country. To extend this line of research, we seek to replicate the findings across different issue contexts for *AP news*—a well-known news brand in the United States. Based on the assumption that news users form judgments of news quality based on heuristic cues (i.e., user comments), we anticipate that incivility in comment threads will dampen news quality perceptions:

> **H1**: Incivility in comment threads will result in lower perceptions of news quality.

To add to the literature, this study specifically looks at two important features of the composition of comment threads—proportion and position of incivility. The general concept of message repetition has received considerable attention in early communication research (entropy in information theory, see Shannon & Weaver, 1949). Empirical evidence shows that message repetition has strong effects on cognitive response, recall, and persuasion (Cacioppo & Petty, 1979). Similarly, the figure-ground hypothesis holds that a higher proportion of negative content in a given text will stand out and have a larger effect on people's perceptions (Kanouse & Hanson, 1972). Accordingly, a higher proportion of incivility was found to cause hostile cognitions (Rösner et al., 2016). Concerning news consumption, it is revealed that a higher proportion of uncivil content in comment threads could decrease news outlet credibility (Masullo et al., 2021). These studies suggest that a higher proportion of incivility will have larger effects on news quality perceptions because it represents the repetition of uncivil content and it holds noticeability based on the figure-ground hypothesis. Here, the following hypothesis is posited:

> **H2a**: Comment threads with a higher proportion of incivility will result in lower perceptions of news quality.

Given that user comment threads on news websites would typically appear as a mix of civil and uncivil messages, we further argue that whether uncivil messages appear at the beginning or the end may also account for differences in news quality perceptions. The position effects of messages have been extensively examined in persuasion literature. The primacy effect, also known as first impression, refers to the mechanism that information placed in the first position in an array of messages matters the most for attitudinal formation, change, and subsequent behavior (Lund, 1925; Schwartz, 2011). The rationale for a primacy effect is grounded in a belief from cognitive psychology that because memory capacity is limited (Waugh & Norman, 1965), people encode information into their long-term memory immediately. Thus, recall would be greatest for items in a series that were learned first (Schwartz, 2011). In contrast, the recency effect refers to the mechanism that information placed in the last position in an ordered list of messages holds more memory advantage because people were exposed to it most recently (O'Keefe, 2002; Schwartz, 2011). Assuming individuals rely on short-term memory for recall, the items placed in the later position may still be available when they recall because they are still salient (Haugtvedt & Wegener, 1994). During web browsing, recency effects are more likely to be observed as people do not spend much cognitive effort (Murphy et al., 2006). Because English speakers, who were the focus in this study, generally read from top to bottom of a page (Kress & Van Leeuwen, 2006), the most recently read comments would be at the end of a thread. Hence, we posit:

> **H2b:** There will be a recency effect of incivility such that comment threads that end with incivility will lead to lower perceptions of news quality compared with comment threads that start with incivility.

Issue obtrusiveness, online incivility, and news quality

Scholars agree that people generally scan through online news articles and tend not to process online information thoroughly to form judgments about news quality (Prochazka et al., 2018). However, it is not always the case across issue contexts, because different issues may entail varying degrees of relevance to individuals and that relevance may shape the way they process such information. Indeed, when considering social issues, some of them are deemed more important and relevant than others based on their direct ramifications to people's personal lives. Research shows the varied media effects across different types of issues. Issue involvement, for instance, could shape the effects of persuasion by enhancing message-relevant cognitive response (see Petty & Cacioppo, 1979). Moreover, agenda-setting scholars identified the "obtrusive contingency" of media effects, in which direct personal experience with an issue could sensitize or prime people's attention toward this issue and a stronger media effect could be observed (Demers et al., 1989).

Given the importance of issue types in conditioning media effects, our goal here is to investigate how issue obtrusiveness—indicating the amount of personal experience with that issue—shape the effects of incivility on news quality perceptions. Conceptually speaking, obtrusive issues are those that affect nearly everyone and with which people can have some kind of personal experience; unobtrusive issues are those being far from reach in people's daily lives and connoting low personal experience. Research shows that obtrusive issues may lead one to devote more attention to the content and in turn heighten media effects (Demers et al., 1989; Erbring et al., 1980). In this study, people may involve high-level message elaboration (i.e., carefully considering a message) and process content more thoroughly when reading news and comments on obtrusive issues. Therefore, given equal proportion of uncivil content, they would be more susceptible to uncivil comments on obtrusive issues than on unobtrusive issues. This leads us to predict a larger effect of incivility on news quality perceptions for obtrusive issues than for unobtrusive ones:

> **H3a**: Issue obtrusiveness will moderate the effects of proportion of incivility on news quality perceptions such that the proportion will have a larger negative effect on news quality perceptions for obtrusive issues than for unobtrusive issues.

Moreover, issue obtrusiveness could change how message position effects operate. In a study of Ohio's 1992 elections, Miller and Krosnick (1998) found that candidate primacy effects only existed when voters were highly involved with the party. Similarly, Haugtvedt and Wegener (1994) revealed that a primacy effect most likely occurred when one was involved in high levels of message elaboration, while recency effects happen if one processed the messages with low levels of elaboration. Applied to this study, we anticipate a primacy effect of incivility on news quality perceptions in obtrusive issues because people may engage in high levels of message elaboration when reading news and comments of personal relevance. On the contrary, we expect a recency effect of incivility on news quality perceptions for unobtrusive issues, because when reading news and comments about unobtrusive issues, people may not seriously consider the messages or process the information thoroughly. As a result, they may rely on the last items they encounter to form judgments:

> **H3b**: Issue obtrusiveness will moderate the effects of the position of incivility on news quality perceptions such that there will be a primacy effect of incivility on news quality perceptions for obtrusive issues and a recency effect of incivility on news quality perceptions for unobtrusive issues.

Method

The study protocol was approved by the Institutional Research Board at the first author's university in August 2020. An online experiment was carried out in the United States in October 2020. The sample for this study was drawn from Prolific, an online panel consisting of a diverse sample of American adults. After removing those who failed the attention check ($n=8$), a total of 291 participants were retained. In the sample, 52.9 percent were female, 60.5 percent were white, with the median age at 35–44 years old, and the median educational level a two-year college degree. Around 25 percent of participants ($n=73$) had not heard of *AP news* before the experiment.

Design and procedure

The experiment adopted a 4 (proportion of incivility: 20, 40, 60, or 80 percent) by 2 (position of incivility: primacy versus recency) by 2 (news topics: obtrusive or unobtrusive issues) mixed-factorial design. After consenting, participants answered a short pre-test survey about their demographic information and if they had heard about *AP news* upon taking the survey. For those who knew *AP news*, we further asked them to rate the overall quality of news published by *AP news*. In the main experiment, participants were instructed to complete a total of four assessment tasks. In each task, they were asked to read a news story accompanying by a randomized comment thread featuring a different proportion and position of incivility. Then the participants answered questions about their assessment of the comment thread and news quality for each of the four stories. The order of the four stories was also randomized. On average, it took eight minutes finishing the experiment. One U.S. dollar was provided to those who followed the instructions and completed the tasks.

Stimulus material

We chose four news articles published during the outbreak of COVID-19 in the United States. Two stories—"Jobless claims rise as cutoff of extra $600 benefit nears" and "1 in 10 Americans think school should reopen this fall without restrictions"— were used to represent obtrusive issues, as people may have had some personal experiences with those issues during the pandemic. For unobtrusive issues, we used "Vice presidential debate to be held with audience in Utah" and "US signs contract with Pfizer for COVID-19 vaccine doses," because of the low amount of direct experience people may have had. To enhance the political neutrality of the news stories, we used real stories from *AP news*, which is perceived as an unbiased news organization by the American public (Gallup & Knight Foundation, 2018), and we removed political cues such as the name of Donald Trump. We also trimmed down all original articles to about 300 words and added an identical timestamp "39 minutes ago" to guarantee the format-level consistency.

Given that *AP news* does not have a comment section on its website, we searched the titles and keywords of all articles and retrieved the relevant comments on Reddit.com, a social media site in the United States. We follow previous research on online incivility to edit the comments with elements, such as upper-case usage, name-calling, and profanity, to represent personal-level incivility (Chen & Lu, 2017; Coe et al., 2014; Muddiman, 2017). Civil comments did not have these attributes. We kept all spelling and grammatical errors in the original comments to reflect realism. To avoid user attributes from confounding the results, we used fictitious profiles with a capitalized letter that indicates the first letter of user names. For each comment thread, five user comments are included. We created eight comment threads, featuring a different proportion and position of online incivility

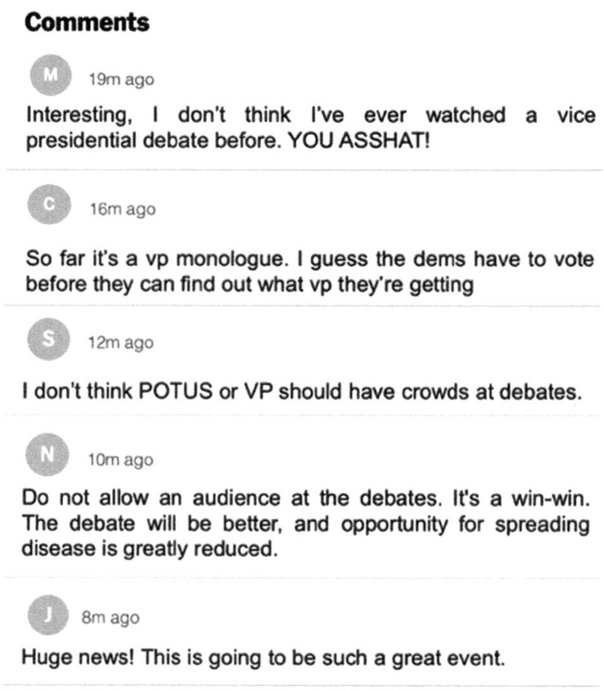

Comments

 19m ago

Interesting, I don't think I've ever watched a vice presidential debate before. YOU ASSHAT!

 16m ago

So far it's a vp monologue. I guess the dems have to vote before they can find out what vp they're getting

 12m ago

I don't think POTUS or VP should have crowds at debates.

 10m ago

Do not allow an audience at the debates. It's a win-win. The debate will be better, and opportunity for spreading disease is greatly reduced.

 8m ago

Huge news! This is going to be such a great event.

FIGURE 5.1 Comment thread following "site announcement for vice presidential debate" (proportion: 20 percent, position: primacy).

for each of the four news stories (see Figure 5.1). Participants were randomly assigned to one of the eight comment threads after reading a news story.

Measures

Perceptions of news quality

Adapting from Prochazka and colleagues (2018) and Urban and Schweiger (2014), we asked participants to rate the quality of news on a 5-point scale (1=*not agree at all*, 5=*very much agree*) on the following statements: "The news story is objective," "The news story reports relevant information," "The news story is comprehensible," "The news story does not insult or discriminate," and "The news story is harmless for children and young people." We averaged the scores to create an index to indicate news quality perceptions, in which the higher scores indicated greater quality. We measured perceptions of news quality both in the pre-test (i.e., overall news quality of *AP news*, Cronbach's α=.84) and the post-test (i.e., the quality of each of the four news stories with user comments, Cronbach's α>.85). Details for the descriptive statistics are reported in the result section.

Reading habits

In the end of the experiment, participants were asked to indicate if they read the comment threads "from the top to the bottom" or "from the bottom to the top." There were three participants reading from the bottom to the top. We reversely coded the position effects for these participants.

Manipulation check

To determine whether the manipulation of online incivility was successful, participants were asked about the extent to which they thought the comment threads were uncivil. We followed Kenski and colleagues (2020) and measured perceived incivility based on a 5-point scale ($1=$*not at all*, $5=$*a great deal*), including "uncivil," "rude," "unnecessary," and "respectful." The four items were averaged into an index with higher scores indicating greater levels of perceived incivility, which yields high reliability across comment threads and news stories (Cronbach's $\alpha>.90$). A Pearson's correlation test showed that the association between proportion of incivility and perceived incivility was statistically significant ($r=.31$, $p<.001$). Therefore, the manipulation check was successful.

Analytical strategy

For **H1**, we used paired-sample t-tests to examine the difference in news quality perceptions between pre-test and post-test ($N=218$). For **H2–3**, we adopted multilevel modeling (nlme package in R) as each participant was presented with four news stories and their ratings of story-level news quality were not an independent observation, but instead nested within a participant. To account for the nested structure of the data, we entered a participant ID as a level-2 independent variable with random intercepts. For a level-1 independent variable, we entered proportion and position of incivility, issue obtrusiveness, and the two-way and three-way interaction terms of the three variables. In Model 1a–b, perceptions of news quality in the post-test were entered as the dependent variable ($N=291$). In Model 2a–b, we employed the change-score approach to estimate the multilevel models among those who knew *AP news* and rated the overall news quality in the pre-test ($N=218$). In Model 2a–b, the difference of news quality ratings between pre-test and post-test was entered as the dependent variable.

Results

H1 posited that incivility in user comments would result in negative perceptions of news quality. The paired-sample t-test showed that participants rated news quality significantly lower after reading uncivil user comments accompanying the news stories ($M=3.40$, $SD=1.03$) than before ($M=3.82$, $SD=0.75$), $t(871)=-9.10$, $p<.001$, supporting **H1**.

76 Shuning Lu, Hai Liang and Gina M. Masullo

H2a predicted that comment threads with a higher proportion of incivility would lead to lower perceptions of news quality. In supporting **H2a,** it showed that proportion significantly negatively predicted news quality perceptions. For post-test-only models, the estimated marginal means of news quality for different conditions were: for 20 percent: M=3.55, SE=0.07; for 40 percent: M=3.45, SE=0.06; for 60 percent, M=3.35, SE=0.06; for 80 percent: M=3.25, SE=0.06. **H2b** posited that position of incivility would lead to lower news quality perceptions. It showed that position did not negatively predict news quality perceptions. For post-test-only models, the estimated marginal means of news quality for the position conditions were about the same: M=3.40, SE=0.06, not supporting **H2b**.

TABLE 5.1 Predicting news quality perceptions using multilevel modeling

	Model 1a	Model 1b	Model 2a	Model 2b
	Posttest only		*Change-score approach*	
Experimental condition				
Proportion of incivility	−0.12(0.02)★★★	−0.15(0.03)★★★	−0.11(0.02)★★★	−0.15(0.04)★★★
Position of incivility (recency=1)	−0.003(0.04)	−0.17(0.18)	−0.04(0.04)	−0.22(0.14)
Issue obtrusiveness	−0.06(0.03)	−0.23(0.12)	−0.05(0.04)	−0.26(0.14)
Interaction terms				
Proportion × position of incivility		0.05(0.05)		0.06(0.05)
Position of incivility × issue obtrusiveness		0.50(0.18)★★		0.50(0.20)★
Proportion of incivility × issue obtrusiveness		0.10(0.05)★		0.11(0.05)★
Proportion × position of incivility × issue obtrusiveness		−0.17(0.06)★		−0.18(0.07)★
Conditional R^2	73.2%	73.4%	76.2%	76.3%
N of observations	1164		872	
N of groups	291		218	

H3a–b anticipated that issue obtrusiveness would moderate the effect of proportion and position of incivility on news quality perceptions. We found a significant three-way interaction effect of position, proportion of incivility, and issue obtrusiveness on perceptions of news. Proportion of incivility exerted larger effects on diminishing news quality perceptions for obtrusive issues than unobtrusive issues. The position effects of incivility on news quality perceptions varied across issue contexts (Figures 5.2 and 5.3). For obtrusive issues, incivility in the primacy position had a larger negative effect than incivility in the recency position when the proportion of incivility was no greater than 40 percent. For unobtrusive issues, incivility in the recency position had a larger negative effect than incivility in the primacy position when the proportion of incivility was no greater than 60 percent. Therefore, **H3a–b** were partially supported.

Discussion

Incivility in user comments on news websites has become an urgent and important question to address because these comments may taint the quality of online discussions and make news websites less attractive to users. To address this concern, we conducted an online experiment to investigate how different arrangements of incivility (i.e., proportion and position) in comment threads diminish news quality perceptions and how such effects vary across obtrusive and unobtrusive issues.

In line with research conducted in Germany (Prochazka et al., 2018), our results show that uncivil comments dampened news quality perceptions of a real news brand (*AP news*) in the United States. As we explicitly gauged brand awareness in the pre-test and analyzed the result with both post-test-only and change-score approaches, we are confident about the robustness of the findings. One notable finding is that when even one in five of comments in a given thread was uncivil, users' perceptions about the quality of the commented-on news articles decreased. This implies that user comments serve as heuristic cues for people to judge journalistic output. Uncivil user comments, in particular, could signal news quality for a real news brand for those who have or have not heard of the brand.

Next, the study provides crucial evidence on the effects of the arrangement of civil and uncivil content in user comments on news quality perceptions. It revealed that proportion of online incivility in user comments dampened perceived news quality. While we did not identify any overall position effects of online incivility on news quality perceptions, we did find that the effects of proportion and position of online incivility on perceived news quality were contingent on issue contexts. One key observation is that the negative effects of proportion of online incivility on news quality perceptions were more pronounced for obtrusive issues than for unobtrusive issues. This indicated that news users were more susceptible to uncivil comments if they appeared on news stories that they have direct experiences with than those with little personal relevance. This corroborates scholarly accounts regarding the connection between obtrusive issues and larger

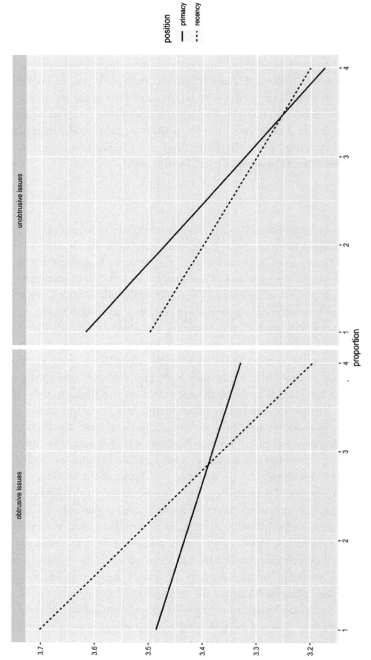

FIGURE 5.2 Predicting news quality perceptions (post-test only).

User comments as news quality **79**

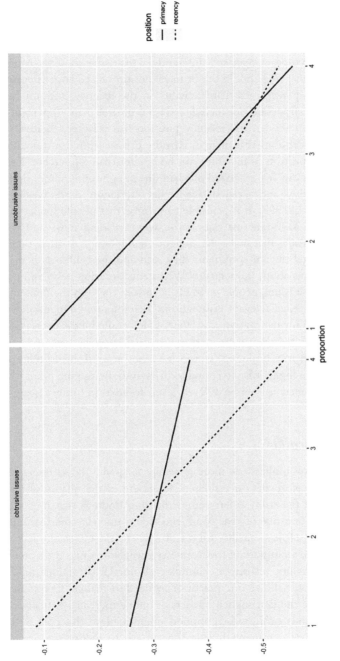

FIGURE 5.3 Predicting news quality perceptions (change-score approach).

media effects (Demers et al., 1989; Erbring et al., 1980). Given that news users may find obtrusive issues personally relevant, they would devote more attention to the relevant content, and that heightened attention in turn strengthened the deleterious effects of online incivility on news quality perceptions.

Another crucial observation is that the position effects of online incivility on news quality perceptions operated differently across issue contexts. More specifically, we found that incivility in the primacy position had a larger negative effect on news quality perceptions than incivility in the recency position for obtrusive issues, when proportion of incivility was no greater than 40 percent. We also observed that incivility in the recency position had a larger negative effect on news quality perceptions than incivility in the primacy position for unobtrusive issues, when proportion of incivility was no greater than 60 percent. This line of findings supports our hypothesized mechanisms in light of literature on message-relevant elaboration and serial message effects (Haugtvedt & Wegener, 1994; Miller & Krosnick, 1998). It is plausible to surmise that people tended to engage in high-level message-relevant elaboration when reading news and comments about obtrusive issues that make the audience feel relevant. As such, they focused on the first several uncivil comments they read and used these as heuristic cues to form judgments about news quality. When encountering news and comments about unobtrusive issues, people were likely to scan through the content quickly, featuring low message-relevant elaboration. Therefore, they judged news quality by recalling the information they saw latest, which could be the last several uncivil user comments in the thread. Although our results are consistent with the theoretical expectation in a bounded fashion (i.e., the proportion of online incivility should not be too high), it is intriguing to delve into the tipping point of position effects of online incivility across different issue contexts in future research.

Practical implications

Our findings have implications more generally for practitioners interested in the impacts of user comments on audiences' judgment of the quality of journalistic content. Overall, the study offers some troubling findings that user comments, even with only one out of five comments being uncivil, could dampen audience perceptions of news quality for a real news brand. Given the fact that user comments remain an important tool for news engagement in today's online media environment, it is not realistic to eliminate all uncivil comments (Chen et al., 2019). Instead, both scholars and practitioners need to change the mindset toward how to minimize the detrimental impacts of online incivility. Actually, our study provides some hints on how practitioners could achieve this goal by tweaking the arrangement of comment threads. One way is to reduce the proportion of incivility in the comment threads through shielding uncivil comments from users. A second suggestion is to reorder the civil and uncivil comments in a given thread depending on the topic of commented-on articles. For obtrusive issues, news organizations and social media companies could manually or automatically de-prioritize uncivil comments to attenuate the negative impacts of incivility on news quality perceptions. For unobtrusive issues, a thread with first several uncivil comments should not be that troublesome. But editors and moderators need to focus on the bottom comments on the first screens to avoid a recency effect of online incivility in dampening news quality perceptions.

Limitations and future directions

Like other research, this study has several limitations. First, the four articles selected in this study, though representing a variety of issues, are all related to the COVID-19 pandemic, which may not be generalized to other types of issues. Second, the study focused on *AP news*, the website of which does not have a comment section, so the findings may not speak well to news brands with comment sections. Third and relatedly, as we looked at a politically neutral news brand, how online incivility dampens news quality of partisan media requires more inquiries. In addition, we only examined the effects of online incivility by using comment threads consisting of five comments. With a fixed number of comments in an experimental setting, users are able to read all the comments and form judgments. It is not clear if this line of findings could be applicable to a longer comment thread, which is more common in the real world. We encourage both researchers and practitioners to employ field experiments to further explore how the different arrangement of civil and uncivil comments would influence users' evaluations of news content.

Note

1 This research was supported by a grant from the Sheila and Robert Challey Institute for Global Innovation and Growth at North Dakota State University. The authors acknowledge that the Challey Institute bears no responsibility for any conclusions drawn in this study.

References

Anderson, A. A., Yeo, S. K., Brossard, D., Scheufele, D. A., & Xenos, M. A. (2018). Toxic talk: How online incivility can undermine perceptions of media. *International Journal of Public Opinion Research*, 30(1), 156–168.

Brown, P., & Levinson, S.C. (1987). *Politeness: Some universals in language usage*. Cambridge University Press.

Cacioppo, J.T., & Petty, R. E. (1979). Effects of message repetition and position on cognitive response, recall, and persuasion. *Journal of Personality and Social Psychology*, 37(1), 97–109.

Chen, G. M. (2017). *Online incivility and public debate: Nasty talk*. Palgrave Macmillan.

Chen, G., & Lu, S. (2017). Online political discourse: Exploring differences in effects of civil and uncivil disagreement in news website comments. *Journal of Broadcasting & Electronic Media*, 61(1), 108–125.

Chen, G., Muddiman, A., Wilner, T., Pariser, E., & Stroud, N. J. (2019). We should not get rid of incivility online. *Social Media + Society, 5*(3), 2056305119862641.

Coe, K., Kenski, K., & Rains, S. A. (2014). Online and uncivil? Patterns and determinants of incivility in newspaper website comments. *Journal of Communication, 64*(4), 658–679.

Conlin, L., & Roberts, C. (2016). Presence of online reader comments lowers news site credibility. *Newspaper Research Journal, 37*(4), 365–376.

Demers, D. P., Craff, D., Choi, Y. H., & Pessin, B. M. (1989). Issue obtrusiveness and the agenda-setting effects of national network news. *Communication Research, 16*(6), 793–812.

Erbring, L., Goldenberg, E. N., & Miller, A. H. (1980). Front-page news and real-world cues: A new look at agenda-setting by the media. *American Journal of Political Science*, 16–49.

Gallup and Knight Foundation. (2018). Indicators of news media trust. https://knightfou ndation.org/reports/indicators-of-news-media-trust/

Graefe, A., Haim, M., Haarmann, B., & Brosius, H. B. (2018). Readers' perception of computer-generated news: Credibility, expertise, and readability. *Journalism, 19*(5), 595–610.

Grieve, T. (2014). Why we're changing our comments policy. www.nationaljournal. com/congress/2014/05/16/why-were-changing-our-comments-policy.

Haugtvedt, C. P., & Wegener, D. T. (1994). Message order effects in persuasion: An attitude strength perspective. *Journal of Consumer Research, 21*(1), 205–218.

Humprecht, E., & Esser, F. (2018). Diversity in online news: On the importance of ownership types and media system types. *Journalism Studies, 19*(12), 1825–1847.

Kanouse, D.E., & Hanson, L.R. (1972). Negativity in evaluation. In E. E. Jones et al. (Eds.), *Attribution: Perceiving the causes of behavior* (pp. 47–62). General Learning Press.

Kenski, K., Coe, K., & Rains, S.A. (2020). Perceptions of uncivil discourse online: An examination of types and predictors. *Communication Research, 47*(6), 795–814.

Kress, G. & Van Leeuwen, T. (2006). *Reading images: The grammar of visual design* (2nd edition). Routledge.

Liang, H., & Zhang, X. (2021). Partisan bias of perceived incivility and its political consequences: Evidence from survey experiments in Hong Kong. *Journal of Communication, 71*(3), 357–379.

Lund, F. (1925). The psychology of belief IV: The law of priming in persuasion. *Journal of Abnormal and Social Psychology, 20*, 183–191.

Masullo, G. M., Tenenboim, O., & Lu, S. (2021). "Toxic atmosphere effect": Uncivil online comments cue negative audience perceptions of news outlet credibility. *Journalism*. https://journals.sagepub.com/doi/abs/10.1177/14648849211064001.

McQuail, D. (1992). *Media performance: Mass communication and the public interest.* Sage Publications.

McQuail, D. (2013). *Journalism and society.* Sage Publications.

Miller, J. M., & Krosnick, J. A. (1998). The impact of candidate name order on election outcomes. *Public Opinion Quarterly, 62*(3), 291–330. https://doi.org/10.1086/297848

Muddiman, A. (2017). Personal and public levels of political incivility. *International Journal of Communication, 11*, 3182–3202.

Murphy, J., Hofacker, C., & Mizerski, R. (2006). Primacy and recency effects on clicking behavior. *Journal of Computer-Mediated Communication, 11*(2), 522–535.

O'Keefe, D. J. (2002). *Persuasion: Theory and research*, Sage.

Papacharissi, Z. (2004). Democracy online: Civility, politeness, and the democratic potential of online political discussion groups. *New Media & Society, 6*(2), 259–283.

Petty, R. E., & Cacioppo, J. T. (1979). Issue involvement can increase or decrease persuasion by enhancing message-relevant cognitive responses. *Journal of Personality and Social Psychology, 37*(10), 1915–1926.

Plasser, F. (2005). From hard to soft news standards? How political journalists in different media systems evaluate the shifting quality of news. *Harvard International Journal of Press/Politics, 10*(2), 47–68.

Prochazka, F., Weber, P., & Schweiger, W. (2018). Effects of civility and reasoning in user comments on perceived journalistic quality. *Journalism Studies, 19*(1), 62–78.

Rösner, L., Winter, S., & Krämer, N. C. (2016). Dangerous minds? Effects of uncivil online comments on aggressive cognitions, emotions, and behavior. *Computers in Human Behavior, 58*, 461–470.

Rossini, P. (2020). Beyond incivility: Understanding patterns of uncivil and intolerant discourse in online political talk. *Communication Research.* https://doi: 10.1177/0093650220921314

Schwartz, B. L. (2011). *Memory: Foundations and applications.* Sage.

Shannon, C. E., & Weaver, W. (1949). *The mathematical theory of communication.* University of Illinois Press.

Stroud, N. J., Van Duyn, E., & Peacock, C. (2016). News commenters and news comment readers. https://mediaengagement.org/wp-content/uploads/2016/03/ ENP-News-Commenters-and-Comment-Readers1.pdf

Urban, J., & Schweiger, W. (2014). News quality from the recipients' perspective: Investigating recipients' ability to judge the normative quality of news. *Journalism Studies, 15*(6), 821–840.

Waddell, T. F. (2020). The authentic (and angry) audience: How comment authenticity and sentiment impact news evaluation. *Digital Journalism, 8*(2), 249–266.

Waugh, N. C., & Norman, D. A. (1965). Primary memory. *Psychological Review, 72*(2), 89–104.

Weber, P., Prochazka, F., & Schweiger, W. (2019). Why user comments affect the perceived quality of journalistic content. *Journal of Media Psychology: Theories, Methods, and Applications, 31*(1), 24–34.

6

BEYOND THE "TRUST" SURVEY

Measuring media attitudes through observation

Zacc Ritter and Jesse Holcomb

Introduction

Public opinion research about media attitudes has advanced over the past several decades (Fawzi et al., 2021). Long gone are the days when a single measure such as credibility, trust, or quality, was considered entirely sufficient. Increasingly, survey researchers use multi-dimensional measures to study such concepts in relation to the media because these related concepts may not be capturing the same underlying construct.

Yet, these positive measurement developments are muted by the limitations of self-reported data on media attitudes. Further still, the self-reporting of media behaviors can be even more problematic. News consumers live in such a complex information ecosystem that it can be difficult to recall one's typical media use. The advent of the consumer internet, along with access to trace data collection through third-party companies, has opened up new opportunities for scholars to observe and document media behaviors, if not attitudes.

Nevertheless, we now know that passive data collection about media use comes with its own set of limitations: it can be messy and prone to error in ways that are difficult to identify, much less correct. And further, collection platforms can be hit-or-miss when it comes to collecting user data across sources, devices, and time (Barthel et al., 2020). Further complicating efforts is the fact that research questions are limited by the type of data available.

Even with these limitations, the appeal of using passive data collection to measure media use is clear. It is one thing for a survey respondent to tell an interviewer that they use a different set of criteria to judge whether a news article is "high quality" than if it is "trustworthy." It is quite another thing, however, to be

DOI: 10.4324/9781003257998-8

able to observe how a user assesses the attributes of a news article without filtering for troublesome issues such as non-attitudes.

This chapter has two aims. First, we intend to answer a research question about how news audiences approach two different but related dimensions of media performance; and second, to illustrate how a methodological innovation can complement both self-reported and observed media use.

We believe that with the full range of research tools, there is a third way to measure media attitudes. Surveys and traditional experiments offer a high degree of control, but are limited in their external validity. Studies utilizing digital trace data have strong external validity, but also significant limitations in what can be measured and studied. In this chapter, we propose further investment in research platforms that simulate the media environment through field experiments, and open up those platforms to scholars.

Literature review

This literature review focuses a few key dimensions of scholarship about media attitudes and behaviors. First, we discuss the evolution of attitudinal measures in self-reported data, namely, surveys. Next, we discuss the evolution of behavioral measures in both self-reported and observed methods, through surveys and through analysis of digital trace data. A fourth dimension—the study of media attitudes leveraging trace data—reveals a gap in the literature that we believe the research described in this chapter helps to fill. Table 6.1 offers a basic roadmap for how we conceptualize the methodological material, as well as the substantive material.

From single measures to multi-dimensional measures

The comparative study of media credibility traces its origins to the Roper surveys of the mid-20th century. From 1959 until the mid-1980s, Burns Roper's surveys asked Americans every two years the following question:

> If you got conflicting or different reports of the same story from radio, television, the magazines and the newspapers, which of the four versions

TABLE 6.1 Structure of literature review

		Methodological approach	
		Survey data	Trace data
Substantive question	News consumption habits	Type 1	Type 2
	Attitudes toward news content.	Type 3	Type 4

would you be most inclined to believe—the one on radio or television or magazines or newspapers?

(Roper, 1985)

The "Roper question" was adopted and widely used by other survey researchers as a sort of standard for media credibility measurement for much of the later 20th century. The question, however, was not without its critics. Gantz in particular critiqued the Roper approach, on the grounds that media credibility cannot reasonably be measured with a single indicator (Gantz, 1981, p. 168).

By the 1970s, researchers were advancing on Roper's work in a way that responded to the critiques leveled by Gantz and others, by using factor analysis to study media credibility as a multidimensional concept (Gaziano & McGrath, 1986; Lee, 1978). (Factor analysis is a statistical method that compares the salience of a group of observed variables to aid in the construction of a smaller number of unobserved constructed variables—in this case, a measure of media trust is the result of analyzing a series of trust-related dimensions.)

At the same time, scholars were applying concepts developed in the study of source credibility specifically to media credibility (Metzger et al., 2003, p. 310).

It was not until the turn of the 21st century, however, that scholars began to develop and test robust scales for measuring media trust. In 2007, Kohring and Matthes introduced a four-dimensional scale, measuring A) trust in the selectivity of topics, B) trust in the selectivity of facts, C) trust in the accuracy of depictions, and D) trust in journalistic assessment (Kohring & Matthes, 2007).

Others have built on this work, including the research team at the American Press Institute, which published a study in 2016 that identified six dimensions of trust in news: A) Accuracy, B) Completeness, C) Presentation, D) Transparency, E) Balance, and F) Convenience or Entertainment (American Press Institute, 2016). More recently, the Knight Foundation with the Gallup organization conducted a conjoint analysis, which identified accuracy and bias—and to a lesser extent, transparency—as the most salient issues among the American public out of a list of 35 potential indicators of media trust (Knight Foundation & Gallup, 2018).

Schmidt and colleagues (2019) build upon these scales and analyses (both factor and conjoint) in an important way, by exploring how people in marginalized communities define trust using their own words. Their study, based on focus groups, found that responsibility, integrity, and inclusiveness are the most salient dimensions.

Importantly, these contributions further incorporate measures of quality assessment, not just trust, into broader measures of news assessments.

In summary, over the past few decades, researchers and practitioners have sought to define and measure the concepts like quality or trust in news. These efforts are critical to identify clearer objective boundaries of what meets the standards of good journalism. While broad consensus exists that trust and quality are multidimensional constructs that encompass different aspects depending on the level of analysis—communication channel, news source, and the article content—these concepts are often treated separately. Yet, the degree to which average news consumers distinguish between them is unclear.

There is reason to suspect these two concepts are distinct, as quality evokes the notion of objectivity while trust elicits more a sense of subjectivity. Specifically, a rater may realize an article is biased against their preferred ideological position and so think the content is untrustworthy, but grudgingly admit the facts are accurate and argument marshaled to support it reasonable. Equally plausible is that respondent-level factors swamp the ability of an online news consumer to make such nuanced assessments at the article-level. For instance, a substantial literature demonstrates that partisan identity strongly mediates general assessments of news—e.g., accuracy, bias, and transparency—at the source-level (Knight, 2018; Ladd, 2011; Mourão et al., 2018; Urban & Schweiger, 2014).

RQ: Do news consumers rate content differently depending on whether the rating metric is trust or quality?

Measurement challenges

Many studies measuring media attitudes, including those that assess trust and quality perceptions, rely on survey data. But there are limitations to self-reported information.

The most instructive case here relates to the perception that news audiences tend to isolate themselves into media bubbles that reflect their partisan priors, a view reinforced most often by survey data.

Guess (2020) critiques what he characterizes as exaggerated concern about filter bubbles and echo chambers. His mixed-methods approach, which combines survey data with digital trace data, shows a more muted degree of media polarization than is suggested by survey data on the topic.

Guess is only the most recent scholar to demonstrate this pattern. Gentzkow and Shapiro (2011) found that online "ideological segregation" is less of an issue online than with national newspapers or in interpersonal face-to-face conversations. Barbara (2014) found, using panel data, that Twitter usage trended toward moderation as opposed to polarization. Flaxman, Goel, and Rao studied the web-browsing histories of Bing users (2016) and found that digital media can actually promote ideological heterogeneity. Finally, Scharkow and colleagues (2020) found that social media and web portals can lead to increased visits to a wider range of news sites using experimental techniques.

But even so, the use of digital trace data to illuminate the public's behaviors comes with its own set of limitations. A major Pew Research Center study in 2020 studied both the self-reported responses, and the observed behaviors, of a representative panel of American news consumers (Pew Research Center, 2020). The researchers found that while the use of passive data shows promise, it contains several shortcomings: news use estimates from passive data collection are consistently lower than self-reported measures, a problem easily traced to the smaller number of consumer devices that can be tracked through passive data collection. On the other hand, the Pew Research report pointed to some passive data collection firms that over-estimated media use. The bottom line, according to Pew, is that while surveys have their own limitations, those limitations are widely understood, and to a degree, can be corrected through weighting and other techniques. Digital trace data are still something of a black box.

Once again, recalling Table 6.1, survey design advancements have developed increasingly granular ways of measuring self-reported media attitudes and behaviors. Still, as Guess and others have found, these approaches are limited in their ability to capture human behavior when it comes to media use. Trace data gleaned from third-party providers offers new insights into media use, but less so, attitudes.

This chapter details a new approach by utilizing a custom news web platform, employing both experimental approaches, but also self-reported measures, to better understand how news consumers respond to news at the article level, specifically, in how they differentiate between their assessments of an article's quality versus its trustworthiness.

Methods

To better understand media consumption habits and attitudes toward news content, the Knight Foundation and the Gallup organization built a custom platform called NewsLens—a digital news aggregation platform that combined survey research and passive measures for tracking behaviors like clicks, impressions, shares, and comments (Knight Foundation & Gallup, 2020).

The platform displayed roughly a hundred daily articles covering the topics of politics, economics, and science randomly selected from ten news outlets across the political spectrum including the Huffington Post, Vox, CNN, NPR, NBC, AP, The Hill, Fox, Breitbart, and One America News (OANN).

We recruited users in three ways. First, Gallup and the Knight Foundation encouraged participation through their respective network of contacts. Second, participants from the Volunteer Science Project at Northeastern University received invitations to join NewsLens. Third, paid advertisements run on Facebook, Twitter, and Google invited U.S. adults from groups that remained under-represented, like Americans without a college degree or political conservatives.

After completing a brief empanelment survey that collects basic demographics, NewsLens users were shown a welcome message asking them to help Gallup learn more about how people decide what news is trustworthy. They were then shown a request to visit the site regularly and read, rate, and share articles.

NewsLens ran for two concurrent research cycles in 2020. The first research cycle ran from July 26 through September 29, and the second research cycle ran from September 30 through November 17. This chapter focuses on data collected during the first research cycle.

Throughout the course of the research cycle, a total of 577 individuals clicked on article content inside the NewsLens platform. Of those users, 312 users rated any articles. Of those 312, 303 users had agreed on the outset to complete the NewsLens empanelment survey, which provided researchers with some key demographic information about those users. Thus, this study is based on results collected from those 303 users, during the summer of 2020.

The NewsLens platform allows for experimental design through random assignment of users to different treatment groups in which they remain for the entire period of research. During the research cycle that is the focus of this chapter, users were introduced to a five-star rating system accompanying each news article they read. Depending on which group a user was randomly assigned to, once an article is opened, users see the full text and can rate the article between one and five stars. Participants were presented with text next to the stars that read, "Submit Your **Trust** Rating" or "Submit Your **Quality** Rating," depending on the treatment group.

Since the user base is drawn from a convenience sample that is not representative of the U.S. adult population, the experimental results reported below focus on effect sizes (the differences between experimental conditions) rather than point estimates (the mean of one of these conditions in isolation).[1]

Results

To assess the main research question, we compare the overall average trust rating for articles with the overall quality rating using an OLS model with clustered standard error around each unique user. The average trust rating for an article is 3.5 stars and the average quality rating is 3.81 stars. While this .31 difference is significant at p<.05 level, statistical significance drops just below p<.1 level if a few outliers—ten NewsLens super-users that account for 20 percent of all the ratings—are omitted from the analysis. Therefore, the evidence does not robustly support the general hypothesis that NewsLens users rate content differently based on whether the metric is quality or trust.

Although there was no a priori hypothesis that different sub-populations would discriminate between these two concepts in systematically different ways, a statistically significant difference arose by party affiliation ideology. Specifically, NewsLens users who identify as independents and conservative respectively rated articles .67 points and .76 points higher on average in the quality condition compared to the trust condition, as shown in Table 6.2. These differences remain statistically significant even if outlier users are omitted. In contrast, the statistical significance for the .36 difference of "somewhat liberal" NewsLens users dropped below p<.01 when outliers are removed.

90 Zacc Ritter and Jesse Holcomb

TABLE 6.2 Results of experiment

Category	Population	Average Trust rating	Average Quality rating	Difference (entire sample)	Difference (outlier cases removed)
Overall	**All Users**	3.50	3.81	.31★	.25
Political party	**Democrat**	3.72	3.76	.04	-.08
affiliation	**Independent**	3.20	3.86	.67★★	.57★
	Republican	3.70	3.92	.22	.22
Political	**Liberal**	3.44	3.57	.13	-.03
ideology	**Somewhat liberal**	3.52	3.88	.36★★	.39
	Moderate	3.47	3.81	.34	.34
	Somewhat conservative	3.51	4.07	.56	.56
	Conservative	3.26	4.02	.76★	.76★
Trust in	**Almost always**	2.93	3.44	.51	.51
journalists	**Most of the time**	3.76	3.97	.21	.02
	About half the time	3.54	3.52	-.01	-.01
	Once in a while	3.16	3.99	.83★★	.83★★
	Almost never	2.57	4.40	1.83★★	1.83★★

† p<.1; ★ p<.05; ★★ p<.01.

These results may be related to the fact that independents and very conservative Americans tend to exhibit low levels of political trust, as well as trust in the media (Hooghe & Oser, 2017; Brenan, 2020). In a survey fielded on the NewsLens platform, we asked respondents how much of the time they think they can trust journalists. We find that respondents with low trust in journalists also tend to rate articles higher when the concept is quality rather than trust. While these results should only be considered suggestive because they are based on only 19 respondents who said they trust journalists "once in a while" or "almost never," the results remain robust at the p<.01 even after removing the top five raters.

To summarize, the results reveal a mixed picture, especially when a small group of outlier "power users" were excluded from the analysis, in order to present a more valid picture. Many NewsLens users rated articles similarly regardless of whether the metric they rated that content was trust or quality. Yet, political independents, conservatives, and those with low trust in journalists gave higher average ratings to articles based on quality than on trust.

Discussion

The findings from this experiment suggest researchers should exercise caution when examining results from public opinion research on attitudes toward the news media based on a single metric. While some consumers may evaluate news content similarly regardless of whether the criteria are based on trustworthiness, quality, credibility, favorability, or some other aspect, others may distinguish between these multi-dimensional concepts. For instance, the experiment discussed in this chapter offers robust evidence that some types of news consumers distinguish between trust and quality in a systematic way, and are able to evaluate news content in such a way as to hold those two concepts independently of each other. In other words, some news consumers—perhaps especially those who are conservative and otherwise distrusting of the news media—might view a news article as high in quality, yet at the same time, not very trustworthy.

Recognition of this fact partly recasts the recent trend in public opinion findings that show a dramatic decline in trust of the media and mainstream news outlets among certain segments of the American public (Knight Foundation & Gallup, 2018). Commentators have critiqued the survey wording in these kinds of polls on the basis that most people can't reasonably evaluate "the news media" as a monolithic whole, because we live in a fractured, high-choice news environment. Our findings here speak to another potential weakness in these kinds of survey questions: the use of the term "trust" may actually prime certain social groups to respond more affectively than others.

Perceptions of overall news quality among members of these groups—especially conservatives—may not follow the same trajectory, as the concept of "trust" may evoke a higher level of expressive responding than "quality," which would imply that general attitudes toward the media have not changed as sharply as public opinion polls suggests. In other words, when pollsters choose a single concept to gauge public opinion about the media, the choice of "trust" language may lead to an especially dire outlook, because of the way that certain social groups react to the word. By contrast, if pollsters were to use terminology related to "quality" in a single measure of public opinion about the news media, the results might paint a slightly more favorable picture overall, especially among conservatives.

More broadly, researchers should avoid conflation of terms like credibility, trust, quality, and favorability (Fawzi et al., 2021). While these concepts are related, they may not measure that same underlying construct when it comes to perceptions of the news media. Most academic studies on this topic are theory-centric, focusing on concept formation, but more empirical studies are warranted to examine whether and under what condition people evaluate news and information differently based on the anchoring concept. Such research could establish common sub-dimensions shared across related multi-dimensional concepts and sub-dimensions unique to a specific concept.

This unique research design made possible through the NewsLens platform revealed some differences in trust and quality of news articles, but there are some limitations to this experiment.

First, the results are based on a non-probability-based sample of 312 study participants, which limits the ability to generalize to the U.S. adult population, or conduct more nuanced sub-group analysis. Second, the NewsLens platform only presented users with text-based news articles, but the results may differ if the stimuli had been audio- or video-based.

The body of scholarly work discussed in this chapter can be boiled down to a set of trade-offs over internal and external validity. Survey approaches to measuring news quality and trust have grown increasingly sophisticated; however, the experiment featured in this chapter suggests that some respondents may not be able to distinguish between these concepts in a questionnaire. On the other hand, a wide range of studies utilizing digital trace data offer strong external validity by way of observational and not self-reported data. But many of these studies suffer from data limitations, some of which are difficult to even identify due to the closed nature of some of the datasets. And further, while trace data is valuable for understanding media behaviors, there have been few studies that leverage trace data for understanding attitudes.

The benefit of a platform like NewsLens is that it allows for observation in a semi-controlled setting, akin to a field experiment. Yet because we had access to the internal architecture of the platform, and worked closely with the research team that engineered it, there were far fewer unknowns in the research process. Even with the limitations in the data (and particularly, the sample), this kind of access is ideal, especially when third-party dataset arrangements reveal flaws late in the game. Another strength of the NewsLens platform is its mixed-methods approach to data collection—not only can researchers collect observational data, but also—through empanelment and ongoing surveys—collect key demographic and attitudinal covariates. Finally, the ability of NewsLens to measure attitudes by way of observation (in the case of this chapter, through the five-star rating system) is noteworthy.

A clear way that this research could be extended and improved upon would be through a more robustly populated news aggregator platform. Access to a nationally representative panel, for instance, would strengthen the findings in this chapter through replication. Additionally, one weakness of the NewsLens platform is that it mimics the digital environment of a news aggregator on a web browser. Increasingly, many people engage with news on social platforms, where their behaviors are telegraphed to their networks via engagement activities. Scholarly access to social platforms, along with the ability to conduct ethical and transparent user experiments related to news assessments, would advance this line of research tremendously. In the end, it seems, it all comes back to the need for robust partnerships that make platform data more accessible to researchers.

Note

1 The demographic composition of the 312 study participants who rated at least one article was 50 percent male, 35 percent over 55 years old, 83 percent with a four-year college education or more, and 51 percent affiliated as Democrats.

References

American Press Institute (2016, April 17). A new understanding: What makes people trust and rely on news. www.americanpressinstitute.org/publications/reports/survey-research/trust-news/

Barberá, P. (2014). How social media reduces mass political polarization. Evidence from Germany, Spain, and the U.S. Working paper. http://pablobarbera.com/static/barbera_polarization_APSA.pdf

Barthel, M., Mitchell, A., Asare-Marfo, D., Kennedy, C., & Worden, K. (2020). Measuring news consumption in a digital era. Pew Research Center. www.pewresearch.org/journalism/2020/12/08/measuring-news-consumption-in-a-digital-era/

Brenan, M. (2020). Americans remain distrustful of mass media. *Gallup.com*. https://news.gallup.com/poll/321116/americans-remain-distrustful-mass-media.aspx

Fawzi, N., Steindl, N., Obermaier, M., Prochazka, F., Arlt, D., Blöbaum, B., ... & Ziegele, M. (2021). Concepts, causes and consequences of trust in news media–a literature review and framework. *Annals of the International Communication Association*, *45*(2), 154–174.

Flaxman, S., Goel, S., and Rao, J. (2016). Filter bubbles, echo chambers, and online news consumption. *Public Opinion Quarterly* 80(S1), 298–320.

Gantz, W. (1981). The influence of researcher methods on television and newspaper news credibility evaluations. *Journal of Broadcasting*, *25*, 155–169.

Gaziano, C., & McGrath, K. (1986). Measuring the concept of credibility. *Journalism Quarterly*, *63*, 451–462.

Gentzkow, M., & Shapiro, J.M. (2011). Ideological segregation online and offline. *The Quarterly Journal of Economics*, 126, 1799–1839.

Hooghe, M., & Oser, J. (2017). Partisan strength, political trust and generalized trust in the United States: An analysis of the General Social Survey, 1972–2014. *Social Science Research*, *68*, 132–146.

Knight Foundation & Gallup (2018). Indicators of news media trust. https://knightfoundation.org/reports/indicators-of-news-media-trust/

Knight Foundation & Gallup (2020). NewsLens 2020: How Americans process the news. https://knightfoundation.org/reports/newslens-2020-how-americans-process-the-news/

Kohring, M., and Matthes, J. (2007). Trust in news media: Development and validation of a multidimensional scale. *Communication Research*, 34(2), 231–252.

Ladd, J. M. (2012). *Why Americans hate the news media and how it matters*. Princeton University Press.

Lee, R. S. H. (1978). Credibility of newspaper and TV news. *Journalism Quarterly*, 55, 282–287.

Metzger, M. J., Flanagin, A. J., Eyal, K., Lemus, D. R., & McCann, R. (2003). Credibility in the 21st century: Integrating perspectives on source, message, and media credibility in the contemporary media environment. In P. Kalbfleisch (Ed.), *Communication Yearbook*, 27 (pp. 293–335). Lawrence Erlbaum.

Mourão, R. R., Thorson, E., Chen, W., & Tham, S. M. (2018). Media repertoires and news trust during the early Trump administration. *Journalism Studies*, *19*(13), 1945–1956.

Roper, B. W. (1985). Public attitudes toward television and other media in a time of change. Television Information Office.

Scharkow, M., Mangold, F., Stier, S., and Breuer, J. (2020). How social network sites and other online intermediaries increase exposure to news. *Proceedings of the National Academy of Sciences*, *117*(6):2761–2763.

Schmidt, T. R., Heyamoto, L., & Milbourn, T. (2019). The social construction of media trust: An exploratory study in underserved communities. *Journal of Applied Journalism & Media Studies, 8*(3), 257–271.

Urban, J. & Schweiger, W. (2014). News quality from the recipients' perspective: Investigating recipients' ability to judge the normative quality of news. *Journalism Studies, 15*(6), 821–840.

PART III

Algorithmic Systems and News Quality

7

ALL THE NEWS THAT'S FIT TO TWEET

Sociotechnical local news distribution from the *New York Times* to Twitter

Jack Bandy and Nicholas Diakopoulos

Introduction

A quality information ecosystem requires steady streams of local news. Studies have shown that local news is associated with higher civic engagement (Hayes & Lawless, 2018), stronger social connections (Barthel et al., 2016), greater economic efficiency (Gao et al., 2020), and other benefits for communities. Yet local journalism is in crisis, as publishers face plummeting revenue, widespread layoffs, and constrained distribution. News consumers also sense that something is wrong: although most U.S. adults (75 percent) have "at least some trust" in local news organizations, the rate is declining, and few (18 percent) express high levels of trust (Pew, 2021). Furthermore, approximately half of U.S. adults (47 percent) say their local news media mostly cover an area other than where they live (Pew, 2019).

With publishers and audiences both dissatisfied, understanding the local news crisis has become a key goal in academic research. Some of this research explores how the malfunctioning local news ecosystem is influenced by new technology, from the internet itself, to aggregators and search engines, to algorithmic feeds on social media. Other related literature—including work within this volume— explores the many non-technological factors at play. Individual cognition, group audience behavior, publishers' goals, organizational structures, and even systemic economic patterns can shape the production and distribution of news, alongside technological factors such as algorithmic platforms.

Considering both social and technological factors, this chapter addresses how publishers and platforms shape the local news ecosystem in tandem. Specifically, we undertake a longitudinal case study of the *New York Times*, analyzing patterns in local news production, editorial curation, and platform curation on Twitter. In

DOI: 10.4324/9781003257998-10

addition to characterizing long-term trends in production and curation, a major focus of our analysis is how algorithms impact the distribution of local news content. We specifically explore how the *Times'* "blossom" algorithm affected the rate of local news shared by the @nytimes Twitter account, and how Twitter's timeline algorithm affected audience engagement with *Times* content.

Overall, evidence suggests a constrained flow of local news from the *Times*, especially in terms of production and editorial curation. Local news production at the *Times* has steadily declined since 2006, and has also declined as a proportion of its overall production since the 1990s. In terms of editorial curation, we find the @nytimes Twitter account was less likely to share local news articles after editors started using the "blossom" algorithm, which recommends articles to share on social media (Wang, 2015). Lastly, in analyzing platform curation and the impact of Twitter's timeline algorithm, we find that the algorithm's introduction coincided with a decreased proportion of followers engaging with tweets from the @nytimes account; however, the decrease was not unique to local news articles. The chapter concludes with a brief discussion of our findings, emphasizing the multi-faceted nature of the local news crisis and potential points of intervention.

Related work

This chapter sits at the intersection of several research topics related to journalism studies and social media platforms. These topics include: theoretical work conceptualizing the flow of news and information; efforts to understand the dynamics of news quality amidst the ongoing local news crisis and technological changes disrupting journalism; and some literature that specifically analyzes the *New York Times*.

Curated flows

Communication scholars have long theorized about how news and information flow in society. One foundational theory was the "two-step flow of communication" (Katz & Lazarsfeld, 1955), which suggests an initial broadcast to mass audiences followed by a second step, wherein "opinion leaders" share news and information to social groups. In this model, interpersonal communication (step two) plays a significant role in how people encounter news and information. Studies testing models of two-step flow and opinion leadership have yielded mixed results, often suggesting the need for more nuanced models (e.g., Robinson, 1976; Nisbet & Kotcher, 2009; Hilbert et al., 2017).

Recent work has proposed several alternative models to capture how news flows in the digital era. Some scholars suggest a "one-step flow" model, since new technology supports sending messages directly to individuals (Bennett & Manheim, 2006). The one-step model emphasizes targeted "narrowcasting" as the main way to reach audiences. Another proposed modification is the expanded "five-step flow" model (Napoli, 2019), which consists of:

1. A news organization producing news
2. The organization curating news to share on social media platforms
3. Social media platforms filtering information for direct news consumers
4. Some direct news consumers re-sharing the news to their personal networks
5. Social media platforms filtering the re-shared news to indirect news consumers

Since the final two steps are repeatable, some characterize it as a "network step" (Hilbert et al., 2017), creating a more dynamic model with limitless repetitions. Furthermore, intermediaries may include not only news producers and social media platforms, but also various types of central "opinion leaders." One large-scale study identified five types of central intermediaries: conversation starters, influencers, active engagers, network builders, and information bridges, each playing a distinct role in disseminating news (Feng, 2016).

This increasing complexity has led some scholars away from linear step-flow models, in favor of a fully networked model: "curated flows" that encompass yet further types of actors, including journalists, strategic communicators, individual media users, social contacts, and algorithmic filters (Thorson & Wells, 2016). The "curated flows" model leverages the concept of "egocentric publics," in which each individual audience member sits at the center of a broad network of actors shaping the individual's media consumption through curation decisions (Wojcieszak & Rojas, 2011).

Thorson and Wells (2016) describe curated flows as each individual receiving news from a personalized, sprawling communication network of "curators" (e.g., people, advertisers, algorithms) that send and/or filter content. This framework prompts several broad research questions for communication studies, including: which news curators have the most impact, and to what extent? In previous studies (e.g., Bandy & Diakopoulos, 2021), we found that Twitter's timeline algorithm had a substantial impact as a platform curator, for example, significantly reducing the rate of external links that appear in user timelines. This chapter aims to further address questions of curation and impact, in this case focusing on local news while accounting for multiple steps in the curated flow.

News quality and social media platforms

With the initial rise of social media, some celebrated its potential benefits to the news ecosystem, suggesting that platforms offered the public "greater access to information, more opportunities to engage in public speech, and an enhanced ability to undertake collective action" (Shirky, 2011, p. 29). A different narrative emerged soon after, highlighting that social media platforms played a role in "enabling increased polarization, rising authoritarianism, and meddling in national elections" (Tufekci,

2018). Scholarship exploring these negative consequences generally focuses on the accuracy/veracity dimension of news quality, and on the low-quality end of that dimension. This body of research has refined various definitions related to low-quality news (e.g., Lazer et al., 2018; Tandoc et al., 2018); however, it leaves open questions regarding the definition and measurement of *high*-quality news.

To identify high-quality news and information, some classification systems label outlets based on professional reputation (Bradshaw et al., 2020), or aggregated credibility scores from organizations like Pew Research and NewsGuard (Guess et al., 2021; Nørregaard et al., 2019). These approaches offer helpful frameworks; however, they treat each publisher as either high-quality or low-quality, and do not account for potential variation within outlets.

In contrast, content-level analysis helps identify specific dimensions of news quality, aside from the status of the news outlet. Crucially, this allows for the possibility that professional news outlets such as the *New York Times* produce a heterogeneous mix of news content that varies in quality and value. Content-level analysis sometimes builds on the news values literature, using concepts like depth and diversity as indicators of high-quality articles (Choi et al., 2021). Another approach is to pinpoint article-level features that indicate quality, such as representative titles and quotes from experts (Zhang et al., 2018).

In this work, we consider *local relevance* as one indicator of quality content. There are many reasons to consider geographic relevance as an indicator of value and an important dimension of quality news. Local relevance is valued both by audiences and journalists (Gladney, 1996; Lacy & Rosenstiel, 2015), defying the "choice gap" that often separates what audiences want to read and what journalists consider important (Boczkowski & Mitchelstein, 2013; Wendelin et al., 2017). Furthermore, a body of research shows that local relevance in news provides unique benefits to communities, including stronger social connections (Barthel et al., 2016; Yamamoto, 2011) and lower environmental pollution (Campa, 2018). Communities also face dire consequences when local news disappears (Abernathy, 2018), including political polarization (Darr et al., 2018), government inefficiencies (Gao et al., 2020), and reduced civic engagement (Hayes & Lawless, 2018).

The New York Times

Given its prominence and reputation as "the paper of record," the *New York Times* has been the subject of numerous research studies. Exploring organizational phenomena at the *Times*, some studies analyze how the newsroom deals with audience metrics (Petre, 2015); how journalists navigate the social processes of business news production (Usher, 2017); and how ownership influences editorial priorities (Chomsky, 2006). Other studies focus more specifically on *Times* content, often narrowing in on a specific section such as science (e.g., Clark & Illman, 2006; Pellechia, 1997), or specific events such as presidential campaigns (e.g., Benoit et al., 2005) and social movements (e.g., Xu, 2013).

Many studies of the *Times* address news quality, at least implicitly. Some use measurements that fit the specific area of interest, such as "broader and more regular coverage" or "more complete and comprehensive" science articles (Pellechia, 1997). Day and Golan (2005) measured author diversity and viewpoint diversity in the opinion section for three topics (affirmative action, the death penalty, and marriage equality). Lewandowsky and colleagues (2020) measured shifts in topical coverage, finding that the *New York Times* was susceptible to political diversion—when former president Trump tweeted about diversionary topics, the *Times* reduced coverage of other key topics.

Despite steady scholarly attention to the *Times* and widespread agreement about the importance of local news, to our knowledge only a limited amount of academic research explores local news at the *Times*. Barkan (2017) offers a journalistic account, reporting on the decline in local reporters and the shift in the *Times'* editorial priorities, as well as a decline in the New York City local news ecosystem more broadly. George and Waldfogel (2006) study the flipside of local news reduction, focusing on the *New York Times* national edition and its impact on over a hundred U.S. cities in the 1990s.

In terms of curation, Wang (2015) reports that the *Times* created an algorithm nicknamed "blossom" to help editors decide which articles to share on social media. Blossom works by using previous social media data to predict which of the day's stories would generate engagement, helping editors choose which of the three hundred or so daily *Times* stories to post. When details of the system were first reported, it worked as a Slack chatbot that responded with a list of stories predicted to perform well. We are not aware of any work analyzing the impact of this algorithm.

Building on related work exploring curated flows, social media platforms, and the *New York Times*, this chapter explores the flow of local news from initial production at the *Times*, to editorial curation on the @nytimes Twitter account, to audience engagement on Twitter (see Figure 7.1 for a visual representation of these flows). More formally, we address the following research questions:

- **RQ1**: How has local news *production* evolved at the *New York Times*?
- **RQ2**: How has *editorial curation* of local news evolved for the *New York Times* on Twitter, and how did the "blossom" algorithm impact this curation?
- **RQ3**: How has *platform curation* of the *New York Times'* local news evolved on Twitter, and how did the platform's algorithms impact this curation?

Data and methods

Data collection

This analysis relies on two data sources to address our research questions: (1) a baseline dataset of all stories published by the *Times* from 1990 to 2020, and (2) a

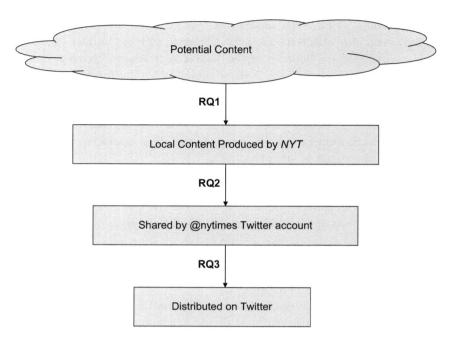

FIGURE 7.1 Diagram of curated flows studied in this work.

dataset of all tweets by the official @nytimes Twitter account. We collected the baseline dataset of stories using the *Times'* archive API,[1] querying and saving all published articles from 1990 to 2020.

For the second dataset of tweets, we collected tweets posted by @nytimes from 2007 (when the account joined) until the end of 2020. Our analysis focuses on the @nytimes account because it has the largest audience on Twitter of any official *Times* account (over 50 million followers as of September 2021). We collected 4,502,465 tweets from the account using the Twitter academic API.

Analyzing production patterns (RQ1) only required the first dataset of stories from the *Times*. Analyzing curation (RQ2 and RQ3), however, required linking the story dataset and the tweet dataset. To do this, we used a python script that followed short links tweeted by the *Times* to their destination URLs (e.g., converting https://nyti.ms/3hecQJj to https://www.nytimes.com/2021/09/08/us/robert-e-lee-statue-virginia.html).

Labeling local news

The chapters in this volume demonstrate several different ways to capture news quality: topic labels, crowdsourced ratings, source reputation, editorial values, and more. One goal of this chapter is to address the limitations of rating news quality at the source level, and instead take a more granular lens. While the *New York Times* is generally considered a reputable, high-quality news source, like any news outlet, it produces different types of content that vary in quality and value. As discussed in the related work section, evidence supports geographic relevance as one important aspect of quality news.

To measure the geographic relevance of articles published by the *Times*, we use section labels provided by the *Times'* archive API. Automated methods could also support this type of analysis, however, our approach has the benefit of human validation: section labels come from human editors who professionally adjudicate the geographic relevance of different news articles. We specifically use labels for three sections that map to local, national, and world news: New York Metro, U.S., and World, respectively.

Notably, as Barkan (2017) discusses, the New York section of the *Times* has changed as the organization has grown. The section has generally covered the New York metropolitan area, but recent years have seen drastic staff cuts (Barkan, 2017) and deliberately reduced coverage of "incremental" news events (Spayd, 2016). In this sense, even the New York section may not represent the kind of local news that researchers have found so beneficial to communities. We explore this limitation further in the discussion.

Analytical framework

Our analysis addresses three main research questions related to local news at the *Times*: (1) production trends, (2) editorial curation trends, and (3) platform curation trends. The first is intended to capture trends in the overall supply of local news from the *Times*, while the second and third explore how algorithms shape "curated flows" along which news travels. We use descriptive measures to capture overall supply (RQ1), namely the number (and proportion) of published words representing local/national/world news at the *Times*.

To analyze curation processes and how new algorithms impacted these processes, we build on the framework of "platform effects" from Malik and Pfeffer (2016). Our longitudinal data allows us to analyze patterns before and after the introduction of algorithms. This type of interrupted time series analysis has proven useful for pinpointing how structural changes can alter system behavior (Malik & Pfeffer, 2016).

The first structural change we explore (RQ2) is the *Times'* introduction of the "blossom" algorithm, a tool that helps editors decide which stories to post on social media (described in the section "The *New York Times*"). In the terminology of curated flows, the blossom algorithm represents a shift away from purely journalistic curation to a hybrid journalistic-algorithm curation, in which the algorithm can suggest stories to editors who make the final decision. The algorithm was first reported in August 2015 (Wang, 2015), so we explore tweet patterns for local, national, and world news articles in the time window spanning August 2014 to August 2016 (i.e., one year before and after the algorithm was reported).[2]

104 Jack Bandy and Nicholas Diakopoulos

TABLE 7.1 Events potentially influencing local news production/curation at the *New York Times*

Date	Event
January 1996	*New York Times* launches nytimes.com (Lichterman, 2016)
July 2006	Twitter introduced to the public
March 2007	*New York Times* joins Twitter as @nytimes
August 2007	*NYT* reduces physical paper size (Dunlap, 2016)
March 2011	Digital paywall instituted on nytimes.com (Sulzberger, 2011)
August 2015	Nieman Lab reports on *NYT*'s "blossom" algorithm (Wang, 2015)
February 2016	BuzzFeed reports Twitter to launch algorithmic timelines (Kantrowitz, 2016)
March 2016	Twitter completes algorithmic timeline rollout to all users (Oremus, 2017)

We also explore the impact of Twitter's timeline algorithm (RQ3), which rolled out to all users in March 2016. We focus on the initial change from chronological to algorithmic timelines; however, Twitter has introduced numerous changes (some known and some unknown) to their platform's algorithms over time (Rashidian et al., 2020) (see Table 7.1). We test the hypothesized change point in March 2016 and run detection for other potential change points using the same causal inference methods from RQ2.

Results

Local news production (RQ1)

Local news has been steadily declining at the *New York Times*, both in terms of total production and proportional production. From the 1990s to the mid-2000s, the New York section of the *Times* steadily published between 800,000 and 1 million words each month. In 2006, the "Empire Zone" blog helped drive a temporary spike in local content production, surpassing 1.4 million words for several months. But by 2020, the New York section was only publishing approximately 200,000 words each month. As shown in Figure 7.2, this reduction in local news production was complemented by increased production of U.S. news, which has exceeded the New York section in total words published since 2015, and has substantially increased since 2018. World news production has been relatively stable, aside from a sharp drop in 2007 that coincides with a reduction in the size of the physical paper and other operational changes (Dunlap, 2016).

Furthermore, as a proportion of total news published by the *Times*, local news production has been declining since the 1990s. In 1995, 23 percent of all words published were in the New York section, but in 2020 that proportion was just 5 percent. In comparison, production for the World section remained fairly

All the news that's fit to tweet **105**

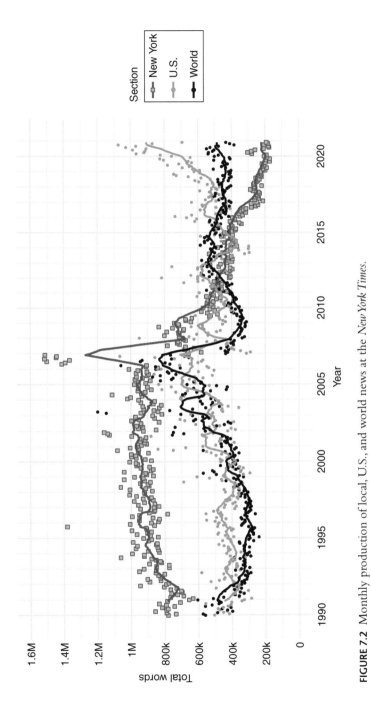

FIGURE 7.2 Monthly production of local, U.S., and world news at the *New York Times*. Measured as the sum of words published by the *Times* each month that were in the New York, U.S., and World news sections. Lines show 12-month rolling mean.

stable, while the U.S. section made notable gains from 2013 (8 percent of words published) to 2020 (20 percent of words published). Figure 7.3 shows the overall trends.

These longitudinal trends strongly suggest declining local news production at the *Times*, and the diminished supply sets up important context for the next two research questions. Algorithms and other curation factors may shape how local news flows from the *Times* to the @nytimes Twitter account (RQ2) and eventually to Twitter users (RQ3), but the *Times* has reduced the initial volume inputted to this flow.

Editorial curation (RQ2)

Our second research question analyzed editorial curation—the step in which *Times* editors choose which articles to share on social media. We focused on changes associated with the "blossom" algorithm that was first reported in August 2015 (Wang, 2015), finding statistically significant changes along several dimensions. At the most basic level, the mean rate of tweeting articles changed for two of the three sections, decreasing for local news (from 0.54 to 0.38), increasing for U.S. news (from 0.71 to 0.95), and holding steady for world news (from 0.70 to 0.70). Bayesian causal impact analysis suggests the changes were statistically significant for local news (p=0.01), marginally significant for U.S. news (p=0.09), and not significant for world news (p=0.21).

In addition to changes at the hypothesized time (August 2015), Bayesian change point analysis suggests a decrease in the tweet rate for local news articles beginning in July 2015. This may indicate when the *Times* expanded usage of the blossom algorithm (which began as early as April 2015, according to an executive we spoke to). See Figure 7.4 for a visual representation of the trends and changes.

Overall, while local news articles were always less likely to be tweeted compared to national and world news articles, the difference expanded in the months after the introduction of the "blossom" algorithm. This suggests that when it was introduced, the *Times'* internal algorithm drove increased social media visibility for articles from the U.S. and World news sections, but not for local news articles from the New York section.

Platform curation (RQ3)

The third research question asked how algorithmic platform curation has shaped engagement with local news from the *Times*. For this analysis, changes revolved around March 2016, when Twitter rolled out algorithmic timelines. After this point, Twitter users saw their timeline sorted algorithmically rather than chronologically, with no more than 2 percent of all users opting out (Oremus, 2017).

As shown in Figure 7.5, one salient effect of the algorithmic timeline was increased variation in engagement. The median number of likes per tweet grew

All the news that's fit to tweet **107**

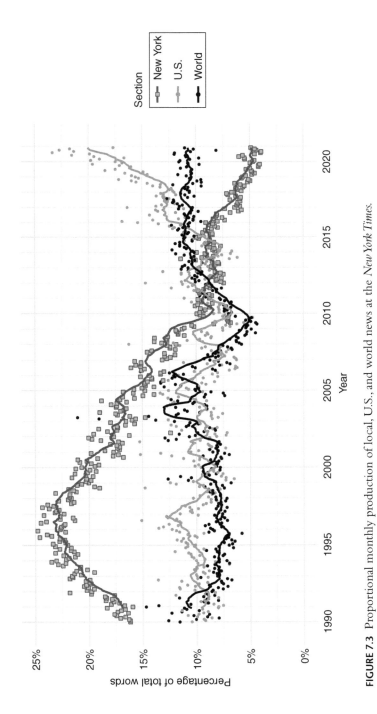

FIGURE 7.3 Proportional monthly production of local, U.S., and world news at the *New York Times*. Measured as the percentage of words published by the *Times* each month that were in the New York, U.S., and World news sections. Lines show the 12-month rolling mean.

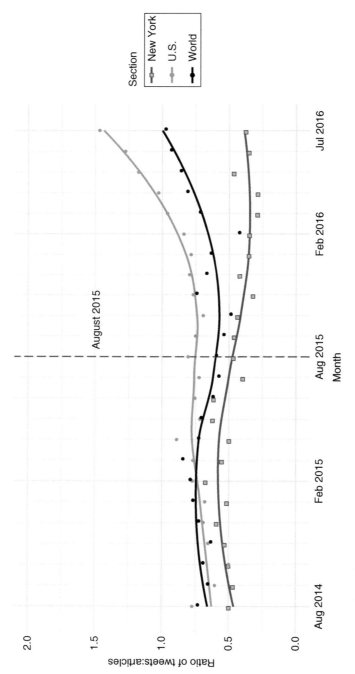

FIGURE 7.4 Editorial curation of local, U.S., and world news on the *New York Times* main Twitter account (@nytimes). Measured as the ratio of tweeted articles to published articles, with smoothed local regressions for trend lines.

All the news that's fit to tweet **109**

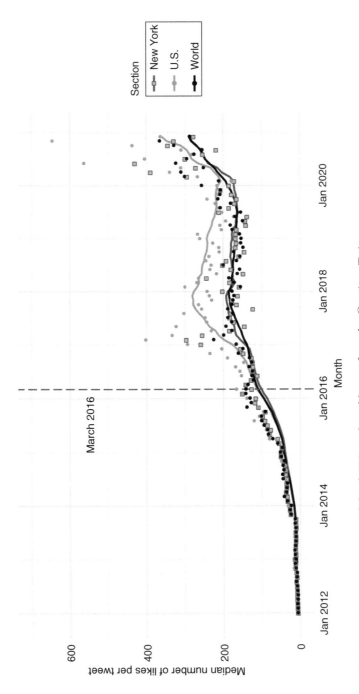

FIGURE 7.5 Raw engagement with local, U.S., and world news from the @nytimes Twitter account. Measured as the number of likes for the median tweet each month. Lines show 12-month rolling mean.

steadily from 2012 onward, but in 2016 the trend became far more dispersed as Twitter rolled out algorithmic timelines.

While engagement grew in terms of total likes after March 2016, the same was not true in proportional terms. The median proportion of followers who liked the *Times'* tweets each month *dropped* after the introduction of algorithmic timelines, as visualized in Figure 7.6. Causal analysis shows the change to be statistically significant for local news (p=0.001), marginally significant for U.S. news (p=0.096), and statistically significant for world news (p=0.001). The effect on U.S. news may have been influenced by the beginning of Donald Trump's presidency in January 2017 and the accompanying news cycle (i.e., the "Trump bump," see Bond, 2017): when excluding the first two months of 2017, the effect of the algorithm is statistically significant (p=0.001).

Discussion and conclusion

The multi-faceted local news crisis

The crisis in the local news industry is often associated with the expansion of the internet and social media platforms. One review article (Siles & Boczkowski, 2012) notes three main ways the internet shaped the crisis: (1) altering traditional values and practices for news production, (2) forcing newspapers to compete with other free digital content sources (e.g., blogs, aggregators, social media influencers, etc.), and (3) drastically reducing advertising revenue as advertisers shifted to DoubleClick, Google, Facebook, and other digital platforms. Another analysis by Toff and Matthews (2021) specifically suggests that social media algorithms have made it difficult for local news outlets to reach audiences.

Our analysis shows how editorial strategy, technological changes, and potentially other systemic changes can all work in concert to constrain the flow of local news. The *Times* produced a smaller volume of local news information over time, and its internal "blossom" algorithm played a further role in diminishing the flow of local news to Twitter. Specifically, after introducing their internal algorithm, the @nytimes account was less likely to feature local news articles from the New York section, and more likely to feature articles on Twitter from the U.S. news section.

While the *Times'* decisions disadvantaged local news, in contrast Twitter's algorithm had a consistent impact on the three sections we analyzed. Our findings suggest that the algorithm does complicate the *Times'* relationship with direct followers (step 3 of the 5-step flow) by reducing direct engagement, while potentially spurring more indirect engagement (via steps 4 and 5 of the 5-step flow). For example, editors might see less engagement when the @nytimes account shares an article, but sporadic spikes of engagement when other users share the same article, leading to overall higher engagement levels and with greater variance.

All the news that's fit to tweet 111

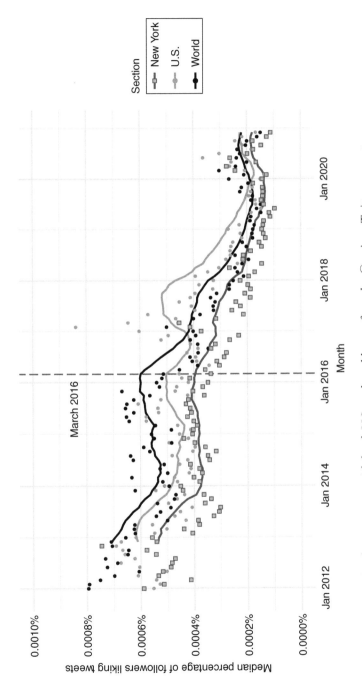

FIGURE 7.6 Proportional engagement with local, U.S., and world news from the @nytimes Twitter account. Measured as the median percentage of followers liking tweets each month. Lines show 12-month rolling mean.

Overall, these findings suggest that the reduction in local news flow is driven more by the *Times'* own content strategy (and algorithmic distribution tools) than by Twitter's algorithms.

Potential interventions

One implication of the multi-faceted crisis is that it offers multiple points of intervention. The flow of local news is a multi-step, sociotechnical process, and intervening at any point could provide improvement. This might include changing the rates of flow, for example, increasing the rate at which the *Times* shares local news, or increasing the rate at which Twitter promotes it. On the demand side, audiences might help by engaging more with local content. But meaningful interventions must involve structural change, not just turning the dials.

One important structural change revolves around the initial supply of local news. The *Times* could hire more local reporters and produce more local content; however, the growth-oriented goals of the company make this unlikely. Simply put, the market for local news does not scale in the way the *Times* wants to scale. This constraint on the news market initially impacted rural areas, as large conglomerate companies bought out smaller local newspapers and diminished local news supply (Abernathy, 2018). Our case study suggests that urban areas may also be impacted: even though the *New York Times* enjoys a large potential audience for local news in New York, they have chosen to focus on building non-local audiences, for example, aiming for 2 million subscribers outside the U.S. by 2025 (*New York Times*, 2021). They thus devote more resources to non-local sections and topics. In light of this, future work might study alternative local news sources in urban areas like New York, and how well they support the local information ecosystem.

Limitations

There are several observed and potential limitations with our work. While we capture several important quantitative trends in the flow of local news from the *Times*, our analysis does not capture more nuanced trends related to the type of local news coverage, such as the push to cover more "consequential" local news (Spayd, 2016). Also, as a case study, our analysis is limited to one outlet; other local news outlets in New York may exhibit different trends and paint a different picture of the local news ecosystem there.

Our case study is also scoped to one specific platform (Twitter) and specific metrics on that platform, introducing further potential limitations. Engagement metrics (i.e., like counts) can only serve as a proxy for distribution, and a more comprehensive analysis would include other metrics such as impressions, clickthrough, and reading time. First-party data from the *Times* could corroborate or qualify our results. Even with more comprehensive engagement metrics, however, another limitation is that engagement is not a uniformly positive signal. For example, the *Times* has experienced engagement spikes when readers "were angered by articles or columns written by [their] journalists" (Roston, 2015).

Finally, many of our findings come from time series analyses, which present other types of limitations. While our work does address common concerns with this method (e.g., by scoping analysis windows), it is possible that we did not account for external events influencing our observations.

Conclusion

This chapter offers a data-driven characterization of the decline of local news at the *New York Times*, finding that production decisions, editorial curation, and platform curation all worked in concert to constrain the supply and flow of local news. These findings paint a more nuanced picture of the local news crisis, suggesting that it stems not only from external technological changes, but perhaps more directly from professional journalists using new internal technologies and shifting their production strategies. Taken as a whole, our work encourages structural changes to help develop healthier local news ecosystems.

Notes

1 https://developer.nytimes.com/docs/archive-product/1/overview
2 To test hypotheses for causal impact, we use the Bayesian framework and R implementation (CausalImpact) provided by Brodersen et al. (2015). We also check for additional potential points of intervention, using the R package (bcp) from Erdman and Emerson (2007).

References

Abernathy, P. M. (2018). *The expanding news desert*. Center for Innovation and Sustainability in Local Media, University of North Carolina at Chapel Hill.

American Press Institute (2018). Americans and the news media: What they do—and don't—understand about each other. *The Media Insight Project*, www.americanpressinstit ute.org/publications/reports/survey-research/americans-and-the-news-media/

Bandy, J., & Diakopoulos, N. (2021). Curating quality? How Twitter's timeline algorithm treats different types of news. *Social Media + Society*, 7(3).

Barkan, R. (2017). The decimation of local news in New York City. *Columbia Journalism Review*. www.cjr.org/united_states_project/local-news-new-york-city.php

Barthel, M., Holcomb, J., Mahone, J., & Mitchell, A. (2016). Civic engagement strongly tied to local news habits. *Pew Research Center*. www.pewresearch.org/journalism/2016/11/03/civic-engagement-strongly-tied-to-local-news-habits/

Bennett, W. L., & Manheim, J. B. (2006). The one-step flow of communication. *The ANNALS of the American Academy of Political and Social Science*, 608(1), 213–232.

Benoit, W. L., Stein, K. A., & Hansen, G. J. (2005). *New York Times* coverage of presidential campaigns. *Journalism & Mass Communication Quarterly*, 82(2), 356–376.

Boczkowski, P. J., & Mitchelstein, E. (2013). *The news gap: When the information preferences of the media and the public diverge*. MIT Press.

Bond, S. (2017). CNN and *New York Times* boosted by 'Trump bump.' *Financial Times*. www.ft.com/content/99039bc0-3011-11e7-9555-23ef563ecf9a

Bradshaw, S., Howard, P. N., Kollanyi, B., & Neudert, L. M. (2020). Sourcing and automation of political news and information over social media in the United States, 2016–2018. *Political Communication, 37*(2), 173–193.

Brodersen, K. H., Gallusser, F., Koehler, J., Remy, N., & Scott, S. L. (2015). Inferring causal impact using Bayesian structural time-series models. *The Annals of Applied Statistics, 9*(1), 247–274.

Campa, P. (2018). Press and leaks: Do newspapers reduce toxic emissions? *Journal of Environmental Economics and Management, 91*, 184–202.

Choi, S., Shin, H., & Kang, S. S. (2021). Predicting audience-rated news quality: Using survey, text mining, and neural network methods. *Digital Journalism, 9*(1), 84–105.

Chomsky, D. (2006). "An interested reader": Measuring ownership control at the *New York Times*. *Critical Studies in Media Communication, 23*(1), 1–18.

Clark, F., & Illman, D. L. (2006). A longitudinal study of the *New York Times* Science Times section. *Science Communication, 27*(4), 496–513.

Darr, J. P., Hitt, M. P., & Dunaway, J. L. (2018). Newspaper closures polarize voting behavior. *Journal of Communication, 68*(6), 1007–1028.

Day, A. G., & Golan, G. (2005). Source and content diversity in Op-Ed Pages: Assessing editorial strategies in the *New York Times* and the *Washington Post*. *Journalism Studies, 6*(1), 61–71.

Dunlap, D. (2016). Honey, I shrunk the Times. *Times Insider*. www.nytimes.com/2016/08/23/insider/2007-honey-i-shrunk-the-times.html

Erdman, C., & Emerson, J. W. (2007). bcp: An R package for performing a Bayesian analysis of change point problems. *Journal of Statistical Software, 23*(1), 1–13.

Feng, Y. (2016). Are you connected? Evaluating information cascades in online discussion about the# RaceTogether campaign. *Computers in Human Behavior, 54*, 45–53.

Gao, P., Lee, C., & Murphy, D. (2020). Financing dies in darkness? The impact of newspaper closures on public finance. *Journal of Financial Economics, 135*(2), 445–467.

George, L. M., & Waldfogel, J. (2006). The *New York Times* and the market for local newspapers. *American Economic Review, 96*(1), 435–447.

Gladney, G. A. (1996). How editors and readers rank and rate the importance of eighteen traditional standards of newspaper excellence. *Journalism & Mass Communication Quarterly, 73*(2), 319–331.

Guess, A., Aslett, K., Tucker, J., Bonneau, R., & Nagler, J. (2021). Cracking open the news feed: Exploring what US Facebook users see and share with large-scale platform data. *Journal of Quantitative Description: Digital Media, 1*, https://doi.org/10.51685/jqd.2021.006

Hayes, D., & Lawless, J. L. (2018). The decline of local news and its effects: New evidence from longitudinal data. *The Journal of Politics, 80*(1), 332–336.

Hilbert, M., Vásquez, J., Halpern, D., Valenzuela, S., & Arriagada, E. (2017). One step, two step, network step? Complementary perspectives on communication flows in Twittered citizen protests. *Social Science Computer Review, 35*(4), 444–461.

Kantrowitz, A. (2016). Twitter to introduce algorithmic timeline as soon as next week. *BuzzFeed News*. www.buzzfeednews.com/article/alexkantrowitz/twitter-to-introduce-algorithmic-timeline-as-soon-as-next-we

Katz, E., & Lazarsfeld, P. F. (1955). *Personal influence: The part played by people in the flow of mass communications.* Free Press.

Lacy, S., & Rosenstiel, T. (2015). Defining and measuring quality journalism. Rutgers School of Communication and Information. www.issuelab.org/resources/31212/31212.pdf

Lazer, D. M., Baum, M. A., Benkler, Y., Berinsky, A. J., Greenhill, K. M., Menczer, F., Metzger, M. J., Nyhan, B., Pennycook, G., & Zittrain, J. L. (2018). The science of fake news. *Science, 359*(6380), 1094–1096.

Lewandowsky, S., Jetter, M., & Ecker, U. K. (2020). Using the president's tweets to understand political diversion in the age of social media. *Nature Communications, 11*(1). https://doi.org/10.1038/s41467-020-19644-6

Lichterman, J. (2016, January 22). 20 years ago today, NYTimes.com debuted "on-line" on the web. *Nieman Lab.* www.niemanlab.org/2016/01/20-years-ago-today-nytimes-com-debuted-on-line-on-the-web/

Malik, M. M., & Pfeffer, J. (2016). Identifying platform effects in social media data. *Proceedings of the Tenth International AAAI Conference on Web and Social Media, 10*(1), 241–249.

Napoli, P. M. (2019). *Social media and the public interest: Media regulation in the disinformation age.* Columbia University Press.

New York Times (2021, November 3). The New York Times reaches 1 million international subscriptions. nytco.com/press/the-new-york-times-reaches-1-million-international-subscriptions/

Nisbet, M. C., & Kotcher, J. E. (2009). A two-step flow of influence? Opinion-leader campaigns on climate change. *Science Communication, 30*(3), 328–354.

Nørregaard, J., Horne, B. D., & Adalı, S. (2019). NELA-GT-2018: A large multi-labelled news dataset for the study of misinformation in news articles. *Proceedings of the International AAAI Conference on Web and Social Media, 13.* https://arxiv.org/pdf/2203.05659.pdf

Oremus, W. (2017, March 5). Twitter's new order. *Slate,* www.slate.com/articles/technology/cover_story/2017/03/twitter_s_timeline_algorithm_and_its_effect_on_us_explained.html

Pellechia, M. G. (1997). Trends in science coverage: A content analysis of three US newspapers. *Public Understanding of Science, 6*(1), 49–68.

Petre, C. (2015, May 7). The traffic factories: Metrics at Chartbeat, Gawker Media, and the *New York Times.* Tow Center for Digital Journalism. www.cjr.org/tow_center_reports/the_traffic_factories_metrics_at_chartbeat_gawker_media_and_the_new_york_times.php

Pew Research Center (2019, March 26). For local news, Americans embrace digital but still want strong community connection. Pew Research Center. www.pewresearch.org/journalism/2019/03/26/for-local-news-americans-embrace-digital-but-still-want-strong-community-connection/

Pew Research Center. (2021, August 30). Partisan divides in media trust widen, driven by a decline among Republicans. Pew Research Center. www.pewresearch.org/fact-tank/2021/08/30/partisan-divides-in-media-trust-widen-driven-by-a-decline-among-republicans/

Rashidian, N., Tsiveriotis, G., Brown, P. D., Bell, E. J., & Hartstone, A. (2020, November 22). Platforms and publishers: The end of an era. Tow Center for Digital Journalism, www.cjr.org/tow_center_reports/platforms-and-publishers-end-of-an-era.php

Robinson, J. P. (1976). Interpersonal influence in election campaigns: Two step-flow hypotheses. *Public Opinion Quarterly*, *40*(3), 304–319.

Roston, M. (2015, January 22). Don't try too hard to please Twitter—and other lessons from the *New York Times'* social media desk. *Nieman Lab*. www.niemanlab.org/2015/01/dont-try-too-hard-to-please-twitter-and-other-lessons-from-the-new-york-times-social-media-desk/

Shirky, C. (2011). The political power of social media: Technology, the public sphere, and political change. *Foreign Affairs*, *90*(1), 28–41.

Siles, I., & Boczkowski, P. J. (2012). Making sense of the newspaper crisis: A critical assessment of existing research and an agenda for future work. *New Media & Society*, *14*(8), 1375–1394.

Spayd, L. (2016, August 6). A "New York" paper takes a look in the mirror. *New York Times*. https://nytimes.com/2016/08/07/public-editor/liz-spayd-new-york-times-public-editor.html

Sulzberger, A. O. (2011, March 7). A letter to our readers about digital subscriptions. *New York Times*. www.nytimes.com/2011/03/18/opinion/l18times.html

Tandoc Jr., E. C., Lim, Z. W., & Ling, R. (2018). Defining "fake news" A typology of scholarly definitions. *Digital Journalism*, *6*(2), 137–153.

Thorson, K., & Wells, C. (2016). Curated flows: A framework for mapping media exposure in the digital age. *Communication Theory*, *26*(3), 309–328.

Toff, B., & Mathews, N. (2021). Is social media killing local news? An examination of engagement and ownership patterns in US community news on Facebook. *Digital Journalism*. https://doi.org/10.1080/21670811.2021.1977668

Tufekci, Z. (2018, August 14). How social media took us from Tahrir Square to Donald Trump. *MIT Technology Review*. www.technologyreview.com/2018/08/14/240325/how-social-media-took-us-from-tahrir-square-to-donald-trump/

Usher, N. (2017). Making business news: A production analysis of the *New York Times*. *International Journal of Communication*, *11*, 363–382.

Wang, S. (2015, August 13). The *New York Times* built a slack bot to help decide which stories to post to social media. *Nieman Lab*. www.niemanlab.org/2015/08/the-new-york-times-built-a-slack-bot-to-help-decide-which-stories-to-post-to-social-media

Wendelin, M., Engelmann, I., & Neubarth, J. (2017). User rankings and journalistic news selection: Comparing news values and topics. *Journalism Studies*, *18*(2), 135–153.

Wojcieszak, M., & Rojas, H. (2011). Correlates of party, ideology and issue based extremity in an era of egocentric publics. *The International Journal of Press/Politics*, *16*(4), 488–507.

Xu, K. (2013). Framing occupy Wall Street: A content analysis of the *New York Times* and *USA Today*. *International Journal of Communication*, *7*, 2412–2432.

Yamamoto, M. (2011). Community newspaper use promotes social cohesion. *Newspaper Research Journal*, *32*(1), 19–33.

Zhang, A. X., Ranganathan, A., Metz, S. E., Appling, S., Sehat, C. M., Gilmore, N., ... & Mina, A. X. (2018). A structured response to misinformation: Defining and annotating credibility indicators in news articles. In *Proceedings of the The Web Conference*. https://homes.cs.washington.edu/~axz/papers/webconf_credco.pdf

8

OUT OF CONTROL?

Using interactive testing to understand user agency in news recommendation systems

Judith Moeller, Felicia Loecherbach, Johanna Möller and Natali Helberger

Introduction

Users of recommender systems on social media and beyond are thought to be involuntarily trapped to hear exclusively a perpetual echo of their existing thoughts and beliefs. In the words of Eli Pariser (2011), this constitutes a "personal ecosystem of information that's been catered by [...] algorithms to who they think you are", the so-called "filter bubble." In the debate about this phenomenon, educating users and giving them more agency is often hailed as one of the key solutions to mitigate negative effects. Many policy makers hold the belief that explaining how algorithms function and giving people options to curate their own information will empower users and help them break out of these bubbles. The Digital Services Act which is the key regulatory framework of online information in the EU is a good example of this approach (Morais Carvalho et al., 2021). The underlying assumption is that users who understand the system and are presented with control options can exercise meaningful control to ensure the curated information stream fits their needs and reflects their interest.

Yet, this assumption has not yet been empirically tested. On the contrary, according to Guzman (2019), scholarship into automatic news dissemination generally lacks an understanding of the technology's communicative role from the point of view of the audience. The notion of empowered users is based on the potential control and theoretical agency that users hold in the context of recommender systems. Indeed, users who are willing and able can often exercise meaningful control over the news environment either through changing the settings of the recommender systems (explicit control), or by steering the system through their selection behavior in feedback loops (implicit control) (Bozdag, 2013), thus making use of the personalization algorithm employed by platforms to meet user

DOI: 10.4324/9781003257998-11

preferences by customizing newsfeeds based on past engagement with content. However, explorative studies in the field (Monzer et al., 2020) show that while users do perceive themselves as active participants when interacting with recommender systems, they also complain about a perceived lack of effective control options (perceived control) This chapter aims to provide insight into the interplay of algorithmic settings and perceived agency. In other words, we want to understand whether different levels of actual control translate into perceived control. Using a novel experimental design (Loecherbach & Trilling, 2020) that allows users to engage with a news recommendation system, we aim to gain insight into how different forms of news personalization are connected to perceived user control and satisfaction with algorithmic news selection.

Studying recommender systems in different fields

The role of the user as an active controller of news recommendation systems is currently insufficiently studied in the different fields that investigate news recommender systems: computer science and social sciences, including normative approaches. This is a direct consequence of the different epistemologies used to understand news consumption in the different fields. In computational and information sciences, which have been the dominant fields for studying (news) recommendation systems, such systems were initially treated as a mathematical issue. In this line of research, the user is conceptualized as the target of recommendations, characterized by stable preferences. This means users are "more the objects than the subjects of this code" (Dahlgren, 2018, p. 23). Recent work has expanded this approach to include measures of diversity, novelty, and serendipity (Karimi et al., 2018), based on a more dynamic image of the user. Another recent development is to move beyond the stable conceptualization of users and test recommenders in live environments (for example, Karimi et al., 2018, or Jugovac & Jannach, 2017). While these developments certainly contribute to a more nuanced understanding of how users interact with algorithmically selected news, there are still both methodological and theoretical shortcomings that speak to an oversimplified conceptualization of the user. The findings are often based on small sample sizes (10–20 respondents) not acknowledging the heterogeneity among users. Additionally, no tests of theoretical assumptions or frameworks are carried out, and the main focus remains on having users give live feedback to improve the algorithms' accuracy and precision (Goossen et al., 2011) as well as marketing-related measures such as click-through rates.

In other fields, the study of recommender systems as a research phenomenon is more recent. In light of the debates about filter bubbles (Pariser, 2011) and the rise of social networking sites as gateways to news, the phenomenon has attracted broader scholarly attention, especially in the social sciences. While these studies employ a more holistic view of the user as an actor situated in a social context, they rarely account for the specific and limited possibilities users have to exercise control over recommendation systems and the dynamics of implicit control through feedback loops. Scholars in the social sciences are mainly focused on testing mechanisms of selective exposure by using one-time selection procedures with content specifically designed for the experimental purpose (Go et al., 2014) and focusing on pro- vs. counter-attitudinal news content (Beam & Kosicki, 2014). Often news stories are presented in a questionnaire format rather than a (real or constructed) news website and remain in one-time selection settings that are not compared to a recommendation algorithm (Zhu & Lee, 2019).

A different strand of research focuses on the user experience and understanding of algorithmic selection. In a qualitative study, Bucher (2017) charted how users perceive the Facebook algorithm through tweets and interviews of 25 ordinary users. She finds that the imaginary of the algorithm shapes how users interact with the system. To some users, this includes the perception that the recommender system has a faulty image of them, an observation that is line with the findings of Monzer and colleagues (2020). Yet many other users are not even aware that news feeds are algorithmically curated (Powers, 2017) and according to a study by Min (2019), only about 13 percent of users are actively challenging algorithmic selection, beyond following or unfollowing certain accounts, whereas about 38 percent do not engage in any form of explicit or implicit control.

From a normative perspective, discussions about recommender systems in the news domain in large part rely on democratic ideals and normative assumptions regarding who should be the gatekeeper and selector of news (Zuiderveen Borgesius et al., 2016; Helberger, 2019). Users are often seen as passive users rather than active actors in the news making and curation process, which also had a lot to do with the one-to-many logic of traditional mass communication services. That being so, with the arrival of more interactive forms of communication and also the growing importance of data, the traditional mass media logic of seeing users essentially as eyeballs has been juxtaposed by the more active control paradigm in data protection law, creating the expectation of users as active controllers of their personal data, if only properly informed and offered the right choices (Hildebrandt, 2019). However, to date there is little empirical research into how to design for meaningful agency and if doing so will indeed result in an increased perception of agency and control from the perspective of users (Strycharz et al., 2020). What both communication science and information law add to the field of computational science is thus the "noisy" element of the recommendation process: the user.

The complicated function of user agency in news consumption

Yet, neither the conceptualization of the stable user as object of the recommender engine, nor that of empowered users, willing and able to shape the news recommender system once they possess enough information and literacy, capture the reality of what it means to be a news consumer in the datafied democratic society. The user is both more and less than either imaginary. To arrive at an integrated conceptualization of users, we thus need to take a step back to understand the factors that differentiate perspectives on how users exercise control when consuming news and what hinders them from doing so. First, we need to explore individuals' relations with media as technologies and their mechanisms of information distribution.

It is important to note that trusting journalistic gatekeepers with the selection of information is necessary and normal in democratic societies (Dahlgren, 2018). This trust is the natural twin sibling of knowledge, as opportunities for taking information and insights for granted enables citizens to cope with demanding information processing work. As this delegation of informational duties has been ritualized for decades, it can be argued that the confidence placed in journalism as gatekeepers is extended to the algorithmic gatekeepers in news recommender systems (see Monzer et al., 2020). That being said, journalistic gatekeeping, which historically took over responsibilities for the choice, verification, and contextualization of information as well as offering opportunities for engagement with news, itself now loses influence, as the internet offers myriad additional channels. Expressed in more positive terms, the news media landscape becomes increasingly "dynamic and varied through the mingling of different news actors" (Russell & Waisbord, 2017, p. 71). At the same time, audience research shows that media consumption is largely ritualized (Lee & Delli Carpini, 2010). Media users compose their media repertoires and contextualization strategies based on habits in their social surrounding (Thorson et al., 2018). News consumers "learn" to trust (or not) media as a systematic resource. Related habits, we assume, persist.

There is also a self-managing element in news consumption (as well as in other dimensions of informed citizenship) that calls for further attention (Livingstone, 2000). Skills, practices, and general trends of self-determined political communication as related to building political knowledge and collecting information were formerly organized within more or less institutionalized publics. Now they increasingly depend on individuals' abilities to understand and cope with technological environments (Hintz et al., 2019). Practices of delegating trust, thus, are called into question and individuals' capacities to understand, reflect on, and critically use technology (Kannengießer, 2020) are at stake. Yet these abilities to critically reflect on technology are not as developed for recommender systems. On the contrary, users' knowledge on algorithms is limited (Cotter & Reisdorf, 2020), and the underlying technology is perceived as too complex to control at least by some of the users (Monzer et al., 2020).

We thus can distinguish three reasons that complicate the motivation and ability to embrace the agency news recommender systems provide to users. First, news users are socialized to delegate the task of selecting relevant news to trusted institutions. This is fostered by the fact that, second, in many regards news consumption is a routine behavior, in which users follow a behavioral pattern, without the motivation to take on an active role to steer the process. Lastly, the complexity of algorithmic recommendation systems and the perceived unresponsiveness of the feedback loop or feeling mis-profiled by the system can lead to disengagement among users (Bucher, 2017; Min, 2019).

User involvement in recommender systems

So how can users exercise control? In general, we can distinguish two forms of control: implicit and explicit control. The notion of explicit and implicit control refers to different strategies of personalization, namely "customization" and "recommendation" (Beam & Kosicki, 2014)—similar to concepts such as explicit and implicit personalization (Bozdag, 2013). Explicit control leaves the control to the user (who has to provide explicit preferences, for example, by stating which topics they like, etc.), while implicit control only allows limited control through the feedback loop. Implicit and explicit can be seen on a continuum from having full control over what is recommended vs. being exposed to recommendations with minimal options to provide feedback. In practice, they are often combined in hybrid forms.

Recommender systems involving the user are often termed "interactive recommender systems". He et al. (2016) mention the main reasons for involving the user in the process: strengthening user involvement and compensating "for deficiencies in recommendation algorithms" (p. 12)—mostly seeing user control as means to increase the accuracy of the predictions yielded by feedback mechanisms. Indeed, insights from other research fields such as gaming studies, marketing, or educational studies support the view that enhanced user control can not only increase the accuracy of the system but also heighten involvement (McNee et al., 2003) and learning perceptions (Ku et al., 2016). However, there are also reasons beyond the optimization of the recommendation process that are of importance to consider here. For example, Sundar (2008), in discussing customizability in computer-mediated communication, states that "greater interactivity allows for greater assertion of one's presence" (p. 62). Thus, in the end, more user control gives back agency—and in the same realm increases transparency of how the recommender works. Additionally, not giving the user the agency to interfere with the recommender in case of erroneous recommendations or a mis-profiling of the user has an impact on the user beyond satisfaction with the system: It can be seen as a threat to first-person authority and self-knowledge (Gertler, 2017). Therefore, adding control mechanisms and opportunities to interfere to the interface can be seen as means to give back the agency to the person who knows best.

> H1a: Explicit personalization (customization) leads to higher perceived user control than implicit personalization.

This does not, however, exclude that some parts of the recommender system should still allow for discovery and unexpected results—since in some cases "people might be interested in things that they did not know they were interested in" (Bozdag, 2013, p. 217). In case no clear preferences are formed yet (such as when people have little experience with or interest in news selection), prompting discoveries can add value to using a recommender system.

Generally, there are different ways in which algorithms can select the news recommended to the user. Usually, a profile of a user is made based on the content they selected in the past and interests they explicitly indicated. In collaborative recommender systems, this profile is matched with a similar user to find items of interest. In content-based systems, articles are selected based on how similar they are with the content the user had read in the past. In this study, we are focusing on content-based systems—and here an important choice is the feature selection, i.e., what information about the article is used for matching it with the user profile. One approach is to use meta-data like the author, source, or genre of a news article or source to find matches that are in line with previous choices of the user. One example of such a meta-data-based recommendation algorithm is a topic-based recommender that deducts a topic preference from user behavior and includes more articles of the same topic in future recommendation sets.

A different approach is automatically analyzing the vocabulary of news articles a user has engaged with in the past and recommending more articles that share linguistic features with these articles (called a similarity-based recommender). The advantage of this approach is that it encompasses many different features of language, for example, if a user has a preference for complex language or specific actors. It is thus more fine-tuned compared to a topic recommender. The disadvantage is that the algorithm is so complex that it is difficult for users to understand how their past choices and behavior have influenced the recommendation sets they are receiving. When being given explicit visual cues on how the information environment has changed—for example, bright color topic tags that change depending on previous selections—the reaction of the recommender to choices of the individual becomes more apparent. Especially since cognitive capabilities are limited, attention can always only be targeted selectively at parts of the information environment (Posner, 1994), often looking for easy visual cues to be detected (Bodenhausen & Hugenberg, 2009). If those cues show a reaction to past choices, it should be easier for users to detect options for indirect control within a recommender system. We thus expect that the higher simplicity of the topic-based recommenders provides users with a larger sense of control.

> H1b: Having a topic-based recommender leads to higher perceived user control than a similarity-based recommender

However, while it can be expected that enhanced user control has beneficial outcomes for both economic and normative aspects of news recommender systems, research in this domain remains rather scarce: in a general overview of studies involving interactive recommender systems, (He et al., 2016), 15 papers are mentioned that specifically designed for or tested controllability. However, none of the studies were about the news domain. Apart from this, as mentioned above, the user studies employed relied on very small sample sizes and remain exploratory in nature. Additionally, most of them have not yet been tested over a longer period of time.

A more specific user profile and a repeated selection of items beyond one-time selection processes are only part of how recommender systems are used in real life. It might, for example, be true that in the short term, customization and enhanced control increase the satisfaction of the user—while in practice people do not use those options due to limited willingness to invest time in customization. It takes mental effort to make customization choices over and over again—since it requires "active exercise of personal choice" (Kang & Sundar, 2013, p. 2273) and thus depletes mental resources. Using one's self-agency can thus also be exhausting, especially when doing it over a longer period of time, possibly leading users not to take advantage of customization options. Indeed, Chung (2008) states: "online audiences are not using interactive features extensively contrary to anticipation by media scholars and the news industry" (p. 672). Nonetheless, based on past research (predominantly in other domains), it can be expected that direct customization requiring active user involvement gives a higher sense of control to the user compared to personalization that relies on behavioral factors without explicit interference by the user.

> H2: Explicit personalization leads to higher satisfaction with a system than implicit personalization.
>
> H3: The effect in H2 is mediated by perceived user control such that explicit personalization positively influences perceived user control which positively influences satisfaction with the system.

Methods

To test the above-mentioned research questions,[1] we used a platform for testing an interactive news recommender system for period of ten days (Loecherbach & Trilling, 2020). It is based on an open-source Python application and presents the user with a web interface showing a selection of nine different news articles in tiles. For each article, the title and a short teaser are shown; additionally, the topic is indicated with a colored tag. The news articles are retrieved from several RSS feeds of different Dutch news providers (similar to strategies employed by Nguyen and Nguyen (2016), or Phelan et al. (2010)). This ensures that the articles presented are recent as well as actual news—a crucial aspect since "in contrast to other domains like movie recommendation, the relevance of news items can change very rapidly" (Karimi et al., 2018, p. 1204). Thus, the website is intended to resemble a news website in a controlled design (i.e., without distracting advertisements and additional cues such as pictures and other tags). Only a set of nine items is used per recommendation round, since the amount and placement of stories plays a crucial role in recommender systems (Jugovac & Jannach, 2017), following an inverted U-shape where too few and too many choice options negatively impact the satisfaction with the system. Additionally, having the tile system allows for displaying all elements on one page without scrolling, limiting positioning effects.

Usage of the website

After the initial questionnaire, participants are redirected to the website where an account needs to be created. During the registration phase, users are assigned to four different experimental conditions:

Random. This group saves as a baseline and control group: Every time the user visits the website, nine random news stories are presented. There are no options to customize the interface and no recommendation algorithm is used, thus the participant simply gets a random selection of current RSS feeds.

Similarity-based behavior recommender. In this condition, stories are selected based on how similar they are to the articles a user has read in the past. It is thus a classic content-based recommender that aims at finding similar items to the user profile. For each article the user has read before, the three most similar new articles are used as potential candidates for new suggestions.[2] Out of this pool of articles, a random selection is made.

Topic-based recommender. The second recommender system is again content-based. However, it does not match the vocabulary of the read stories but rather their topics, in that it relies on specific tags or keywords for recommending the news stories and is less bound to specific content read but rather the broad overall interests of a person. In case a person has a specific interest in one topic, they will be shown more from this topic even if the articles do not match vocabulary-wise (i.e., from different types of sports); when having a broad interest in many different topics, the recommender will reflect that broadness. This recommender more clearly "reacts" to the selection of a person in that the topic tags indicate the personalization at one glance.

Customization. This condition by default shows only random stories— unless the user decides to customize the interface. Without interference, no personalization takes place. The option to customize essentially picks up the topic-based recommender: The user can decide for up to three topics to be recommended more often. This is similar to making a static user profile as it used to be an option in the old interface of Google News (Jugovac & Jannach, 2017, p. 12)—however, it can be changed by the user at any time. A different number of stories is shown for each selected topic, depending on whether one (six recommended stories per topic), two (three stories), or three (two stories) favorite domains were selected. Therefore, direct consequences of the customization should be noticeable for the user.

In all personalization conditions (two recommenders and customization), three of the nine stories remain randomly selected to always offer the possibility to select non-personalized stories and thus change the outcomes of the recommender system even if no customization options are given. Thus, two-thirds of the stories are personalized, without indicating to the user which are and which are not.

Other interface elements

The overall interface additionally includes elements of gamification to ensure interaction with the system and keep participants entertained enough to continue using the website over a longer period of time: With every interaction, a number of points are collected (for logging in, reading articles, rating articles) with daily limits to avoid the situation where all points can be collected in one go. This system allows the user to estimate how much interaction is still needed until finishing the study. Lastly, other feedback elements such as reporting articles that were displayed incorrectly (to avoid low ratings not due to content) and a contact form are given.

Final questionnaire

After having gathered eighty interaction points and having logged in on at least seven different days, participants are prompted to fill in a final questionnaire. It includes scales for measuring perceived control (Knijnenburg et al., 2011), satisfaction with the system (Chen et al., 2011), and behavioral intention ("If we were to launch an official version of this website, how likely is it that you would use it again?," 7-point scale—see Figure 8.1).

Explorative addition

Apart from testing the preregistered hypotheses, this study also included an additional exploration of the question of whether actual control is the determining factor when it comes to news personalization, or whether the feeling of being in control (i.e., having explicit visible control options) is enough. So the larger question is not which type of control creates more user satisfaction, but whether it is really only the illusion of control that provides perceived agency and thus satisfaction with the system. This question has not gotten much scholarly attention, but it is crucial to understand to make sense of the causal process at play. For this reason, participants in the two recommendation conditions (topic-based and

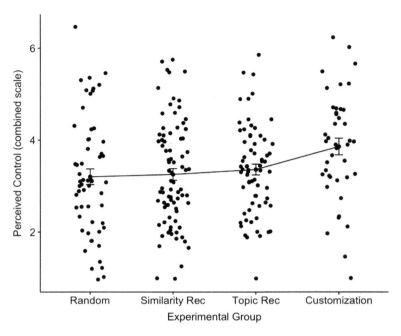

FIGURE 8.1 Perceived control (7-point-scale) in the different experimental groups.

similarity-based) were asked to continue the study for an additional three days and were being given additional control options they did not have before: All got a slider to control how many out of the nine stories on a page should be personalized. Additionally, users in the similarity-based recommender condition got a "diversity" slider to adjust how similar or dissimilar the recommendations should be to the content they read in the past. The users in the topic-based recommender condition got the same panel for indicating topic preferences that was given to the customization condition in the first part of the study. However, the control options actually worked only for half of the participants in this second part of the study—for the other half, they were just sliders without any real use, giving users the illusion that they were in control. After three days, participants were again asked for their feelings of control and satisfaction to be able to compare the impact of added controls to those variables and to see whether participants spotted if their control features did not work.

Results

The data collection took place between October and December 2019. In total, 1,753 users filled in the initial questionnaire, of those 1,585 agreed to proceed, 1,160 made an account on the website, and 1,029 activated their account by confirming their email. In total, 298 respondents qualified for the final questionnaire (enough interaction and days logged in). As specified in the preregistration, respondents who (1) had a standard deviation of 0 on one of the dependent variables, or (2) spent on average less than five seconds reading the news articles were excluded from the analysis, leading to a final sample of 248 respondents. Of those, 57 were in the random baseline group, 81 in the similarity recommender group, 68 got the topic recommender, and 42 could customize their settings. They are between 18 and 86 years old (M=46.19, SD=14.89), 54 percent identify as female and 53.6 %percent finished higher education. Randomization checks show no differences between any of the groups regarding socio-demographics or variables related to news consumption and political interest.

Of the 42 users who were given the option to customize their settings by selecting topics that they were particularly interested in, 16 did not use the option at all. Another twelve only used the option once and after that left the settings unchanged, meaning that two-thirds of respondents only sparsely made use of the control options given. The other users used the tool up to 16 times—however, again most of the activity happened within the first two days of signing up to the system. Additionally, users often inserted the same topic choices multiple times and did not change their preferences again.

Hypotheses testing

Looking at H1a and H1b, the differences between the groups regarding perceived control were examined. The seven items used to measure perceived control form a reliable scale (α=0.9). The items were thus averaged into one measure (M=3.37, SD=1.14). Since the normality assumptions are violated for perceived control, a Kruskal-Wallis test is used for analysis. A significant difference was found ($\chi2(3,N=248)=10.43$, p=0.015,$\eta2$=0.038). Pairwise comparisons using the Wilcoxon rank sum test show significant differences between the customization group and all other groups (baseline p=0.017; similarity-based recommender, p=0.017; topic-based recommender, p=0.029). This shows that the customization condition with its explicit control indeed lead to higher perceived control among respondents compared to the baseline and the two recommender systems (implicit control). H1b received no support: the two recommender systems were not perceived differently in terms of controllability.

For H2, the two recommender groups are compared to the customization group regarding several satisfaction measures: explicit satisfaction (satisfaction with the website), implicit satisfaction (rating individual articles), and behavioral intention to return to the website. Since normality assumptions are violated, the Mann Whitney U test is used for comparison. The customization group compared to both recommendation groups combined does not show any higher explicit satisfaction (U=3501.5, p=0.24), similar results are found when comparing the customization to each recommender individually (topic recommender: U=1162.5, p=0.10; similarity-based recommender: U=1594, p=0.57). Regarding the ratings,

128 Judith Moeller et al.

again no differences could be found for comparing the customization group with the combined recommendation group (t(78.977)=0.21, p=0.83), the topic recommendation (t(95.845)=0.08, p=0.92) or the similarity-based recommendation (t(102.98)=-0.40, p=0.68). Lastly, regarding the behavioral intention for coming back to the website, no differences could be found for any of the comparisons (combined recommenders: U=3609.5, p=0.12; topic recommender: U=1191.5.5, p=0.14; similarity-based recommender: U=1457, p=0.18). Overall, this shows that no differences between the customization conditions and the recommender conditions could be found regarding any of the satisfaction measures, lending no support to H2. Since the direct effect could thus not be established, the mediation proposed in H3 was not tested.

Control vs. the feeling of being in control

To explore whether the illusion of control or actual control are related to satisfaction with the system, we analyzed how measures of satisfaction and perceived control changed after adding responsive or unresponsive control options. We used a mixed model ANOVA with perceived control and satisfaction as dependent variables and with the measurement point (t1, t2) as within factor and experimental group (topic recommender or content-based recommender), as well as control (fake or real) as between factors. For perceived control, no significant results for any of the variables or interactions could be found. The results for satisfaction show that while there are no main effects of any of the independent variables (group: $F(1, 129)=0.196$, $p=0.659$, control: $F(1,129)=1.370$, $p=0.224$, measurement: $F(1,129)=0.081$, $p=0.776$), a small significant interaction effect of measurement point and control can be found ($F(1,129)=6,440$, $p=0.012$). As Figure 8.2 shows, respondents who received actual control gained slightly in satisfaction between t1 and t2, while those who got non-working sliders showed a decline in satisfaction. In other words, when control is promised but not realized, users become more dissatisfied with the recommender system.

Discussion

In this chapter, we set out to understand how and if the possibility to control a news recommender system translates into perceived control and agency. From the perspective of engineers developing recommender systems, the user is conceptualized (1) as an entity that has to be modeled, that has to be represented in a mathematical way to select fitting items to it, or (2) as a consumer that needs to be satisfied and come back to the website frequently. In this sense, users are seen as bundles of information reacting to the input of the recommender system—which to some extent ignores the role of users as autonomous citizens or agents that should have the opportunity to control their information diets and selection options. Yet research in the social sciences indicates that users face specific ritualized, technical,

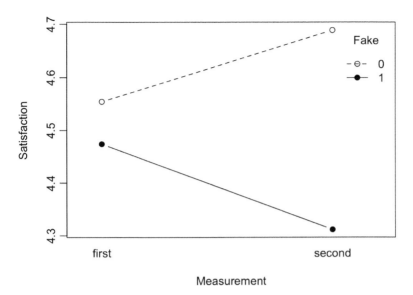

FIGURE 8.2 Interaction of measurement, control, and satisfaction.

and motivational barriers that hinder them from playing an active role in shaping a news recommender system so that it reflects their needs and wishes (Monzer et al., 2020; Powers, 2017). Moreover, customizable interfaces ask investment of time and energy of the respondent—something that does not necessarily go hand in hand with an easy-to-use system and enhanced user satisfaction. Actively customizing a recommender is a clear path towards agency; however, the next question is whether or not the effects of the customization can even be perceived, given the complexity of algorithmic recommendation systems.

In this study, we find that providing the functionality of explicit control of a news recommender system to users indeed leads to higher levels of perceived control. Yet this does not necessarily translate into high levels of usage of explicit control settings. On the contrary, in our study, participants barely engaged with the control panels, and if they did the engagement was not sustained. This raises questions for future research: first, what are the reasons for the lack of user interest in controlling a news recommender system? Second, does actively exercising control add to their feeling of agency, or is merely the perception of agency already enough to feel empowered? Third, more qualitative research is needed to understand how users exercise agency in news consumption, i.e., via communicative relations within news consumption networks. This also raises questions about how this could translate into the design of digital news consumption infrastructures.

Moreover, higher levels of control also did not lead to higher levels of user satisfaction. Concretely, this means that the economic incentives to offer more control may be limited. If there are no economic incentives to provide more user control, the only option to ensure controllability is to demand it by law. This could point to a role for the law in demanding more meaningful control options if such options are not offered otherwise. Yet these control options would need to be carefully designed to be empowering and intuitive enough so that users would at least try them from time to time. Having said that, we also found that providing an illusion of control that is not matched with actual control decreases satisfaction with the recommender system significantly. So, while adding control options does not add to user satisfaction, being dishonest about control translates into a negative evaluation of the system in general.

In this study, we employed a novel research design in which we could observe and survey users interacting with a recommender system in which we systematically controlled the parameters of the system. The advantage of this system is that it overcomes issues of external validity in experimental research, yet it also limits the generalizability of our results. First, our recommender only recommended news items, whereas in the reality of platform-afforded communication, news is mixed with private information and ads. Second, the limited sample size did not allow us to test one of the most commonly used algorithms for news selection, which is collaborative filtering. This algorithm matches users with other users that have engaged with similar content and recommends items these users also engaged with; to realistically simulate collaborative filtering we would have needed to include thousands of data points which is the beyond the scope of our experiment. Third, we did not include individual-level factors such as motivation to exercise control or digital literacy, to understand whether the willingness to exercise control and its effects are conditional on user types. Future studies should also test more and different types of control options to the users, in particular, options that are more intuitive and adaptive to the user. It could be that the limited enthusiasm of exercising control has been a function of the way control was designed and operationalized.

Nevertheless, our study provides valuable first insights into the conditions under which users exercise control in the context of a complex AI system. How far are humans really willing and able to use the opportunities the technology provides them to become the human in the loop in the process of news production, dissemination, and consumption? Our findings suggest that realizing the communicative role of technology (Guzman, 2019) is a complex endeavor. Possibly, the conceptualization of the user as a static object by those building recommender systems (Dahlgren, 2018) has led to an acceptance of that very role by users themselves—an acceptance that cannot simply be fixed by a normative need for users to be more than that, even if it is a crucial precondition for functioning democracies in a datafied society.

From a more optimistic point of view, it should be noted that extant work has established that users are in principle motivated to play a more active role (Monzer et al., 2020). However, this role is a departure from the delegation of trust towards journalistic gatekeepers that media users were socialized into. Thus, to realize user agency vis-à-vis recommender systems—and probably all AI systems—norms and practices of self-determined political communication as related to building political knowledge and collecting information need to be fostered in new ways (Hintz et al., 2019). This process is likely to take time. Yet, designing technology with this goal in mind could accelerate our capacities to understand, reflect on, and critically use technology, in order to feel like we are in control of our political information use in today's datafied society.

Notes

1 All hypotheses and analyses have been preregistered. The report can be found at https://aspredicted.org/t7hw5.pdf
2 The similarity was determined by using Soft Cosine Similarity (Sidorov et al., 2014).

References

Beam, M. A., & Kosicki, G. M. (2014). Personalized news portals: Filtering systems and increased news exposure. *Journalism & Mass Communication Quarterly*, *91*(1), 59–77. https://doi.org/10.1177/1077699013514411

Bodenhausen, G. V., & Hugenberg, K. (2009). Attention, perception, and social cognition. In F. Strack & J. Förster (Eds.), *Social cognition: The basis of human interaction* (pp. 1–22). Psychology Press.

Bozdag, E. (2013). Bias in algorithmic filtering and personalization. *Ethics and Information Technology*, *15*(3), 209–227.

Bucher, T. (2017). The algorithmic imaginary: Exploring the ordinary effects of Facebook algorithms. *Information Communication and Society*, *20*(1), 30–44.

Chen, G. M., Chock, T. M., Gozigian, H., Rogers, R., Sen, A., Schweisberger, V. N., … & Wang, Y. (2011). Personalizing news websites attracts young readers. *Newspaper Research Journal*, *32*(4), 22–38. https://doi.org/10.1177/073953291103200403

Chung, D. S. (2008). Interactive features of online newspapers: Identifying patterns and predicting use of engaged readers. *Journal of Computer-Mediated Communication*, *13*(3), 658–679.

Cotter, K., & Reisdorf, B. C. (2020). Algorithmic knowledge gaps: A new dimension of (digital) inequality. *International Journal of Communication*, *14*, 745–765.

Dahlgren, P. (2018). Media, knowledge and trust: The deepening epistemic crisis of democracy, *Javnost – The Public*, *25*(1–2), 20–27

Gertler, B. (2017). Self-knowledge. In E. N. Zalta (Ed.), *The Stanford encyclopedia of philosophy* (Fall 2017 ed.). Metaphysics Research Lab, Stanford University.

Go, E., Jung, E. H., & Wu, M. (2014). The effects of source cues on online news perception. *Computers in Human Behavior*, *38*, 358–367. https://doi.org/10.1016/j.chb.2014.05.044

Goossen, F., IJntema, W., Frasincar, F., Hogenboom, F., & Kaymak, U. (2011). News personalization using the CF-IDF semantic recommender. *Proceedings of the International Conference on Web Intelligence, Mining and Semantics*. https://doi.org/10.1145/1988688.1988701

Guzman, A. L. (2019). Prioritizing the audience's view of automation in journalism. *Digital Journalism*, *7*(8), 1185–1190.

He, C., Parra, D., & Verbert, K. (2016). Interactive recommender systems: A survey of the state of the art and future research challenges and opportunities. *Expert Systems with Applications, 56*, 9–27.

Helberger, N. (2019). On the democratic role of news recommenders. *Digital Journalism, 7*(8), 993–1012.

Hildebrandt, M. (2019). Privacy as protection of the incomputable self: From agnostic to agonistic machine learning. *Theoretical Inquiries in Law, 19*(1), 83–121.

Hintz, A., Dencik, L., & Wahl-Jorgensen, K. (2019). *Digital citizenship in a datafied society.* Polity Press.

Jugovac, M., & Jannach, D. (2017). Interacting with recommenders – overview and research directions. *ACM Transactions on Interactive Intelligent Systems (TiiS), 7*(3), 1–46. https://doi.org/10.1145/3001837

Kang, H., & Sundar, S. S. (2013). Depleted egos and affirmed selves: The two faces of customization. *Computers in Human Behavior, 29*(6), 2273–2280.

Kannengießer, S. (2020). Engaging with and reflecting on the materiality of digital media technologies: Repair and fair production. *New Media & Society, 22*(1), 123–139.

Karimi, M., Jannach, D., & Jugovac, M. (2018). News recommender systems – survey and roads ahead. *Information Processing & Management, 54*(6), 1203–1227. https://doi.org/10.1016/j.ipm.2018.04.008

Knijnenburg, B. P., Reijmer, N. J., & Willemsen, M. C. (2011, October). Each to his own: How different users call for different interaction methods in recommender systems. Proceedings of the Fifth ACM Conference on Recommender Systems (pp. 141–148). https://doi.org/10.1145/2043932.2043960

Ku, O., Hou, C.-C., & Chen, S.Y. (2016). Incorporating customization and personalization into game-based learning: A cognitive style perspective. *Computers in Human Behavior, 65*, 359–368.

Lee, A., & Delli Carpini, M. X. (2010). News consumption revisited: Examining the power of habits in the 21st century. Paper presented at the 11th International Symposium on Online Journalism, Austin, Texas, April 23–24, 2010. https://isoj.org/wp-content/uploads/2018/01/LeeCarpini10-1.pdf.

Livingstone, S. (2000). Television and the active audience. In D. Fleming (Ed.), *Formations: A 21st century media studies textbook* (pp. 175–195). Manchester University Press

Loecherbach, F., & Trilling, D. (2020). 3bij3—Developing a framework for researching recommender systems and their effects. *Computational Communication Research, 2*(1), 53–79. https://doi.org/10.5117/ccr2020.1.003.loec

McNee, S. M., Lam, S. K., Konstan, J. A., & Riedl, J. (2003). Interfaces for eliciting new user preferences in recommender systems. *Lecture Notes in Computer Science*, 178–187.

Min, S. J. (2019). From algorithmic disengagement to algorithmic activism: Charting social media users' responses to news filtering algorithms. *Telematics and Informatics, 43*, 101251. https://doi.org/10.1016/j.tele.2019.101251

Monzer, C., Moeller, J., Helberger, N., & Eskens, S. (2020). User perspectives on the news personalisation process: Agency, trust and utility as building blocks. *Digital Journalism, 8*(9), 1142–1162.

Morais Carvalho, J., Arga e Lima, F., & Farinha, M. (2021). Introduction to the Digital Services Act, content moderation and consumer protection. *Revista de Direito e Tecnologia, 3*(1), 71–104.

Nguyen, T. H., & Nguyen, V. A. (2016). Implicit feedback mechanism to manage user profile applied in Vietnamese news recommender system. *International Journal of*

Computer and Communication Engineering, 5(4), 276–285. https://doi.org/10.17706/ijcce.2016.5.4.276-285

Pariser, E. (2011). *The filter bubble: What the internet is hiding from you*. Penguin. https://doi.org/10.3139/9783446431164

Phelan, O., McCarthy, K., Smyth B. (2010). Buzzer – online real-time topical news article and source recommender. In L. Coyle & J. Freyne (Eds.), *Artificial intelligence and cognitive science: Lecture notes in computer science*, vol 6206 (pp. 251–261). Springer.

Posner, M. I. (1994). Attention: The mechanisms of consciousness. *Proceedings of the National Academy of Sciences*, 91(16), 7398–7403.

Powers, E. (2017). My news feed is filtered?: Awareness of news personalization among college students. *Digital Journalism*, 5(10), 1315–1335. https://doi.org/10.1080/21670811.2017.1286943

Russell, A., & Waisbord, S .(2017). The Snowden revelations and the networked fourth estate. *International Journal of Communication*, 11, 858–878, https://ijoc.org/index.php/ijoc/article/view/5526

Sidorov, G., Gelbukh, A., Gómez-Adorno, H., & Pinto, D. (2014). Soft similarity and soft cosine measure: Similarity of features in vector space model. *Computación y Sistemas*, 18(3), 491–504. https://doi.org/10.13053/cys-18-3-2043

Strycharz, J., Ausloos, J., & Helberger, N. (2020). Data protection or data frustration? Individual perceptions and attitudes towards the GDPR. *European Data Protection Law Review*, 6(3), 407–421

Sundar, S. S. (2008). Self as source: Agency and customization in interactive media. In E. A. Konijn, S. Utz, M. Tanis, & S. B. Barnes (Eds.). *Mediated interpersonal communication* (pp. 58–74). Routledge.

Thorson, K., Xu, Y., & Edgerly, S. (2018). Political inequalities start at home: Parents, children, and the socialization of civic infrastructure online. *Political Communication*, 35(2), 178–195.

Thurman, N., Moeller, J., Helberger, N., & Trilling, D. (2019). My friends, editors, algorithms, and I: Examining audience attitudes to news selection. *Digital Journalism*, 7(4), 447–469.

Zhu, D., & Lee, S. (2019). Autonomous readers: The impact of news customisation on audiences' psychological and behavioural outcomes. *Communication Research and Practice*, 6(2), 125–142. https://doi.org/10.1080/22041451.2019.1644586

Zuiderveen Borgesius, F. J., Trilling, D., Möller, J., Bodó, B., de Vreese, C. H., & Helberger, N. (2016). Should we worry about filter bubbles? *Internet Policy Review*, 5(1), 1–16.

9

GAMING AI

Algorithmic journalism in Nigeria

Emeka Umejei

Introduction

In November 2019, the Opera web browser launched an open platform for people to consume, create, and share content. The platform uses recommendation algorithms that help content creators target audience and helps users find the content that matches their interests. Opera's news hub is arguably the first platform using recommendation algorithms to review stories before they are published in sub-Saharan Africa. The hub uses an automated gatekeeping process in which recommendation algorithms review content before it is published. Every post must first go through the Opera News Review System before it can reach millions of Opera News users. Their Review System ensures that all users are provided with high-quality content and a premium experience. Each post published on Opera News is first examined by machines and human editors against their content standards.

In order to provide content for the platform, Opera recruited Nigerian journalists, who had trained and worked in the traditional media as content creators for the Nigerian audience. There are broadly two categories of content creators: salaried and commissioned. While commissioned content creators solely depend on the impression and clicks that their stories generate on the platform to earn income, others are paid based on agreed number of stories to be produced weekly. However, paid creators also have an opportunity to earn more income depending on the number of impressions and clicks generated by their stories on the hub. Studies on the relationship between algorithms and journalism have largely occurred in countries in the Global North where there is an advanced form of democracy. This is not the case in Africa, where there is little knowledge about individual African journalists, who are "working with limited or no press

DOI: 10.4324/9781003257998-12

freedom" (Weaver, 2015, p. 9). This study is a novel attempt to bridge this gap in the academic literature on the relationship between algorithms and journalism in a transitional democracy such as Nigeria, where journalism professionalization straddles traditional and digital media orbits.

The role of algorithms in news distribution and production

According to Wilding and colleagues (2018, p. 2), digital platforms have fundamentally reshaped the consumption, distribution, and production of news and now provide access to news—"a function formerly performed by media companies".

Pre-digital media, in its conception and operation, vertically integrated news production and distribution (Napoli, 2019). This mode of operation limited monopolistic or oligopolistic tendencies within the legacy media ecology. However, the intrusion of digital technology on the media has decoupled production from distribution. This decoupling is facilitated by the "applications and platforms that were layered onto the internet such as aggregators, search engines and social media platforms" (Napoli, 2019, p. 59).

Despite news consisting of production and distribution components, the dominant academic literature has focused on algorithmic gatekeeping of distributed news on social media platforms such as Google News, Facebook, Apple News, and Hotmail News that redistribute already published news items (see, for instance, Bodo et al., 2019; Thurman et al., 2019; Trielli & Diakopoulos, 2020). Bodo and colleagues (2019, p. 206) show that quality news organizations that pursue reader loyalty and trust have a strong incentive to implement personalization algorithms that help them achieve these particular goals by considering diversity, expecting user attitudes, and providing high-quality recommendations. In their examination of the effect of multiple recommender systems on different diversity dimensions, Möller and colleagues (2018, p. 959) concluded that "basing recommendations on user histories can substantially increase topic diversity within a recommendation set." For their part, Trielli and Diakopoulos (2020) show that the Google search engine partly neutralizes differentiation by providing common results to people from different ideological backgrounds. However, Thurman and colleagues (2019, p. 451) and Hansen et al. (2017, p. 2) emphasize that one of the major limitations of algorithmic selection of news is that it could result in limited diversity, filter bubbles, and echo chambers.

On the other hand, Bandy and Diakopoulos (2020, p. 9), in a comparative analysis of the human-curated top stories section with the algorithmically curated trending stories sections of Apple News, concluded that "human curation outperformed algorithmic curation in several measures of source diversity, concentration, and evenness." They also found that algorithmic curation featured more "soft news" about celebrities and entertainment, while editorial curation featured more news about policy and international events.

136 Emeka Umejei

Nechushtai and Lewis (2018, p. 7) point out there are two interrelated issues critical to the role of machines as gatekeepers: news personalization and news diversity. The first, algorithmic news personalization, could result in a "narrower range of news content thereby isolating individuals from a broader set of information that might challenge their beliefs by giving personalised recommendation based on past history." Additionally, algorithmic recommendation may result in a "fragmented set of news sources."

While these studies have focused on the role of recommender algorithms in the gatekeeping of distributed news, there is less emphasis on the role of algorithmic recommendation in the selection of news produced by journalists. This study examines how content creators on Opera News Hub, who have been socialized in the traditional media, perceive the role of recommender algorithms in news production and how these systems influence their understanding of journalism.

Algorithms and journalism

The "algorithmic turn" (Napoli, 2014) in journalism has disrupted news production processes with consequences for the way and manner journalists analyze, gather, and distribute information. Carlson (2014, p. 1) explains that automation has altered news production practices and "affects larger understandings of what journalism is and how it ought to operate." For his part, van Dalen (2012, pp. 652–653) explains that "automated journalism" has some advantages over humans, including low marginal costs, speed of writing up articles, and the extensive area of coverage that it can provide with a particular genre such as sports journalism. He, however, added that human journalists have certain advantage over algorithms, including the "ability to write with humour and come up with more complex and varied sentences are seen as two of their main competitive advantages." Similarly, Linden, in his examination of the "algorithmic turn" in news production at three separate news outlets, found that the

> impact of automated news is, first, increased efficiency and job satisfaction with automation of monotonous and error-prone routine tasks; second, automation of journalism routine tasks resulting in losses of journalist jobs; and third, new forms of work that require computational thinking.
>
> (Linden, 2017, p. 60)

Clerwall (2014), Wolker and Powell (2018), and Graefe and colleagues (2018) have researched the perception of automated and human-written news through diverse approaches and reached the same conclusion that there are minimal differences between them. For instance, Graefe and colleagues (2018) explain that machine-written news stories are rated higher than human-written news in terms of credibility. However, they pointed out that audiences get more "pleasure out of reading human-written as opposed to computer-written content." Lastly, "differences in terms of perceived credibility and expertise tend to be small." They pointed out that a possible explanation for the differences is "that algorithms strictly follow standard conventions of news writing and, as a result, computer-written stories reflect these conventions" (Graefe et al., 2018, p. 604).

For their parts, Carlson (2015, p. 5), Milosavljevic and Vobic (2019, p. 1), and Hansen and colleagues (2017) contend that algorithms will not replace human journalists, but will enhance the work of human journalists. In their study of how US-based journalists make sense of these algorithms, Peterson-Salahuddin and Diakopoulos (2020, p. 28) conclude that "journalists' understandings of platform algorithms create new considerations for gatekeeping practices." However, they note also that the "extent to which these algorithmic understandings influence their gatekeeping practices is often negotiated against traditional journalistic conceptions of newsworthiness and journalistic autonomy." Most of these studies have focused on machine-written news with limited focus on algorithmic selection of news content produced by journalists.

Evolution of gatekeeping

The term "gatekeeper" has its origin in social psychology as conceptualized by Kurt Lewin (Schudson, 1989). The concept, borrowed like numerous other journalistic concepts, has been adopted by many social scientists in journalism studies. These include White (1950) and Gieber (1964). In the "gatekeeper" David Manning White (1950) studied a wire editor at the *Peoria Star,* a morning newspaper. Manning kept a record of why the editor chose some stories and discarded others. For a period of one week, Mr Gates (as White called him) provided a record of every piece of wire copy including those he rejected as well as the ones he accepted for publication in the newspaper (Schudson, 1989; Reese & Ballinger, 2001). However, by his own admission, Mr Gates admitted subjectivity in his news judgement (Reese & Ballinger, 2001, p. 646; Schudson, 1989, p. 265). A re-analysis of White's pioneering research on gatekeeping suggests that types and proportion of stories that made it through the gatekeeping process were similar to the types and proportion of stories provided by the wire service (Hirsch, 1977). However, White's study was contradicted by Walter Gieber's 1956 study of 16 wire editors in Wisconsin. This study determined that all the wire editors selected news items in generally the same way. Gieber (1964) then concluded mechanical pressures are informed by media routines and professional relations rather than individual journalistic decisions (Schudson, 1989, p. 265).

Studies focusing on gatekeeping have evolved over time from White's conceptualization of gatekeeping as an individual judgement and news selection to factors both internal and external to media organizations that influence the selection of news (Shoemaker & Reese, 1996). The diverse forces that influence the selection of news within a media organization have constelled under gatekeeping theory, in which factors such as such as markets, audiences, advertisers, financial markets, sources, public relations, governments, interest groups, other media, and news consultants "influence both the selection and shaping of messages as they approach and pass or do not pass through news gates" (Shoemaker & Vos 2009, p. 76). The advent of digital technology, in which audiences have become producers of news, has put to question the continued relevance of gatekeeping theory. There is a sense that gatekeeping is in "transit" and requires rethinking in the era of digital media (Vos, 2015). For her part, Shoemaker (2020) proposes that gatekeeping theory should go beyond to instead consider the entire web of gatekeepers as a whole or system composed of elements (gatekeepers), interactions (relationships among them), and a goal or function.

In the digital media environment, the new "gatekeeping model is outside the control of journalism just as traditional gatekeeping was mainly outside the control of audiences" (Russell, 2019, p. 633). Digital platforms such as Google, Facebook, and Twitter use algorithms in news production and distribution, a process that has been described as the "algorithmification of gatekeeping" (Heinderyckx, 2015, p. 257). These algorithms "assign relevance, value, and prominence of knowledge to blend a cocktail of news, information, and entertainment tailored to individual users" (Hermida, 2020, p. 476).

Role conception versus role performance

The concept of journalistic role performance examines the relationship between normative ideals of journalism and the actual practice of journalism (Mellado, 2015). Most studies of journalistic role conception have been based on an assumption that the way journalists define their roles has a bearing on media content. However, empirical evidence remains, at best, inconclusive (Mellado, 2015). While some commentators maintain that how journalists think about themselves has an impact on their work (Van Dalen, 2012, p. 905; Mellado & Dalen, 2014, p. 860), others contend the relationship is not automatic considering the numerous forces that influence the actual practice of journalism (Shoemaker & Reese 1996; Preston, 2009).

Mellado (2015) identifies three frameworks for examining these roles that manifest in media content: the presence of the journalistic voice in the news item, the power relations domain, and the audience dimension. Several studies have pointed out that the gap between role conception and role performance is informed by the institution of journalism. Mellado and Dalen (2014, p. 859) in a study of Chilean journalists concluded that there is a "significant gap between role conception and performance, particularly for the service, civic and watchdog roles." However, they found a larger gap in the watchdog role than others which they attributed to external factors influencing the actual practice of journalism (Mellado & Dalen, 2014, p. 863). Conversely, Weischenberg and Scholl (1998) concluded that while there is a "large gap between the role conception of 'explaining complex issues' and the extent to which German journalists put this ideal into practice, both aspects were significantly correlated." Other studies have also indicated that the gap between role conception and performance could be attributed to commercial pressures (Preston, 2009). The gap between role conception and role performance is defined as the "degree of congruency or discrepancy" between journalistic role conception and the actual performance of journalism (Mellado et al., 2017, p. 8).

Josephi (2005), and Mwesige (2004) have shown the gap is greater in transitional democracies and developing countries. Hallin (2017, p. xii) explains that understanding the gap is important for the analysis of the forces that impact the actual practice of journalism as well as "differences in the media system and processes of historical change in journalism."

However, there have been limited studies focusing on the influence of digital affordances on the performance of journalism. In one such study, Mellado et al. (2018: 16) examined the extent to which media platforms account for differences in the performance of key journalistic roles, and concluded that their result provided partial support to the "expectations of differences arising from different media affordances." In this study, I am not going to use the three variables for examining manifest roles in media content identified by Mellado (2015), that is, the presence of the journalistic voice in the news item, the power relations domain, and audience dimension. I am interested in how content creators on Opera News Hub perceive algorithmic gatekeeping at the input and throughput and output stages and how it may influence their understanding of journalism.

The study has the following research questions:

RQ1 How do Nigerian traditional journalists perceive the role of recommendation algorithms in news production processes?

RQ2 What is the influence of recommendation algorithm on the journalistic role conception of content creators on Opera News Hub?

Methodology

The purpose of this qualitative study is to elicit, report, and analyze the perception of and experience of algorithmic gatekeeping among traditional journalists working in a sociotechnical gatekeeping process for the first time and how it may affect their understanding of journalism. The 13 journalists selected for this study were segmented into three dominant roles: Watchdog, Disseminator, and Entertainment.

The watchdog role of the press, with roots in libertarian-democratic traditions, is concerned with providing a check and balance on every level of leadership in society (Christians et al., 2009, p. 149). In its disseminator role, the main concern of the press is to pass information to the public (Mellado & Dalen, 2014); while journalists who adhere to the entertainer role aim to entertain their audience through the use of, for example, sensationalist wording or the depiction of emotions (Mellado & Humanes, 2012; Mellado, 2015).

The study employed semi-structured interviews with the 13 journalists in Lagos, Nigeria between January and February 2020. In order to elicit responses from the journalists, an interview guide was developed comprising 14 questions in relation to their experience and perception of the sociotechnical gatekeeping process at Opera News Hub. The goal of the semi-structured interviews was to understand through the original accounts of content creators on Opera News Hub their perception of the role of algorithm gatekeeping in news production processes (Lindloff & Taylor, 2002, p. 170).

I asked a set of questions with the aim of comprehending their perception of algorithmic gatekeeping in news production processes, and how they navigate between normative expectations and the actual practice of journalism on the hub. Some of the questions asked were:

- ✓ What is your perception of the algorithmic recommendation systems on Opera News Hub?
- ✓ What is your perception of recommendation algorithms in the selection of content for publication on Opera News Hub?
- ✓ In your estimation, are there differences between algorithmic journalism and traditional journalism? Do you think algorithmic journalism will make journalists lazy or efficient?
- ✓ Would the introduction of algorithms into journalism improve business efficiency in the media landscape in Nigeria?
- ✓ How has algorithmic gatekeeping affected your understanding of journalism?
- ✓ Are you able to perform the kind of journalism you would have wanted working as a content creator on Opera News Hub?
- ✓ What is the reason for your inability to perform this role on the hub?

The 13 journalists were interviewed individually at an agreed destination. The interviews lasted between 22 minutes and 36 minutes and interviewees agreed to an anonymity clause with the researcher because they didn't want to lose their source of livelihood. Furthermore, an editorial staffer of Opera News was also interviewed to get an insider perspective on the operations of the platform. The interviews were conducted through person-to-person sessions except for two of the interviews, one of which was conducted with a content creator who was resident outside of Lagos, and the other with a subject who could not keep an in-person appointment with the researcher.

Findings

Algorithmic gatekeeping, quality as casualty

The ranking criteria informing the platform's algorithm include content (controversial/ sensational, not porn or video content), audience response to a specific story such as time spent on a story, and likes, comments, and shares generated by the story. The quality of content is the least considered factor influencing algorithmic gatekeeping on the hub. This indicates there is dissonance between the ranking criteria of the hub's algorithms and traditional news values.

Furthermore, an editorial staffer at Opera News explained the gatekeeping in the news production processes on the hub involves two stages. The first stage of gatekeeping is solely conducted by an algorithm, after which human editors check through the stories that might be considered sensational or clickbait. According to the staff, stories that are deemed sensational or clickbait are removed from the hub. However, this does not seem to help in any way, as respondents complain that even when their stories are rejected, they find that all they have to do is tweak the headline a bit and it is accepted. So, in their opinions, there is no human factor involved or maybe, they pointed, the role of human editors is to monitor the algorithm. Respondents also mentioned that there has never been a time when a story that was rejected was embellished by the so-called human editors, which in their estimation, suggests that the human editors are largely docile or were recruited for public relations, as this would enable Opera to lay claim to human editors. However, another respondent added that the challenge facing the human editors could have emanated from the fact that there are too many stories waiting for editorial attention and hence, it would be difficult for human editors to engage with most of the stories. Hence, respondents acknowledged it could be possible that what the human editors do is random editing of stories on the hub. However, the general consensus of content creators is that algorithmic gatekeeping in the news production process on the hub is tardy and in need of a review. One respondent noted that he has seen stories published on the hub that he would not publish on his own blog, but the algorithm allows them to pass for publication. For instance, there was a particular story involving the wedding of two children that gained traction on the hub, but the story merely comprised pictures of the children wearing wedding attire without any information regarding where it happened. Later, it turned out it was a scene from a Nigerian Nollywood movie, but, as the editorial staff from Opera News mentioned, "fictional stories are allowed as far as they are not libellous." This tends to reinforce Bandy and Diakopoulos' (2020) finding that the sections curated by algorithm comprised the majority of soft news, while those of human editors are hard news and serious stories. Another respondent added that there is the challenge of clickbaiting on the hub, with stories that are shallow and poorly written being passed for publication by the algorithm. He noted that "There are some stories that will bait you and you click on it and it is very empty." He explained further that some of the content creators on the hub know how to bait the algorithm with sensational headlines:

> I will know if my story is rejected or accepted by the way I caption the headline; they don't care about the body of the story. They don't care if the

story is credible, if the story is well-written, or well-researched. There's no depth in those stories.

(Interview with P1, Lagos, Nigeria)

This suggests that the quality of content on Opera News Hub is the likely casualty of the hub's algorithm ranking criteria. Therefore, content creators are able to game the hub's recommendation algorithm because they know "what it wants and write for it while monetising the performance of their stories on the hub." This suggests an economic logic is at play because content creators need to write stories that will elicit audience engagement on the hub in order to earn extra income, as well as generate income for the hub's ownership.

Role performance on the hub

Participants who identified as watchdogs and disseminators reported that the recommendation algorithm on Opera News Hub constrains the performance of their roles while it facilitates the entertainment role. Participants point out that the recommendation algorithm on the hub has biases for trending, entertainment, sensational, and controversial stories. This means that if a content creator wants to do other kinds of stories such as investigative or business reporting, they might be constrained by the algorithmic reviewing system on the hub, unless such stories are sensationalized. One disseminator said that the recommendation algorithm tries to "pigeon hole" content creators to specific stories that are considered sensational. Another respondent noted that the algorithm does not like stories that are deep and intellectually challenging to read. He said that sometimes if you write a story that is intellectually engaging it might seem as if you are just wasting your efforts, because you might be left with less than 300 clicks:

When you want to do a story, for instance, to analyze the budget and to compare with previous health budgets in the last four years, it might not be appreciated by many people on the hub. It is very frustrating because I rarely write sensational stories, I write serious things and serious stories don't get clicks.

(Interview with P1, Lagos, Nigeria)

This is another indication that quality is compromised at the expense of business by both content creators as well as the hub's ownership. Another respondent, a watchdog journalist, emphasized that it is not ideal that news stories should be rewarded on the basis of the number of clicks they attract on the hub, because it encourages clickbaiting. He noted that when journalists submit their stories for awards, the awards panel is not interested in the number of clicks that the story attracted but on quality and content:

I think that what should be done is not paying people per clicks because when you do so, you will only be encouraging clickbait. When you put up a story for [an] award, the award panels don't care about the clicks. Once you can craft a headline to appeal to people's emotions, you will get the click which results in exaggerating things out of the ordinary. These are the things we don't do in journalism because we deal with facts in journalism.

(Interview with P1, Lagos, Nigeria)

However, the watchdog journalist above said he had learned the hard way, and decided to readjust his understanding of journalism so that it would be acceptable to the algorithm. He noted that if he wants his story to be published on Opera News Hub, he has to readjust it to suit the kind of stories that the algorithm likes: "the recommendation algorithm now determines what we write; our training and our experience no longer count." Hence, to write what the recommendation algorithm on the hub likes, he explained that he has to bring in entertainment or sensationalize it if it must pass the algorithmic gatekeeping on the hub:

So, we can still write about health issues or budget analysis, but we must use a celebrity in the headline. Perhaps you could interview celebrities to complain about health or the budget so it will garner clicks. So, we can talk serious issues but use celebrities to headline it, but if you go and get activists or medical doctors to talk about heath or the budget, you won't get clicks on the hub.

(Interview with P2, Lagos, Nigeria)

Another watchdog journalist added that a journalist who is hungry to win awards should not rely on recommendation algorithms because you won't be able to conduct investigative reporting or in-depth reporting. He noted that he used to produce hard, serious stories until he found out that the recommendation algorithm on the hub has biases for soft stories:

I know what the algorithm wants on Opera News Hub; it wants sensationalism and human-interest stories. I used to write serious stories until I realized that nobody was reading them. I came to know that the algorithm on the hub wants those trending stories with [a] Waoh! effect. Even though the hard news stories that I wrote had some clicks, but [they were] not as much as the ones I did on human interest stories.

(Interview with P3, Lagos, Nigeria)

These responses tend to reinforce the findings of Bandy and Diakopoulos (2020) that algorithmic curation featured more "soft news" about celebrities and entertainment, while editorial curation featured more news about policy and international events.

Entertainment journalists have a different perception of the recommendation algorithm on Opera News Hub. They perceive it to provide a very viable approach to news reporting because it privileges soft news:

> I don't see any difficulty with the algorithmic review on Opera News Hub. Once I send my story, it is published and I am paid as of when due. I think the algorithm is doing a very good job for entertainment reporting and hope other media organizations should copy it.
>
> (Interview with P4)

An editorial staff at Opera News Hub explained that entertainment stories are the preferred stories on the hub because they attract audience participation and engagement on the hub. He further explained that trending sensational stories are acceptable even in mainstream media as long as they are well-written. He noted that it is also possible to write fictional stories as long as they are not libellous:

> There are people who do exclusive content; they try to sensationalize relationships between a man and woman; the algorithm passes it and people jump on it. There is someone whose story is going to get as much as 700,000 naira based on the story he writes on the hub, which are mostly fiction.
>
> (Interview with P5, Lagos, Nigeria)

On the other hand, the reason content creators readjust their journalistic role perception, to be able to write stories for the hub is largely economic. Content creators, whose payments are based on the performance of their stories on the hub, are left with no choice but to dance to the tune of the recommendation algorithm. One respondent explained that he cannot write serious stories if he wants to maximize his presence on the hub. He said that the monetization of clicks on the hub "puts pressure on you." For instance, one content creator who disclosed that he refused to write "what the algorithm wants," said he lost money because he did not make as much money as he would have made from the hub:

> Fortunately, I can say that 99 percent of the stories that I have written are things that I can defend. I did not pander to the demand of the algorithm, but that has also cost me money because I didn't earn as much as I would have earned because of the poor performance of these stories on the hub.
>
> (Interview with P6, Lagos, Nigeria)

This speaks to the economic logic that influences the sociotechnical gatekeeping processes on Opera News Hub. This is not only from the perspective of content creators, as an editorial staff at Opera News Hub explained that the algorithm prefers certain genre of stories because that is what is trending and attracts audience participation on the hub.

News personalization on the hub

There is general agreement among content creators on Opera News Hub that algorithmic recommendation systems are viable for media owners and audiences, as they help media owners to monetize their content as well as compel journalists to produce niche content for a specific audience. One respondent said that it will help journalists to "understand the mood, the street, the market and know news and celebrities that are trending in the country." They emphasized that distribution of news through a recommendation system is good "because it will help you to understand your target audience and feed them with the kind of stories that they require, unlike the conventional media where you have to write for everybody and most times nobody reads it." However, privileging soft stories over hard stories, respondents emphasized, limits diversity and compromises the quality of the stories on the hub. An editorial staff at Opera News agreed that the news recommendation system limits diversity by focusing on entertainment and sensational stories:

> Yes, it does limit diversity. That is why there is a problem with using algorithms because there are times that I might not want to read entertainment news. But that is where the human factor is required. So, I now take my time to go beyond that to check for the kind of news that I want.
>
> (Interview with P6, Lagos, Nigeria)

This is one of the many challenges that have been identified in the study of news recommendation systems—for example, that they could lead to filter bubbles (Pariser, 2011) or echo chambers (Sunstein, 2001).

Fact-checking, fake news, and democracy

There is a consensus that Opera News Hub could become a hub for disseminating misinformation and disinformation in the country if it does not fact-check stories before they are published. Respondents said that the biggest challenge facing the hub is that it may lose the trust of audiences because of the poor quality of stories that are published on the hub:

> They may lose trust of audiences because of the quality of stories that are published on the hub. If the gatekeeping continues to be shabby, people will begin to doubt the authenticity of their stories and that will be bad for Opera News Hub.
>
> (Interview with P8, Lagos, Nigeria)

146 Emeka Umejei

Another respondent encapsulated the challenges thus: "Some of the stories are not professionally written; you get to see errors, misinformation and disinformation on the hub." The findings of this section emphasize that if the "tools and design of platforms do not have civic purposes as well as commercial purposes, it will result in crisis for sustainable journalism" (Rashidian et al., 2020). In this case, misinformation is one of those crises of sustainable journalism in the world, and much more so in transitional democracies in sub-Saharan Africa. Hence, the publication of stories that are considered today on the hub could provide a space for the thriving of misinformation and disinformation, which has implications for Nigeria's fragile democracy.

Conclusion

This study examined Nigerian journalists' perceptions of, and experiences with, recommendation algorithms in news production on Opera News Hub, and how they may influence the journalistic role conception of traditional-journalists-turned-content-creator on the hub. The study employed qualitative research interviews with 13 journalists, drawn from the roles of watchdog, disseminator, and entertainment. The findings suggest that automation of gatekeeping on Opera News Hub has a profound impact on the role performance of content creators, especially those subscribing to the watchdog and disseminator roles. While the hub's gatekeeper algorithm limits the performance of watchdog and disseminator roles, it shows a bias toward the entertainment role.

While the ranking criteria of the hub's algorithm and the priorities of the ownership of the hub are central to the mode of operation on the platform, the priorities, preferences, and behaviors of audiences are complicit. This is because the activities of these three broad actors intersect and influence one another in the contemporary algorithmic gatekeeping process (see, for instance, Napoli, 2019, p. 66). The demand of news consumers on the hub has a bearing on the pattern of content curation on the hub. Since consumers are more likely to engage with entertainment, sensational, and controversial stories, the hub's algorithms privilege soft stories over hard stories. Hence, content creators are likely to write stories that elicit audience attention to generate clicks, likes, and shares on the hub and these are entertainment or controversial stories. In a bid to comply with the hub's content ranking criteria, content creators readjust their role conception to entertainment-investigative journalists or entertainment-disseminator journalists, as they must tweak their stories to accommodate celebrities in the headline, so the stories can pass through the gatekeeping on the hub. This finding correlates with the conclusions of other studies on the impact of algorithmic gatekeeping on journalism professionalization (see, for instance, van Dalen, 2012, p. 649; Dorr, 2016, p. 702; Carlson, 2015, p. 8). While Dorr (2016) emphasized that the "algorithmic turn" would result in a new professional role where journalists are "migrating from a direct to an indirect role," van Dalen (2012) noted that automation "will change the way journalists conduct their work and force them to re-examine their core skills." For his part, Carlson (2015, p. 8) pointed out that automation will result in new roles for journalists such as "meta-writer" or "meta-journalists" to facilitate automated stories.

On the other hand, Jones and Jones (2019) found that journalists are "writing for machines" by converting unstructured information into structured data to enable automated recombination and future re-use of content, which impacts editorial control by delegating responsibility to either the algorithm or the audience, in the name of choice. In the case of Opera News Hub, journalists were compelled to "write for machine," because it is the only way their stories could attract audience participation on the hub for monetization. In order to achieve this, they must write stories that will elicit audience engagement and interaction while creating profit for the ownership of the hub.

While Carlson (2015, p. 12) pointed out the "authority of automated news" becomes that of the thinking of a machine capable of objectively sorting through data, content creators on Opera News Hub do not consider the algorithm to possess news sense because it approves stories that are deemed soft, sensational, and trending. However, this reinforces the findings of Bandy and Diakopoulos (2020), that while algorithmically curated stories focus on "soft news" pieces about celebrities and entertainment, editorially curated news featured "hard news" topics including international stories and news about political policy.

However, this study found that the economic logic is critical to the sociotechnical gatekeeping processes on Opera News Hub. The economic logic is influential both on the side of content creators and Opera News Hub. Opera News Hub configures the algorithm on the basis of metrics that will attract more clicks from the audience in terms of performance, while content creators readjust their understanding of journalism to write what audiences want, because that suits the content-ranking criteria of the hub's algorithm. Journalists who refuse to write content to elicit audience engagement lose money because their stories might get rejected or won't attract clicks on the hub. This suggests that beyond the editorial and algorithmic logics identified by Gillespie (2014), the economic logic is critical in a sociotechnical gatekeeping process of news production. On the other hand, algorithmic gatekeeping on Opera News Hub is fraught with challenges, resulting in the dissemination of sensational stories, misinformation, and disinformation on the hub. Unless the process of gatekeeping on the hub is reformed to include fact-checking, it has implications for Nigeria's fragile democracy.

This research provides a starting point for other researchers to investigate the relevance of algorithmic gatekeeping in news production processes in Africa. Algorithmic news has been celebrated in some quarters for being objective and devoid of bias. It would be interesting to research how it may impact journalism professionalizsation in Africa, where biases such as racism, ethnicity, and religion influence news production processes.

References

Bandy, J., & Diakopoulos, N. (2020). Auditing news curation systems: A case study examining algorithmic and editorial logic in apple news. *Proceedings of the International AAAI Conference on Web and Social Media*, *14*, 36–47.

Bodó, B., Helberger, N., Eskens, S., & Möller, J. (2019). Interested in diversity: The role of user attitudes, algorithmic feedback loops, and policy in news personalization. *Digital Journalism*, *7*(2), 206–229.

Carlson, M. (2015). The robotic reporter: Automated journalism and the redefinition of labor, compositional forms, and journalistic authority. *Digital Journalism*, *3*(3), 416–430. https://doi.org/10.1080/21670811.2014.976412

Carlson, M. (2018). Automating judgment? Algorithmic judgment, news knowledge, and journalistic professionalism. *New Media & Society*, *20*(5), 1755–1772.

Christians, C. G., Glasser, T., McQuail, M., Nordenstreng, K., & White, R. (2009). Normative theories of the media: Journalism in democratic societies. University of Illinois Press.

Clerwall, C. (2014). Enter the robot journalist: User perceptions of automated content. *Journalism Practice*, *8*(5), 519–531. https://doi.org/10.1080/17512786.2014.883116

Dorr, K. L. (2016). Mapping the field of algorithmic journalism. *Digital Journalism*, *4*(6), 700–722. https://doi.org/10.1080/21670811.2015.1096748

Gieber, W. (1956). Across the desk: A study of 16 telegraph editors. *Journalism & Mass Communication Quarterly*, *33*(4), 423–432. https://doi.org/10.1177/10776990560 3300401

Gieber, W. (1964). News is what newspapermen make it. In L. A. Dexter, & D. Manning (Eds.), *People, society and mass communications* (pp. 173–180). Free Press of Glencoe.

Gillespie, T. (2014). The relevance of algorithms. In T. Gillespie, P. J. Boczkowski, & K. A. Foot (Eds.), *Media technologies: Essays on communication, materiality, and society* (pp. 167–194). Cambridge University Press.

Graefe, A., Haim, M., Haarmann, B., & Brosius, H. B. (2018). Readers' perception of computer-generated news: Credibility, expertise, and readability. *Journalism*, *19*(5), 595–610.

Hallin, D. C. (2017). Preface. In C. Mellado, L. Hellmueller, & W. Donsbach (Eds.), *Journalistic role performance: Concepts, contexts, and methods* (pp. xi–xvi). Routledge.

Hansen, M., Roca-Sales, M., Keegan, J., & King, G. (2015). *Artificial intelligence: Practice and implications for journalism*. Tow Center for Digital Journalism, Columbia University. https://academiccommons.columbia.edu/doi/10.7916/D8X92PRD

Heinderyckx, F. (2015). Gatekeeping theory redux. In T. P. Vos & F. Heinderyckx (Eds.), *Gatekeeping in transition* (pp. 253–267). Routledge.

Heinderyckx, F., & Vos, T. P. (2016). Reformed gatekeeping. *CM: Communication and Media*, *11*(36), 29–46.

Hermida, A. (2020). Post-publication gatekeeping: The interplay of publics, platforms, paraphernalia, and practices in the circulation of news. *Journalism & Mass Communication Quarterly*, *97*(2), 469–491.

Hirsch, P. (1977). Occupational, organizational and institutional models in mass media research: Toward an integrated framework. In P. M. Hirsch, P. Miller, & F. G. Kline (Eds.), *Strategies for communication research* (pp. 13–42). Sage.

Jones, R., & Jones, B. (2019). Atomising the news: The (in)flexibility of structured journalism. *Digital Journalism*, *7*(8), 1157–1179.

Josephi, B. (2005). Journalism in the global age: Between normative and empirical. *Gazzette, 67*(6), 575–590. https://doi.org/10.1177/0016549205057564

Linden, T. C. (2017). Algorithms for journalism: The future of news work. *Journal of Media Innovations, 4*(1), 60–76. https://doi.org/10.5617/jmi.v4i1.2420

Lindloff, T. R., & Taylor, B. C. (2002). *Qualitative communication research methods* (2nd ed.). Sage.

Mellado, C. (2015). Professional roles in news content: Six dimensions of professional role performance. *Journalism Studies, 16*(4), 596–614. https://doi.org/10.1080/1461670X.2014.922276

Mellado, C., & Dalen, A. V. (2014). Between rhetoric and practice: Explaining the gap between role conceptions and performance in journalism. *Journalism Studies, 15*(6), 859–868. https://doi.org/10.1080/1461670X.2013.838046

Mellado, C., Hellmeuller, L., Marquez-Ramirez, M., Humanes, M. L., Sparks, C., Stepinska, A., Pasti, S., Schielcke, A., Tandoc, E., & Wahg, H. (2017). The hybridization of journalistic cultures: A comparative study of journalistic role performance. *Journal of Communication, 67*(6), 944–967. https://doi.org/10.1111/jcom.12339

Mellado, C., & Humanes, M. L. (2012). Modeling perceived professional autonomy in Chilean journalism. *Journalism, 13*(8), 985–1003. https://doi.org/10.1177/1464884912442294

Mellado, C., Humanes, M. L.., Scherman, A., & Ovando, A. (2021). Do digital platforms really make a difference in content? Mapping journalistic role performance in Chilean print and online news. *Journalism, 22*(2), 358–377. https://doi.org/10.1177/1464884918792386

Milosavljevic, M., & Vobic, I. (2019). Humans still in the loop: Editors reconsider the ideals of professional journalism through automation. *Digital Journalism, 7*(8), 1098–1116. https://doi.org/10.1080/21670811.2019.1601576

Möller, J., Trilling, D., Helberger, N., & van Es, B. (2018). Do not blame it on the algorithm: An empirical assessment of multiple recommender systems and their impact on content diversity. *Information, Communication & Society, 21*(7), 959–977.

Mwesige, P. G.. (2004). Disseminators, advocates, and watchdogs: A profile of Ugandan journalists in the new millennium. *Journalism, 5*(1), 69–96. https://doi.org/10.1177/1464884904039556

Napoli, P. M. (2014). Automated media: An institutional theory perspective on algorithmic media production and consumption. *Communication Theory, 24*(3), 340–360. https://doi.org/10.1111/comt.12039

Napoli, P. M. (2019). *Social media and the public interest: Media regulation in the disinformation age*. Columbia University Press.

Nechushtai, E., & Lewis, S. C. (2018). Personalization and diversity in recommendations on Google News. Paper presented at the 12th International AAAI Conference on Web and Social Media, Palo Alto, CA.

Nechushtai, E., & Lewis, S. C. (2019). What kind of news gatekeepers do we want machines to be? Filter bubbles, fragmentation, and the normative dimensions of algorithmic recommendations. *Computers in Human Behavior, 90*, 298–307.

Operahub (2020). FAQ: How can I get more reach? *Opera News Hub*, https://hub.opera.com/login?redirect=%2Fhome%2Fdashboard

OperaNewsHubAcademy (2020). Opera News Hub: Frequently asked questions. https://ng.opera.news/ng/en/covid/604be2b3074ab88125391721c8ad673e_ng

Pariser, E. (2011). *The filter bubble: What the Internet is hiding from you*. Penguin.

Peterson-Salahuddin, C., & Diakopoulos, N. (2020). Negotiated autonomy: The role of social media algorithms in editorial decision making. *Media and Communication*, *8*(3), 27–38.

Preston, P. (2009). *Making the news: Journalism and news cultures in Europe*. Routledge.

Rashidian, N., Tsiveriotis, G., Brown, P. D., Bell, E. J., & Hartstone, A. (2020). *Platforms and publishers: The end of an era*. Tow Centre for Digital Journalism, www.cjr.org/tow_cen ter_reports/platforms-and-publishers-end-of-an-era.php

Reese, S. D., & Ballinger, J. (2001). The roots of a sociology of news: Remembering Mr. Gates and social control in the newsroom. *Journalism & Mass Communication Quarterly*, *78*(4), 641–658.

Russell, F. M. (2019). The new gatekeepers: An institutional-level view of Silicon Valley and the disruption of journalism. *Journalism Studies*, *20*(5), 631–648.

Schudson, M. (1989). The sociology of news production. *Media, Culture & Society*, *11*(3), 263–282.

Shoemaker, P. J. (2020). Gatekeeping and journalism. In *Oxford research encyclopedia of communication*. https://oxfordre.com/communication/view/10.1093/acrefore/978019 0228613.001.0001/acrefore-9780190228613-e-819(Jan,2020).10.1093/acrefore/ 9780190228613.013.819

Shoemaker, P. J., & Reese, S. D. (1996). *Mediating the message: Theories of influences on mass media content*. Longman.

Shoemaker, P. J., & Vos, T. (2009). *Gatekeeping theory*. Routledge.

Sunstein, C. R. (2001). *Echo chambers: Bush v. Gore, impeachment, and beyond*. Princeton University Press.

Thurman, N., Moeller, J., Helberger, N., & Trilling, D. (2019). My friends, editors, algorithms, and I: Examining audience attitudes to news selection. *Digital Journalism*, *7*(4), 447–469.

Trielli, D., & Diakopoulos, N. (2020). Partisan search behavior and Google results in the 2018 US midterm elections. *Information, Communication & Society*, *25*(1), 145–161.

Weaver, D. H. (2015). Studying journalists and journalism across four decades: A sociology of occupations approach. *Mass Communication and Society*, *18*(1), 4–16.

Weischenberg, S., & Scholl, A. (1998). Die Wahr-Sager. In: K. Kamps & M. Meckel (Eds.), *Fernsehnachrichten*. VS Verlag für Sozialwissenschaften. https://doi.org/10.1007/978-3-663-07643-8_9

White, D. M. (1950). The "gate keeper": A case study in the selection of news. *Journalism Quarterly*, *27*(4), 383–390.

Wilding, D., Fray, P., Molitorisz, S. & McKewon, E. (2018). The impact of digital platforms on news and journalistic content, University of Technology Sydney, NSW, www.uts. edu.au/node/247996/projects-and-research/impact-digital-platforms-news-and-journ alistic-content

Wolker, A., & Powell, T. E. (2021). Algorithms in the newsroom: News readers' perceived credibility and selection of automated journalism. *Journalism*, *22*(1), 86–103. https://doi. org/10.1177/1464884918757072

Van Dalen, A. (2012). The algorithms behind the headlines: How machine-written news redefines the core skills of human journalists. *Journalism Practice*, *6*(5–6), 648–658.

Vos, T. P. (2015). Revisiting gatekeeping theory during a time of transition. In T. Vos & F. Heinderyckx (Eds.), *Gatekeeping in transition* (pp. 3–24). Routledge.

Zamith, R. (2019). Algorithms and journalism. In *Oxford research encyclopedia of communication*. https://doi.org/10.1093/acrefore/9780190228613.013.779

10

EDITORIAL VALUES FOR NEWS RECOMMENDERS

Translating principles to engineering

Jonathan Stray

Introduction

News recommendation systems are operated both by publishers and by platforms and have become one of the primary ways that journalism finds its way to audiences. Communication scholars have argued that these systems should embody a variety of values such as informedness, accuracy, comprehensiveness, autonomy, inclusiveness, participation, representation, diversity, deliberation, and tolerance (Helberger, 2019; Nechushtai & Lewis, 2019). While the recommendation technical community has developed a wide variety of values-driven metrics and algorithms (Celis et al., 2019; Kunaver & Požrl, 2017; Stray, 2020), these do not generally align with the conceptions of journalists and scholars. Building recommenders that enact editorial values is a deeply interdisciplinary pursuit, and few individuals (or organizations) have both a deep grasp of editorial values and the technical skill to design novel recommender systems.

In short, different communities are talking about the same problem in different languages. On one side, journalists, scholars, critics, and regulators have largely discussed these systems in terms of their normative concerns and societal outcomes. On the other side, computer scientists, product managers, AI researchers, and others have built ever more sophisticated news recommender systems. This is a caricature; in reality there are not two clear "sides," but a complex network of overlaps and interconnections between people and ideas. Yet this divide is immediately recognizable to workers in the field, and useful for framing the problem.

DOI: 10.4324/9781003257998-13

With this divide in mind, this chapter proposes narrowing the *journalist-technologist gap* through interdisciplinary collaboration to create four types of artifacts:

- Metrics. What should be measured, and what counts as an acceptable result?
- Data sets. These can be used to train algorithms, or to evaluate and compare their performance.
- Feedback methods. There are emerging methods to enable users and other stakeholders to provide algorithmically actionable feedback to a recommender system.
- Evaluation protocols. Understanding the consequences of news recommendation algorithms is essentially social science research, which would benefit from repeatable methods.

While a great deal of scholarship has focused on principles, both for news recommenders (Helberger, 2019; Vrijenhoek et al., 2020) and responsible AI in general (Fjeld et al., 2020), there has been less attention to metrics, data sets, feedback, and evaluation specifically. Collaboratively produced artifacts could be a key way for *journalists* and *technologists* to work toward the shared goals of embedding editorial values into news recommender systems.

Related work

Editorial values are significant for any recommender system that handles news content, with potentially profound effects on democracy (Fields et al., 2018; Helberger, 2019; Vrijenhoek et al., 2020). This includes recommenders operated by a single news organization such as that which produces personalized suggestions in the *New York Times* app, news aggregators such as Google News, and social media recommenders which also handle news items such as the Facebook News Feed. For simplicity, I will refer to all of these types of systems as "news recommenders." I use "news" fairly narrowly to mean the output of conventional news organizations, though there are analogous editorial concerns about any recommender which selects media items.

This chapter takes a design orientation towards journalistic algorithms, as articulated by Diakopoulos (2019). My foremost concern is the real-world deployment of news recommenders that embody important editorial values. Merely explicating these values is not enough, which is why "developing evaluation methods and metrics" (Diakopoulos, 2019, p. 4) is so central to advancing journalism automation.

Participatory design is an orientation and a set of practices that attempts to actively involve all stakeholders in a system design process (Simonsen & Robertson, 2012). The stakeholders in this case include journalists as content creators, technologists as system designers and operators, audience members, and perhaps society in general.

The related field of *value sensitive design* is "a theoretically grounded approach to the design of technology that accounts for human values in a principled and systematic manner throughout the design process" (Friedman et al., 2017). Most specifically, *multi-stakeholder recommendation* studies the design and evaluation of recommender systems that must simultaneously serve the interests of multiple groups (Abdollahpouri et al., 2020).

Other work examines the values actually implemented in production recommenders. Nechushtai and Lewis (2019) undertake a crowdsourced audit of Google News while Bandy and Diakopoulos (2019) study Apple News, evaluating the output of these systems with respect to values such as diversity, local news content, etc. DeVito (2017) infers the values of the Facebook News Feed by reading public documents to determine which factors are used as inputs.

Yet none of this work specifies how values are to be translated into algorithms. Though methods like participatory design provide high-level descriptions of design processes, more specialized technical approaches are necessary to construct operational recommender systems. The state of the art of recommender values engineering is the creation of hand-crafted metrics or machine learning classifiers to identify various wanted and unwanted aspects of content or recommendations, used in a three-part process (Stray et al., 2020):

- Identification: System designers become aware of a negative outcome associated with the system and identify a concept associated with it—for example, discovering that users are getting drawn into low-quality content and developing a corresponding definition of "clickbait."
- Operationalization: A concrete procedure is developed to identify instances of the abstract concept in the recommender system. This may involve the development of hand-crafted metrics, but most systems rely on some form of machine learning, trained on human-labeled data.
- Adjustment: system designers modify the recommender system in order to increase or decrease the prevalence of the target concept. This could involve A/B testing with respect to an evaluation protocol, incorporating a metric into model training, or adding code that re-orders ("re-ranks") results prior to presenting them to the user.

The actual processes used to engineer values into producing news recommender systems today involve various technical artifacts such as metrics, data sets, and evaluation protocols. These have a deep role in defining the character and enacted values of such systems. Yet these artifacts are much more amenable to the involvement of non-experts than core recommendation algorithms *per se*.

Finally, it is important to conceive of this process as more than "embodying editorial values in technology." When journalists are asked to translate their practices into the definitions and data required for algorithmic implementation, they often discover that naturalized concepts like "newsworthy" or "authoritative" are not as clear or uncontested as they thought (Stray, 2019). As the News Quality Initiative put it, "any confusion that existed among journalists regarding principles, standards, definitions, and ethics has only travelled downstream to platforms" (Vincent et al., 2020).

In many cases, there is no existing normative consensus on exactly which journalistic values a recommendation system should support, how these should trade off against each other, and how the results should be evaluated (Nechushtai & Lewis, 2019). Therefore, the synthesis of journalism and technology will force articulation and clarification of core editorial concerns, up to and including journalism's ultimate societal goals.

Principles do not define behavior

By "principles," I mean written descriptions of the values that technical systems should uphold. Such descriptions are, so far, the primary method by which the ethical behavior of technical systems have been specified by scholars and critics. Fjeld and colleagues (2020) map the content of several dozen AI principles documents, finding themes such as privacy, accountability, safety, transparency, fairness, human control, and responsibility. There are also ongoing standards efforts around the values which apply to particular technical domains, such as the IEEE Ethically Aligned Design series (Shahriari & Shahriari, 2017).

Likewise, *journalists* (and allied scholars and non-technical experts) have mostly attempted to specify the operation of news recommenders through written descriptions of the values that such systems should uphold. Existing critiques of AI ethics principles typically focus on the lack of incentives for implementation and the dangers of superficial "ethics washing" (e.g., Floridi, 2019), but here I critique principles from a different direction: they are typically not precise enough to define the behavior of a technical system.

As an example, consider how the value of "diversity" is implemented in recommender systems. Diversity is perhaps the most widely discussed value in the news recommender literature produced by *journalists*. But what is it?

Regulatory discussions typically consider *source diversity*, that is, they are concerned with the mix of news organizations in the content recommended to each person (e.g., Helberger et al., 2019). Several researchers who have audited news recommender systems are correspondingly concerned with source diversity (Bandy & Diakopoulos, 2019; Nechushtai & Lewis, 2019). But users may still encounter only a small number of topics or perspectives even though they consume diverse sources, so other authors have been concerned with *content diversity* (Möller et al., 2018). Helberger and colleagues (2018) suggest that we should think instead in terms of the goals of a news recommender, and outline *liberal*, *deliberative* and *adversarial* notions of diversity. This is appealing, but these are concepts at an even higher level of abstraction.

Meanwhile, *diversity* has been extensively studied in the technical context of recommender design. A review by Kunaver and Požrl (2017) lists eight different diversification algorithms and nine different formulas to measure the diversity of a set of items, mostly based on evaluating a *similarity function*. This is an algorithm for computing the relative sameness of two different items, for example, the classic *cosine similarity* method for comparing text documents based on word frequencies, which has been used in search engines since the 1970s (Manning et al., 2008). *Cosine similarity* is essentially a measure of topical similarity, but similarity metrics can be designed to capture many other axes of variation, for example, source diversity or demographic diversity.

Recommender systems actually in use by news organizations employ further definitions of diversity. One large news organization has designed their recommender to consider diversity in terms of media format, so that the user sees a mix of articles, videos, podcasts, etc. Another uses the topical diversity algorithm of Ziegler and colleagues (2005) so as to prevent all of the top-ranked news stories from being about the same popular topic, for example, President Trump. Further afield in music recommendation, Spotify uses a popularity-based diversity metric in an effort to give a fair level of exposure to all artists who provide content (Hansen et al., 2021; Mehrotra et al., 2018).

As these examples show, there is no end to the normative and technical definitions of diversity that might be employed. A review of the concept of diversity across communications scholarship, social science, and computer science concludes that "research on this topic has been held back by the lack of conceptual clarity about media diversity and by a slow adoption of methods to measure and analyze it" (Loecherbach et al., 2020, p. 606). Hence, merely stating that a news recommender system should be "diverse" is not enough. There is still considerable work to be done in a) choosing a conception of diversity, and then b) choosing a specific algorithmic operationalization of that concept.

In other words, there is a very large gap between a principle such as "represent diverse viewpoints" and a specification such as "ensure that no one news source accounts for more than 20 percent of the recommended items." The latter is concrete enough to be implemented. It also necessarily captures only a small portion of the rich concept of "diverse viewpoints." While it is true that a narrow mechanical process can never account for all the contextual richness of human experience, all principles must claim *some* power of generalization if they are to serve as a guide to future behavior. It is necessary to commit to specific definitions, phrased in algorithmic terms, in order to build real recommenders.

This is why "principles" are not a satisfactory method for specifying the desired behavior of a news recommender. When inspected closely, most "principles" for recommender design admit many possible algorithmic translations. If the work of making the abstract concrete is not done by *journalists*, it must be done by *technologists*, which is closer to delegation than collaboration.

156 Jonathan Stray

Metrics

Metrics are a key tool for translating principles to practice because they span the divide between the conceptual and the empirical. In the context of AI systems, they are used both at the level of management (e.g., "key performance indicators") and encoded algorithmically (e.g., "objective functions.") Well-being metrics are already being used by large platforms in this dual role (Stray, 2020). Metrics can also contribute to transparency and provide regulatory affordances, as they define a common language for comparing recommender performance.

Aside from the well-known issues with using metrics in a management context generally (Jackson, 2005), metrics pose a problem for AI systems in particular because most AI systems are built around strongly optimizing for a narrow objective (Thomas & Uminsky, 2020). Poor use of metrics can result in a damaging emphasis on short-term outcomes, manipulation and gaming, and unwanted side effects. Even a successful metric cannot remain static, as the structure of the world will change over time; many machine learning models broke when the onset of the COVID-19 pandemic caused mass changes in behavior (Heaven, 2020). Yet metrics are an essential component of modern recommender systems, and offer rich possibilities for *journalist-technologist* collaboration.

There are two major questions that must be answered in the design of a metric: what is important, and how to measure it. This starts with the question of which values a particular system should enact, which must then be "operationalized" into practical metrics (Jacobs & Wallach, 2021). *Technologists* will need to be included in discussions of which values matter, because it is necessary to consider both the constraints of technical possibility and the empirical behavior of the audience-platform system. *Journalists* will need to be involved in the operationalization and validation of metrics, because these decisions ultimately define what, exactly, is measured. The issue of who actually carries out these measurements is also significant—it need not be the platform itself (Wu & Taneja, 2020).

Returning to the example of diversity, Helberger and colleagues (2018) propose several metrics that might help us evaluate different axes of diversity in recommender systems:

> It is conceivable to design metrics that would focus, for example, on user engagement with opposing political views, cross-ideological references in public debates or social media connections between people who represent different ideological positions.
>
> (Helberger et al., 2018, p. 195)

All of these suggestions are technically realizable. It is possible to infer an individual's ideological position from their posts, social network structure, and/or news consumption data (Bodrunova et al., 2019; Garcia et al., 2015; Garimella

& Weber, 2017), and this could be used to define "cross-ideological" engagement. Such metrics can drive news recommender design at the managerial level when given as targets to a product team, who may further choose to translate these metrics technically by incorporating them into the objective functions of their algorithms (Stray, 2020).

It remains to decide what value of such a metric counts as a "good" outcome; the numerical result of measuring something doesn't mean much if we cannot say what an acceptable number is. Nechushtai and Lewis (2019) grapple with this problem in their study of source diversity in Google News:

> If every news story recommended by a search engine were false, or if a search engine referred readers to one news organization alone, it would be clear that the algorithm is falling short as a news provider acting in the public interest. But, in most cases, public-facing algorithms of this sort do not function catastrophically or perfectly, but somewhere in between. Precisely where they fall on such a spectrum remains open for debate. What standards should be used to assess their performance?
>
> (Nechushtai & Lewis, 2019)

Translating news values into metrics and numerical thresholds is likely to be an uncomfortable process for *journalists*, because it requires examination of naturalized values in extremely explicit terms. Consider the concept of "newsworthiness," which might be the fundamental value underlying content ranking. Even for stories which are already data-driven, involving crime statistics, earthquakes, or corporate earnings, it is difficult to say exactly what number counts as "news." Previous efforts have tried to infer a numeric threshold which matches what journalists already do, set the threshold so as not to overwhelm editors or audiences with too many stories, or simply picked a "reasonable" threshold arbitrarily (Stray, 2019). None of these options is completely satisfactory.

Metrics also have an important role to play in regulation. A metric can be considered a "regulatory affordance," a common language for the regulator, the regulated, and the public. For example, Facebook has proposed regulation of unwanted content based on a "prevalence" metric (Bickert, 2020), that would define some acceptably small percentage of views of prohibited content such as hate speech. Without both a metric and an acceptable limit, it is difficult to answer the question of whether there is "too much" unacceptable content. Quantification is especially important when judging tradeoffs between different values; given the limited accuracy of automated classifiers, removing more hate speech will necessarily impinge on freedom of expression as false positives also increase (Duarte et al., 2017). Metrics are thus a key component of evaluation protocols (see below).

Metrics work best for concepts that have straightforward observable counterparts, like source diversity. It is difficult to capture more complex notions in a simple metric. A number of metrics have been used over the years to detect

158 Jonathan Stray

"clickbait," including dwell time (Yi et al., 2014) and click-to-share ratio (El-Arini & Tang, 2014). But neither of these measures is a very good operationalization, as neither really captures what is meant by "clickbait." Modern systems instead use machine learning classifiers trained on custom data sets.

Data sets

Data sets can embody values in a variety of ways. While this embeddedness is usually studied in the context of fairness (e.g., Barocas et al., 2018), custom data sets are also used to define and promote positive outcomes. Data sets at the level of sources, items, or sets of items could provide valuable normative direction for news recommendations.

Recommender systems that select user posts must remove clickbait and spam. Because there is no one metric that can reliably detect this unwanted content, in practice platforms solve this problem through machine learning (ML) models trained on data sets containing examples of both clickbait and non-clickbait content (Cora, 2017; Peysakhovich & Hendrix, 2016). Hate speech is similarly hard to measure using hand-crafted metrics, so ML classifiers are used instead (Fortuna & Nunes, 2018). In short, data sets can encode more subtle and complex values than hand-crafted metrics. A classifier trained on such data outputs a numerical score for each item, which can be considered a type of algorithmically constructed metric.

One of the simplest kinds of news-relevant data sets is a list of organizations which meet certain standards for process and quality. A news aggregator must first solve the problem of which sources produce "news," and even general social media platforms must be able to identify when users post news if they wish to treat it differently—for example, if they wish to subject it to evaluation, ranking, and labeling according to quality standards. For this reason, there are commercial organizations like NewsGuard that maintain a list of news organizations rated for credibility. Facebook has assembled source-level credibility data through crowdsourced surveys, a technique which other researchers have independently validated (Mosseri, 2018; Pennycook & Rand, 2018; Zhang et al., 2020).

Collections of labels at the level of individual news items (articles, videos, etc.) could in principle be used to embody various dimensions of item quality and credibility. While many "fake news classifiers" have been built from article-level data sets, in practice credibility classifiers built this way typically pick up on source or topic and do not generalize well (Bozarth & Budak, 2020). A classifier can only detect a concept if the necessary data are actually available to the system; it is not possible to identify "misinformation" with a classifier alone because determining whether something is true or not can require open-ended human research (Silverman, 2020). Still, it is useful to combine various content and contextual cues to evaluate credibility, and credibility rating data sets are used by platforms as one signal to rank content lower, rather than remove it.

Annotated *sets* of articles may also be an important data source. The News Quality Initiative has scraped the daily top stories from several news aggregators and asked journalists to "re-rank" the stories according to their editorial judgement and record their reasoning (Sehat, 2020). This data set, though small and partially qualitative, suggests that ranked sets of articles could be used to evaluate or perhaps even train news recommenders to match professional editorial values. The Reuters Tracer system relies on a similar approach to flag tweets with potential breaking news value for human review. It employs a "newsworthiness" classifier trained on the stories that reporters actually chose to write (Liu et al., 2016).

Given the lack of a precise theory of the aims of journalism, much less a theory of the aims of news recommenders which produce personalized results, whether or not news recommenders *should* attempt to match traditional editorial judgements is an open question. There may be greater agreement on which sorts of content should *not* be selected by recommenders, which speaks to the relationship between ranking (deciding what should be shown) and moderation (deciding what should not be shown).

Feedback methods

Interactive feedback is an emerging method to control the output of AI systems in general, and recommenders in particular. In this approach, users or experts are asked to provide feedback on the actual output of a running system. This has the advantages of adaptability and ecological validity as compared to static data sets. Like metrics and data sets, this method of algorithmic tuning is also suitable for non-expert collaboration. The humble "like" button is a type of interactive feedback, but far more is possible.

Structured feedback has proven useful for training information filtering systems. For a document summarization task, OpenAI has demonstrated that guiding a reinforcement learning algorithm, by repeatedly asking humans which of two summaries is better, dramatically improves the quality of the results. Notably, including pairwise feedback produces much better summaries than training only on human-written reference summaries (Stiennon et al., 2020).

Pairwise feedback has also been used to design a multi-stakeholder ranking system. Lee and colleagues (2019) demonstrate the use of a similar pairwise-comparison protocol for participatory design of a ranking algorithm. The goal was to design a system for a non-profit which collects donated food and delivers it, via volunteer drivers, to local food charities. Representatives from different stakeholder groups were repeatedly shown a pair of donor-driver-recipient matches and asked to choose which they preferred. This feedback was used to construct a quantitative model of the preferences of each participant, with these models aggregated at run-time to produce the final ranking. The resulting algorithm improved both efficiency and distributional fairness, as judged by stakeholders.

160 Jonathan Stray

For news recommendation in particular, semi-structured feedback has enabled successful collaborations between technologists and journalists. During the iterative development of their in-house recommender systems, the BBC uses "a custom-designed qualitative scale and free text" to collect feedback from editors on each recommended item (Boididou et al., 2021).

This type of semi-structured feedback is not necessarily machine readable, meaning that only a small number of people (in this case, editors) can be served in this way, but a number of researchers are investigating *conversational* methods which interact using natural language (Radlinski & Craswell, 2017; Sun & Zhang, 2018). Such a recommender might ask a user whether a particular article was a good choice for them and pose follow-up questions to try to learn why.

The design of interactive feedback methods is an opportunity for *journalist-technologist* collaboration. There are a variety of feedback paradigms that might yield useful information on how the system is enacting journalistic values. Journalists or users might be asked to do pairwise comparisons, rate individual articles, or provide natural language feedback. They could rate hypothetical recommendations, or recommendations actually provided. Retrospective, deliberative judgement on the items previously presented might be an especially powerful technique, as it could align short-term and long-term incentives (Stray et al., 2020). If natural language feedback is possible, what sorts of questions should the algorithm ask?

Evaluation protocols

News recommenders operate in a dynamic environment, interacting with large numbers of people. Offline evaluations of recommender performance—that is, testing against prepared data sets—often do not meaningfully predict online performance (Jeunen, 2019). Thus, evaluation within a real-world setting is essential.

The most straightforward way to evaluate a news recommender is to measure its output against some metric. Such evaluation is a normal part of the process of recommender construction and operation, and engineers already repeatedly evaluate the output of recommender systems according to standard metrics like "accuracy," the ability to predict which items the user will actually engage with or otherwise rate as valuable. There is no reason why, for example, a suitable "diversity" metric could not be used similarly.

Standardized metrics would also allow external stakeholders to evaluate news recommenders, including users, researchers, and regulators. An evaluation protocol would specify which metric to use and how to collect the data to be evaluated. Data collection is a complex issue for recommender systems because most of them provide personalized results. Existing approaches include crowdsourced data collection from a demographically balanced sample of users (Nechushtai & Lewis, 2019) and using multiple new, non-personalized user accounts (Ledwich &

Zaitsev, 2020). A standardized protocol is beneficial because it would allow longitudinal analysis, cross-recommender comparisons, and regulatory consistency.

Evaluation protocols can also go beyond assessing the output of a recommender system to consider the effect on users. Understanding the broader human consequences of these systems is essentially social science research which would benefit from repeatable methods. For example, the IEEE 7010 standard for well-being assessment (Schiff et al., 2020) proposes gathering baseline well-being metrics data for both expected users and non-users for a particular product, then collecting the same metrics over time for both groups.

As an example, we might want to test whether a particular news recommender increases or decreases political polarization. Affective polarization, a dislike and distrust of the outgroup, is a central part of the identity-based polarization that is occurring in modern democracies (Iyengar et al., 2019) and can be measured by simple survey instruments (Iyengar & Westwood, 2015). It might be possible to measure affective polarization of users and non-users before making some algorithmic change intended to reduce polarization, then re-measure for these two groups several months after deployment. The difference in the change in affective polarization between the two groups can be attributed to the recommender change, under certain assumptions. This is essentially a difference-in-differences research design (Angrist & Pischke, 2009, p. 227).

Evaluation protocols are the most general type of collaborative artifact studied here, and may specify the use of particular principles, metrics, data sets, and feedback methods. As above, different stakeholders may use such protocols in different ways. Recommender designers can use them to create and monitor their systems, while external stakeholders can use them to audit and compare different products.

Conclusion

While a number of authors have envisioned algorithms that embed values, much less has been said about how this is to be accomplished in practice. If *journalists* and *technologists* want to collaborate to produce better news recommenders, they will need to co-produce more than principles or guidelines. It is not reasonable to expect *journalists* to become algorithmic experts and participate directly in technical design processes. Rather, these two groups could collaborate in the production of specific technical artifacts that are already used in contemporary recommender values engineering: metrics, data sets, feedback methods, and evaluation protocols.

References

Abdollahpouri, H., Adomavicius, G., Burke, R., Guy, I., Jannach, D., Kamishima, T., Krasnodebski, J., & Pizzato, L. (2020). Multistakeholder recommendation: Survey and research directions. *User Modeling and User-Adapted Interaction*, *30*(1), 127–158. https://doi.org/10.1007/s11257-019-09256-1

Angrist, J. D., & Pischke, J.-S. (2009). *Mostly harmless econometrics: An empiricist's companion.* Princeton University Press.

Bandy, J., & Diakopoulos, N. (2019). Auditing news curation systems: A case study examining algorithmic and editorial logic in Apple News. *Proceedings of the Fourteenth International AAAI Conference on Web and Social Media.* http://arxiv.org/abs/1908.00456

Barocas, S., Hardt, M., & Narayanan, A. (2018). *Fairness and machine learning: Limitations and opportunities.* http://fairmlbook.org

Bickert, M. (2020). Online content regulation policy. https://about.fb.com/wp-content/uploads/2020/02/Charting-A-Way-Forward_Online-Content-Regulation-White-Paper-1.pdf

Bodrunova, S. S., Blekanov, I., Smoliarova, A., & Litvinenko, A. (2019). Beyond left and right: Real-world political polarization in Twitter discussions on inter-ethnic conflicts. *Media and Communication, 7*(3), 119–132. https://doi.org/10.17645/mac.v7i3.1934

Boididou, C., Sheng, D., Mercer Moss, F. J., & Piscopo, A. (2021). Building public service recommenders: Logbook of a journey. *RecSys 2021 – 15th ACM Conference on Recommender Systems,* 538–540. https://doi.org/10.1145/3460231.3474614

Bozarth, L., & Budak, C. (2020). Toward a better performance evaluation framework for fake news classification. *Proceedings of the International AAAI Conference on Web and Social Media, 14*(Icwsm), 60–71.

Celis, L. E., Kapoor, S., Salehi, F., & Vishnoi, N. (2019). Controlling polarization in personalization. *FAT* '19: Conference on Fairness, Accountability, and Transparency,* pp. 160–169. https://doi.org/10.1145/3287560.3287601

Cora, M. V. (2017). Detecting trustworthy domains—Flipboard engineering. Flipboard. https://engineering.flipboard.com/2017/04/domainranking

DeVito, M. A. (2017). From editors to algorithms: A values-based approach to understanding story selection in the Facebook news feed. *Digital Journalism, 5*(6), 753–773. https://doi.org/10.1080/21670811.2016.1178592

Diakopoulos, N. (2019). Towards a design orientation on algorithms and automation in news production. *Digital Journalism, 7*(8), 1180–1184. https://doi.org/10.1080/21670811.2019.1682938

Duarte, N., Llanso, E., & Loup, A. (2017). Mixed messages? The limits of automated social media content analysis. Center for Democracy and Technology. https://cdt.org/insights/mixed-messages-the-limits-of-automated-social-media-content-analysis/

El-Arini, K., & Tang, J. (2014). Click-baiting. Facebook. https://about.fb.com/news/2014/08/news-feed-fyi-click-baiting/

Fields, B., Jones, R., & Cowlishaw, T. (2018). The case for public service recommender algorithms. https://piret.gitlab.io/fatrec2018/program/fatrec2018-fields.pdf

Fjeld, J., Achten, N., Hilligoss, H., Nagy, A., & Srikumar, M. (2020). Principled artificial intelligence: Mapping consensus in ethical and rights-based approaches to principles for AI. *SSRN Electronic Journal.* https://doi.org/10.2139/ssrn.3518482

Floridi, L. (2019). Translating principles into practices of digital ethics: Five risks of being unethical. *Philosophy and Technology, 32*(2), 185–193. https://doi.org/10.1007/s13347-019-00354-x

Fortuna, P., & Nunes, S. (2018). A survey on automatic detection of hate speech in text. *ACM Computing Surveys, 51*(4), 85:3–85:24. https://doi.org/10.1145/3232676

Friedman, B., Hendry, D. G., & Borning, A. (2017). A survey of value sensitive design methods. *Foundations and Trends in Human-Computer Interaction, 11*(23), 63–125. https://doi.org/10.1561/1100000015

Garcia, D., Abisheva, A., Schweighofer, S., Serdült, U., & Schweitzer, F. (2015). Network polarization in online politics participatory media. *Policy & Internet, 7*(1), 46–79.

Garimella, V. R. K., & Weber, I. (2017). A long-term analysis of polarization on Twitter. *Proceedings of the 11th International Conference on Web and Social Media, ICWSM 2017*, 528–531. www.aaai.org/ocs/index.php/ICWSM/ICWSM17/paper/view/15592

Hansen, C., Mehrotra, R., Hansen, C., Brost, B., Maystre, L., & Lalmas, M. (2021). Shifting consumption towards diverse content on music streaming platforms. *WSDM '21: Proceedings of the 14th ACM International Conference on Web Search and Data Mining*, 238–246.

Heaven, W. D. (2020). Our weird behavior during the pandemic is messing with AI models. *MIT Technology Review.* www.technologyreview.com/2020/05/11/1001 563/covid-pandemic-broken-ai-machine-learning-amazon-retail-fraud-hum ans-in-the-loop/

Helberger, N. (2019). On the democratic role of news recommenders. *Digital Journalism, 7*(8), 993–1012. https://doi.org/10.1080/21670811.2019.1623700

Helberger, N., Karppinen, K., & D'Acunto, L. (2018). Exposure diversity as a design principle for recommender systems. *Information Communication and Society, 21*(2), 191–207. https://doi.org/10.1080/1369118X.2016.1271900

Helberger, N., Leerssen, P., & Van Drunen, M. (2019). Germany proposes Europe's first diversity rules for social media platforms. *Media@LSE Blog.* https://blogs.lse.ac.uk/ medialse/2019/05/29/germany-proposes-europes-first-diversity-rules-for-social-media-platforms/

Iyengar, S., & Westwood, S. J. (2015). Fear and loathing across party lines: New evidence on group polarization. *American Journal of Political Science, 59*(3), 690–707. https://doi.org/ 10.1111/ajps.12152

Iyengar, S., Lelkes, Y., Levendusky, M., Malhotra, N., & Westwood, S. J. (2019). The origins and consequences of affective polarization in the United States. *Annual Review of Political Science, 22*, 129–146. https://doi.org/10.1146/annurev-polisci-051117-073034

Jackson, A. (2005). Falling from a great height: Principles of good practice in performance measurement and the perils of top down determination of performance indicators. *Local Government Studies, 31*(1), 21–38. https://doi.org/10.1080/0300393042000332837

Jacobs, A. Z., & Wallach, H. (2021). Measurement and fairness. FAccT Conference, http:// arxiv.org/abs/1912.05511

Jeunen, O. (2019). Revisiting offline evaluation for implicit-feedback recommender systems. *RecSys 2019 – 13th ACM Conference on Recommender Systems, 3*, 596–600. https://doi. org/10.1145/3298689.3347069

Kunaver, M., & Požrl, T. (2017). Diversity in recommender systems – A survey. *Knowledge-Based Systems, 123*, 154–162. https://doi.org/10.1016/j.knosys.2017.02.009

Ledwich, M., & Zaitsev, A. (2020). Algorithmic extremism: Examining YouTube's rabbit hole of radicalization. *First Monday, 25*(3). https://doi.org/10.5210/fm.v25i3.10419

Lee, M. K., Kusbit, D., Kahng, A., Kim, J. T., Yuan, X., Chan, A., See, D., Noothigattu, R., Lee, S., Psomas, A., & Procaccia, A. D. (2019). Webuildai: Participatory framework for algorithmic governance. *Proceedings of the ACM on Human-Computer Interaction, 3*. https:// doi.org/10.1145/3359283

Liu, X., Wudali, R., Martin, R., Duprey, J., Vachher, A., Keenan, W., Shah, S., Li, Q., Nourbakhsh, A., Fang, R., Thomas, M., Anderson, K., Kociuba, R., Vedder, M., & Pomerville, S. (2016). Reuters Tracer: A large scale system of detecting & verifying real-time news events from Twitter. *Proceedings of the 25th ACM International on Conference on*

Information and Knowledge Management – CIKM, '16, 207–216. https://doi.org/10.1145/2983323.2983363

Loecherbach, F., Moeller, J., Trilling, D., & van Atteveldt, W. (2020). The unified framework of media diversity: A systematic literature review. *Digital Journalism*, *8*(5), 605–642. https://doi.org/10.1080/21670811.2020.1764374

Manning, C. D., Raghavan, P., & Schütze, H. (2008). In C. D. Manning, P. Raghavan, & H. Schütze (Eds.), The vector space model for scoring, *Introduction to information retrieval* (pp. 109–126). Cambridge University Press.

Mehrotra, R., McInerney, J., Bouchard, H., Lalmas, M., & Diaz, F. (2018). Towards a fair marketplace. *Proceedings of the 27th ACM International Conference on Information and Knowledge Management*, 2243–2251. https://doi.org/10.1145/3269206.3272027

Möller, J., Trilling, D., Helberger, N., & van Es, B. (2018). Do not blame it on the algorithm: An empirical assessment of multiple recommender systems and their impact on content diversity. *Information, Communication & Society*, *21*(7), 959–977. https://doi.org/10.1080/1369118X.2018.1444076

Mosseri, A. (2018). Helping ensure news on Facebook is from trusted sources. Facebook. https://about.fb.com/news/2018/01/trusted-sources/

Nechushtai, E., & Lewis, S. C. (2019). What kind of news gatekeepers do we want machines to be? Filter bubbles, fragmentation, and the normative dimensions of algorithmic recommendations. *Computers in Human Behavior*, *90*, 298–307. https://doi.org/10.1016/j.chb.2018.07.043

Pennycook, G., & Rand, D. G. (2018). Crowdsourcing judgments of news source quality. *SSRN Electronic Journal*. https://doi.org/10.2139/ssrn.3118471

Peysakhovich, A., & Hendrix, K. (2016). Further reducing clickbait in feed. Facebook. https://about.fb.com/news/2016/08/news-feed-fyi-further-reducing-clickbait-in-feed/

Radlinski, F., & Craswell, N. (2017). A theoretical framework for conversational search. *Proceedings of the 2017 Conference on Conference Human Information Interaction and Retrieval*, 117–126. https://doi.org/10.1145/3020165.3020183

Schiff, D., Ayesh, A., Musikanski, L., & Havens, J. C. (2020). IEEE 7010: A new standard for assessing the well-being implications of artificial intelligence. http://arxiv.org/abs/2005.06620

Sehat, C. M. (2020). NewsQ review panel reports 2020. News Quality Initiative. https://newsq.net/newsq-review-panel-reports-2020/

Shahriari, K., & Shahriari, M. (2017). IEEE standard review – Ethically aligned design: A vision for prioritizing human wellbeing with artificial intelligence and autonomous systems. *IHTC 2017 – IEEE Canada International Humanitarian Technology Conference 2017*, 197–201. https://doi.org/10.1109/IHTC.2017.8058187

Silverman, C. (Ed.). (2020). *The verification handbook for disinformation and media manipulation*. European Journalism Center. https://datajournalism.com/read/handbook/verification-3

Simonsen, J., & Robertson, T. (2012). *Routledge international handbook of participatory design* (1st edition). Routledge. https://doi.org/10.4324/9780203108543

Stiennon, N., Ouyang, L., Wu, J., Ziegler, D. M., Lowe, R., Voss, C., Radford, A., Amodei, D., & Christiano, P. (2020). Learning to summarize from human feedback. http://arxiv.org/abs/2009.01325

Stray, J. (2019). Making artificial intelligence work for investigative journalism. *Digital Journalism*, *7*(8), 1076–1097. https://doi.org/10.1080/21670811.2019.1630289

Stray, J. (2020). Aligning AI optimization to community well-being. *International Journal of Community Well-Being, 3*, 443–463, https://doi.org/10.1007/s42413-020-00086-3

Stray, J., Adler, S., & Hadfield-Menell, D. (2020). What are you optimizing for? Aligning recommender systems with human values. *Participatory Approaches to Machine Learning Workshop, ICML 2020*. https://participatoryml.github.io/papers/2020/42.pdf

Sun, Y., & Zhang, Y. (2018). Conversational recommender system. *41st International ACM SIGIR Conference on Research and Development in Information Retrieval, SIGIR 2018*, 235–244. https://doi.org/10.1145/3209978.3210002

Thomas, R. L., & Uminsky, D. (2020). Reliance on metrics is a fundamental challenge for AI. *Ethics of Data Science Conference*. https://arxiv.org/abs/2002.08512

Vincent, S., Lopez, P., Allen, L., Allsop, J., Riley, R., & Traister, R. (2020). Our opinion: recommendations for publishing opinion journalism on digital platforms. News Quality Initiative. https://newsq.net/wp-content/uploads/2020/11/NewsQ-Opinion-Panel-2020-nov30-FINAL.pdf

Vrijenhoek, S., Kaya, M., Metoui, N., Möller, J., Odijk, D., & Helberger, N. (2020). Recommenders with a mission: assessing diversity in newsrecommendations. *Proceedings of ACM Conference (Conference'17), 1*(1), 554–561. https://doi.org/10.1007/978-3-030-65965-3_38

Wu, A. X., & Taneja, H. (2020). Platform enclosure of human behavior and its measurement: Using behavioral trace data against platform episteme. *New Media and Society, 23*(9), 2650–2667, https://doi.org/10.1177/1461444820933547

Yi, X., Hong, L., Zhong, E., Liu, N. N., & Rajan, S. (2014). Beyond clicks: Dwell time for personalization. *RecSys 2014 – Proceedings of the 8th ACM Conference on Recommender Systems*, 113–120. https://doi.org/10.1145/2645710.2645724

Zhang, A. M. Y. X., Sehat, C. M., & Mitra, T. (2020). Investigating differences in crowdsourced news credibility assessment: Raters, tasks, and expert criteria. *Proceedings of the ACM on Human-Computer Interaction, 4*(CSCW2), 1–26, https://doi.org/10.1145/3415164

Ziegler, C.-N., McNee, S. M., Konstan, J. A., & Lausen, G. (2005). Improving recommendation lists through topic diversification. *Proceedings of the 14th International Conference on World Wide Web – WWW 05, January 22*. https://doi.org/10.1145/1060745.1060754

PART IV

News Quality, Government, and Media Policy

11

HOW AUSTRALIA'S COMPETITION REGULATOR IS SUPPORTING NEWS, BUT NOT QUALITY

Chrisanthi Giotis, Sacha Molitorisz and Derek Wilding

Introduction

On 15 August 2018, Australia's competition watchdog held an evening forum as part of its Digital Platforms Inquiry for journalists in Sydney. On stage were three of the statutory office-holders with the Australian Competition and Consumer Commission (ACCC): chair Rod Sims, deputy chair Delia Rickard, and commissioner Roger Featherston. Among other things, the evening's agenda was to ask, 'Is government intervention needed to support quality journalism in Australia? If so, what initiatives or measures could government (or others) consider to support the provision of quality journalism in Australia?' One attendee suggested a better-funded public broadcaster, while another suggested that the government ought to fund quality journalism directly (ACCC, 2018). However, the most telling exchange came when one senior journalist stood up to challenge the difficulty of defining quality. Is this, he asked, what the ACCC was aiming to do – to define quality journalism, and then to support it? In response, the ACCC was succinct and unequivocal. The Digital Platforms Inquiry (the Inquiry) would not be limiting itself to quality journalism. And so it has played out. Passed into law in February 2021, Australia's News Media Bargaining Code (the Code) seeks to force digital platforms to pay media businesses for news content, but the notion of 'quality' is almost entirely absent.

The importance of quality news is not in dispute. In economic terms, it is a 'merit good' with 'an inherent value for society that extends beyond what can be measured or expressed in market terms' (Doyle, 2013, p. 94). As the ACCC explained in 2020:

DOI: 10.4324/9781003257998-15

> … intervention is necessary to address the bargaining power imbalance because of the public benefit provided by the production and dissemination of news and the importance of a strong independent media in a well-functioning democracy.
>
> (ACCC, 2020a, p. 3)

In other words, the ACCC found that digital platforms make money from news content, but the news providers do not receive a commensurate payment for the effort put into the production. Missing from this scheme is a method of quantifying the value of news to platforms, and to the public; neither is there a mechanism for calculating the value to publishers of referrals from platforms to their news sites. Instead, the Code proceeds on the understanding that Google and Facebook 'use' the news content of publishers and imposes a compulsory arbitration process to determine how much Google and Facebook must pay for this use of news content.

During development of the Code, Google and Facebook were deeply unhappy (Google, 2020; Facebook, 2020a). They waged a public relations war against the Code, with Google threatening to remove its search engine from Australia, and Facebook removing news from its platform at the eleventh hour (Leaver, 2021). The development of the legislation also raised the vexatious prospect of putting into black letter law exactly what it was the government was trying to protect. Nonetheless, by early 2022, the new law had resulted in a significant redistribution of revenue from platforms to publishers – even though the underlying uncertainty concerning the value of news remained.

In this chapter, we describe the Digital Platforms Inquiry, in which Australia's competition regulator identified an unfair value exchange between news media businesses, on the one hand, and Google and Facebook on the other. We also describe the law and the Code that ensued. Despite sustained pressure from Google and Facebook, the Australian legislation looks likely to set a global precedent, with Canada and the UK contemplating similar reforms. We analyze the Code to show that although it aims to promote public interest journalism (including by prompting payments from Google and Facebook), the notion of quality journalism is largely absent. Drawing on our previous research commissioned by the ACCC for the Inquiry, we take an expansive approach to the concept of 'quality' that recognizes traditional news standards such as accuracy, fairness, transparency and the protection of privacy, but also encompasses aspects such as originality, geographic relevance, civic function and social diversity (Wilding et. al., 2018). Unfortunately, as it stands, the Code has the potential to incentivize journalism that is inaccurate, misleading or otherwise of poor quality. In this regard, the Code's professional standards test, under which news media businesses must adhere to professional news standards, is a missed opportunity. Ultimately, we note that such a Code for journalism developed by a competition regulator can only ever be limited in impact. What is needed is a more thorough accounting of the social value of news. By using social utility as a metric of quality, we will be better placed to protect quality journalism.

News deserts and a legislative first

The ACCC is a federal statutory authority that administers both anti-trust law and consumer protection law. It shares responsibility for media mergers with the Australian Communications and Media Authority (ACMA), another federal statutory authority that is responsible for other media sector-specific regulation, including licensing and content regulation. In December 2017, the federal government directed the ACCC to begin an inquiry in the face of growing concerns that Google, Facebook and other digital platforms were affecting traditional media's ability to fund journalism and that this was impacting the 'level of choice and quality of news and content being produced by Australian journalists' (see Flew & Wilding, 2020). This became known as the Digital Platforms Inquiry.

Australia has a relatively small but culturally diverse population of about 26 million across a large continent; at 7.69 million sq km, Australia is the world's sixth largest country (DFAT, 2020). However, Australians are not avid consumers of news: with a 'news interest' rating of 51 per cent in the *Reuters Institute Digital News Report 2021*, Australia was below the 24-market average of 58 per cent, with interest in news declining by 12 percentage points over the past five years (Newman et al, 2021, p. 13). And choice is limited. In terms of pluralism and ownership, Australia has one of the world's most concentrated media markets (see Dwyer et al., 2021; Brevini & Ward, 2021; Papandrea & Tiffen, 2016). The Australian commercial news landscape is dominated by two large players: Nine Entertainment (2021 revenue A\$2.3 billion) and News Corp (Australian revenue unavailable: Burrowes, 2021a). Both own tabloid and broadsheet newspapers and their digital equivalents; and while Rupert Murdoch's News Corp controls Australia's only pay TV network, Nine controls a leading commercial free-to-air network as well as influential radio stations. A third commercial media company is Seven West Media (2021 revenue A\$1.3bn). Australia also has a large and relatively well-funded public broadcaster, the Australian Broadcasting Corporation, modelled on the UK's BBC (2021 government funding \$1.1bn).

In June 2019, the ACCC handed down the Final Report of its Inquiry. The ACCC identified, for the first time in Australia, news deserts. It found that the net total of unique Australian local and regional newspaper titles had declined by 15 per cent between 2008–09 and 2017–18, which translates to 106 papers. Closures during this period left 21 'local government areas' (that is, one of the 500-plus local areas under the control of a council) without a single local or regional newspaper, 16 of those in regional Australia. This key finding, echoing developments in countries including the US, confirmed long-held concerns about news provision. The ACCC found that public interest journalism was becoming scarce, with fewer reporters dedicated to full-time coverage of local government and fewer reporters dedicated to attending court proceedings. ACCC chair Rod Sims emphasized that 'public interest journalism is essential for a well-functioning society', and that 'costly investigative journalism, journalism that can take some months to put together, is often not rewarded as the algorithms don't prioritize original material' (Sims, 2019).

The ACCC concluded, 'There is not yet any indication of a business model that can effectively replace the advertiser model, which has historically funded the production of these types of journalism in Australia' (ACCC, 2019, p. 1). The ACCC proposed that Google and Facebook work with Australian news businesses to develop and implement a voluntary code of conduct. Over the next nine months, discussions between digital platforms and news media businesses revealed some goodwill, but also the difficulty of reaching consensus on the key question of how to value the benefits publishers receive from platforms, let alone the benefits platforms receive from publishers.

In April 2020, when the ACCC delivered a progress report to the government, Australia had just emerged from a bushfire crisis to find itself in a global pandemic. Thirst for news was high, yet local and regional titles were continuing to fold: between March 2020 and September 2021, another 200 newsrooms closed or contracted (PIJI, 2021). The ACCC indicated that the core issue of payment for content was unlikely to be resolved through a voluntary process, due in part to the 'opacity' of the 'ad tech supply chain', which clouds the finances of digital platforms and makes it extremely difficult for advertisers to know where their dollars go (ACCC, 2019, p. 2). With news media businesses similarly unwilling to make their financial operations fully transparent, news media businesses and digital platforms started making wildly different claims. Google Australia managing director Mel Silva claimed that the value it received from news services per annum was A$9.8 million (approximately US$7 million) (Cheik-Hussein, 2020). By contrast, News Corp Australasia boss Michael Miller said revenue lost to the tech giants was up to A$1 billion annually, and Nine chairman Peter Costello estimated lost revenue at A$600 million (Mason, 2020).

On 20 April 2020, the Government intervened, announcing its intention to implement a mandatory code before the end of that year. Controversially, it prescribed mandatory 'final offer arbitration' if no agreement could be reached as to value exchange. That is, the digital platform makes an offer; the news media business makes an offer; the arbitrator picks the one that seems fairest. It also included a set of 'minimum standards' for digital platforms stipulating that Google and Facebook share user data about how people interact with the content of news media businesses; Google and Facebook give advance notice of any upcoming changes to their algorithms that affect news; and Google and Facebook appropriately recognize original news content in ranking and in display. Google and Facebook responded diplomatically, then militantly (Google, 2020; Facebook, 2020a; Leaver, 2021; Lee & Molitorisz, 2021). For a week in late February, Facebook Australia raised the stakes by removing news from its platform for Australian users, and removing news produced by Australian news media for all Facebook users internationally.

On 25 February 2021, the *Treasury Laws Amendment (News Media and Digital Platforms Mandatory Bargaining Code) Act 2021* was voted into law. It retained provisions for final offer arbitration and minimum standards, but these were significantly diluted. And in the wake of threats from Google and Facebook, the biggest concessions destined the Code to a degree of irrelevance. Under the law, the Code applied to 'registered' news media businesses and 'designated' digital services. As of 17 February 2022, 28 news businesses had registered with the communications regulator to receive the benefits of the Code (ACMA, 2022). However, the Treasurer has not designated a single digital platform or service as covered by the law. What's more, this situation is likely to continue. The Treasurer won't trigger the legislation by naming the digital platforms, as long as he is satisfied that, in the words of the legislation, the digital platform has made 'a significant contribution to the sustainability of the Australian news industry through agreements relating to news content of Australian news businesses (including agreements to remunerate those businesses for the news content)' (Lee & Molitorisz, 2021). In effect, then, the new law is a threat from the government to Google and Facebook: pay money to news media businesses, or else we'll activate the Code. So far, deals have been struck with the biggest news outlets, and with some medium and small outlets, which, according to ACCC chair Rod Sims, has led to 'well north of A\$200m a year' flowing to Australian news businesses (Butler, 2021). For some, this means the Code qualifies as a major success, even if it is effectively a big stick that may never be used; for others, the Code is a failure because it favours old established media and threatens to exclude small players and to stifle innovation, and also because it creates an opaque and secretive system of deals (Lee & Molitorisz, 2021). In September 2021, it emerged that Facebook was not negotiating with Australia's second national broadcaster, SBS, which specifically services Australia's diverse communities (Burrowes, 2021b).

Further criticisms include that the deals struck have been explicitly for the use of news content on Google News Showcase and Facebook News Tab, rather than across all Google's services and Facebook's services; it would seem that striking deals for the use of news content on Showcase and News Tab is a strategic move by which digital platforms are able to gloss over the value that news content brings to their best-known and best-used services. There is also no requirement, either under the Code or in the deals struck, for news media businesses to channel any money received directly into journalism.

Our specific concern here, however, is in the way the Code, as legislated, may go some way to promoting public interest journalism, but stands very little chance of promoting quality journalism, and may even work against it. To be clear: the provisions of the Code matter, even if they are not invoked. Presumably the digital platforms will seek to avoid being designated under the Code by taking steps to satisfy its provisions.

Can public interest journalism exist without quality?

Neither in public discourse nor in Australian law is the definition of news or journalism clear (Wilding et al., 2018, pp. 16–17). Similarly, there is no accepted definition of 'public interest journalism' or 'quality journalism' or how they interact. In the Final Report of its Inquiry, the ACCC defined 'public interest journalism' as:

> Journalism with the primary purpose of recording, investigating and explaining issues of public significance in order to engage citizens in public debate and inform democratic decision-making at all levels of government.
>
> (ACCC, 2019, p. 283)

This definition didn't include quality as a necessary ingredient. That's perhaps surprising, given that a stated concern of the Inquiry was the potential for digital platform distribution to erode the ability of news organizations to produce quality journalism. Overall, despite the prominence of 'choice and quality' in the Inquiry's terms of reference, the ACCC's Final Report has few mentions of quality. However, it did explicitly address the difference between quality journalism and public interest journalism:

> It is important to distinguish 'high quality journalism' from 'public interest journalism' … journalism may be produced with the purpose of examining matters of public significance, meeting the definition of 'public interest journalism', without meeting minimum quality standards – for example by failing to be accurate or failing to clearly distinguish reporting from the presentation of opinion.
>
> (ACCC, 2019, p. 287)

It also observed that 'poor quality news and journalism is also seen and heard outside of digital platforms' (ACCC 2019, p. 354), and recorded the results of its commissioned survey that showed that 'around 92% of the respondents … had some concern about the quality of news and journalism they were consuming' (ACCC, 2019, p. 355). However, the ACCC had little to say about ways of addressing quality of news and journalism *per se*. Instead, it discussed the dimensions of quality represented by practices such as fake news, atomization (where news has been broken down into its constituent parts, so that it is distributed and consumed on a story-by-story basis rather than as part of a news package) and algorithmic presentation of extreme views, and settled on an approach based on helping 'consumers to evaluate the veracity, trustworthiness and quality of the news content they receive online' (ACCC, 2019, p. 358). This was how the ACCC arrived at its proposal for a disinformation code (Recommendation 15, p. 370) to be developed by Australia's media regulator; hence the development of a code of practice on

How Australia's competition regulator supports news, not quality   **175**

disinformation and misinformation, along with the topic of 'flagging quality journalism', was to be overseen by the Australian Communications and Media Authority (ACMA). In doing so, the ACCC explained that stakeholder responses to its Preliminary Report, released in December 2018, prompted it to abandon the suggestion of a regulatory requirement for 'badging' of all news and journalism by digital platforms, noting (among other reasons) that it would be difficult to apply disincentives to the inclusion of content that breached journalism standards (ACCC, 2019, p. 364). True to its comments to journalists in August 2018 as described at the start of this chapter, the ACCC ultimately gave quality little more than a cameo role in its Final Report.

The ACCC's lack of focus on quality carried through into the Code. The only element of quality in the ACCC's scheme is that journalists must meet minimum standards set out in the various media industry codes and standards administered by bodies such as the media regulator, ACMA. In Australia, unlike in the US, there are various sets of standards (such as the Commercial Television Industry Code of Practice) that are policed by bodies including the ACMA.

The ACCC (2019, p. 286, footnote omitted) noted:

These codes and standards almost universally require that journalism:

- presents factual material accurately
- corrects significant or material factual errors
- presents news fairly and impartially
- clearly distinguishes reporting from commentary and analysis.

Accordingly, s52P of the Bargaining Code prescribes a 'professional standards test' that must be satisfied for news businesses to be registered under the Code. Section 52P(1)(a)(iv) refers, rather obliquely, to 'the provision of quality journalism' as the basis for this professional standards requirement. This is the single time that the word 'quality' appears in the *Treasury Laws Amendment (News Media and Digital Platforms Mandatory Bargaining Code) Act 2021*, an expansive piece of legislation that runs to 33 pages. We return to s52P below.

Instead, the definitions contained in the Code create two categories of news: 'core news' and 'covered news'. With this approach, the ACCC adopted a definition of public interest news without ever invoking the phrase 'public interest news'. Core news is a threshold concept, determining which companies get through the door and qualify to be covered by the legislation. According to s52A:

Core news content means content that reports, investigates or explains:

- issues or events that are relevant in engaging Australians in public debate and in informing democratic decision-making; or
- current issues or events of public significance for Australians at a local, regional or national level

This definition retains the essence of the ACCC's 2019 definition of public interest journalism, chiefly in the phrase 'informing democratic decision-making'. However, it also broadens out to include matters 'of public significance … at a local, regional or national level'. This is a clear concession to arguments from local and regional news outlets that public interest journalism is about more than upholding democracy, but also about locally significant matters. That includes the community-building function of news. There is recognition here by the ACCC of the twin functions of local news content widely acknowledged in both academic and policy literature (Wilding et al., 2020; ACMA, 2020b).

The legislation then complements 'core news' with a category of 'covered news', which encompasses a broader range of content. While 'core' content determines whether a business qualifies to be covered by the Code, 'covered news' designates the content that is recognized under the Code once a business has qualified. 'Covered' content is defined as 'core content', as well as 'content that reports, investigates or explains current issues or events of interest to Australians'.

For 'covered news', the distinction is the focus on '*of* interest' to the public, whereas 'core news' can be considered closer to journalism that is *in* the public interest. The explanatory materials released with the draft legislation in July 2020 showed the ACCC accepted an understanding of news business economics that includes cross-subsidy of democracy/community-enhancing news through more commercial/popular news products:

> Many news businesses use other news content to cross-subsidize the production of core news content. This means it is important that registered news businesses receive information relating to, and can bargain over, a broader range of content than just their core news content.
>
> (ACCC, 2020b, p. 14)

By designating both core and covered content as subject to the benefits of the legislation, without including an explicit requirement for quality, the legislation opens the possibility of incentivizing poor-quality journalism, including poor-quality public interest journalism. For instance, news about a major new housing development is clearly in the public interest. However, if the reporting merely regurgitates a rapacious developer's press release, or if it is discussed in an emotive, partial and misleading way to provoke reactions and be favoured by algorithms, does such journalism deserve regulatory intervention and financial support? The answer at this point would seem to be 'yes', because it satisfies the definition of 'core news'. On politics, a news outlet might choose only to cover volatile and divisive issues. Or a news outlet might focus on issues that are racially divisive, as occurred with the dubious reporting of crime said to be perpetrated by African-Australian 'gangs' in Melbourne in 2018, in a way that stretched the truth and inflamed tensions (Media Watch, 2018). These issues are all in the public interest, and they all satisfy the definition of 'core news', but they would fail to meet important criteria of *quality*.

One way quality could be rewarded under the Code is in s52X, which states digital services 'designated' under the Code are required to develop 'a proposal … to recognize original covered news content when it makes available and distributes that content'. As Wilding (2021, p. 34) notes, this requirement is somewhat inconsistent with the ACCC's previously stated position (noted above) that 'flagging quality journalism' was to be left to the disinformation code overseen by the ACMA. This intervention by the ACCC was likely in response to the arguments made by publishers during the Inquiry that they did not receive significant recognition for their original content, with re-purposed stories by their competitors often ranking higher than their original investigative pieces. During the development of the Code, however, Google and Facebook fiercely resisted any attempts to enforce algorithmic oversight, or transparency (Google, 2020; Facebook, 2020a). In its Preliminary Report in late 2018, the ACCC recommended that a regulator ought to oversee the ranking of news and advertising; the ACCC's Final Report, however, dispensed with this recommendation. And, again, given that no digital service has been designated, s52X is not in effect, just like the rest of the Code.

In any case, even before the Code passed into law, Google and Facebook had announced moves to prioritize original reporting. In 2019, soon after the ACCC handed down its Final Report, Google announced it was 'elevating original reporting in Search' (Gingras, 2019). And in 2020, Facebook announced that its algorithm would favour original news content in its News Feed; this has subsequently been updated with further commitments to originality (Brown and Levin, 2020). However, we cannot know the extent or effectiveness of these commitments, given that Google and Facebook ensure there is very little transparency about their algorithms and their impacts.

Standards as a missed opportunity

At this point in our analysis, it is important to make explicit why we believe there is value in some regulatory mechanism to encourage quality, and how this would be consistent with other aspects of media regulation in Australia, as it would in some other countries, such as Canada and the UK, although not the US. In Australia specifically, much of media content regulation, including news standards, is achieved by way of 'co-regulation' (Lee & Wilding 2022). In brief, this means that industry associations draft the rules that appear in codes of practice, but the regulator (the ACMA) accepts unresolved complaints and can take enforcement action. It is also important to understand that Australia's system of media oversight is highly fragmented, consisting of 14 different media standards schemes (Wilding et al., 2018, p. 88). It is not just different media platforms that have their own scheme. Rather, each category of broadcasting (commercial radio, commercial television) has its own code of practice, as does each of the two publicly funded broadcasters, the ABC and SBS.

Among the mess of these 14 standards schemes, the Code imposes a 'professional standards test' in s52P. To be registered under the Code as a 'news media business', a news organization needs to establish that each of its participating news outlets is subject to:

- one of two industry schemes established by the print/online news sector;
- one of two statutory codes of practice drafted by industry but enforced by the media regulator, the ACMA (not the ACCC); or
- 'rules substantially equivalent to those mentioned [above] regarding internal editorial standards that relate to the provision of quality journalism'.

While the ACCC has at least succeeded in incorporating some reference to media standards, there are two problems with this approach. First, it leaves intact – in fact, it endorses – the fragmentation of media standards. As it is entirely reasonable that the beneficiaries of a very substantive legislative intervention should themselves meet minimum standards, the development of the Code presented an opportunity – now a lost opportunity – to consolidate media standards through a requirement to participate in an independent standards scheme. To this end, both the competition regulator in developing the Code and the media regulator overseeing the development of the disinformation code have overlooked the potential for standards councils to combat 'fake news' through the promotion of trusted and accountable journalistic sources (Podger, 2019).

Second, by permitting *in-house* codes of ethics (via 'internal editorial standards') based on the undefined concept of 'quality journalism', with no requirement for independent complaint handling, it risks harming the very aspect it seeks to support. Under this approach, 14 schemes could become 28 or more. In this scenario, the leverage held by Australian governments over many years, and which underpins the industry scheme operated independently by the Australian Press Council (which oversees print and digital newspapers) – in effect, 'keep your house in order, and we'll leave you alone' would disappear. It could thus add to the risk that quality news will be dis-incentivized under the scheme. And while much of this last aspect is specific to Australian conditions, it may become increasingly relevant in a global media environment where national schemes come face-to-face with businesses operating across national borders. As part of its submission on the ACCC's Concepts Paper, Facebook suggested the idea of a new industry-based standards forum. The 'Australian Digital News Council' proposed by Facebook would:

> exchange information about product roadmaps and industry trends, consider issues or concerns around dealings between publishers and platforms,

and to air and mediate complaints and concerns from publishers about their relationship with digital platforms.

(Facebook, 2020b, p. 31)

Further, Facebook said it 'would welcome the opportunity to contribute funds towards this Council to support a secretariat that can resolve any complaints and concerns'. While Facebook's proposed council would not address issues of quality and standards in a comprehensive way, it's nevertheless interesting to see a digital platform propose to be involved in a standards forum.

How social accounting might promote quality

An omission from both the conceptual framework and legislative enactment of the Code is the recognition of the *social* value of news. The legislation underpinning the Code has been drafted as part of commercial and competition law and framed around bargaining power. But is commercial exchange all that should be on the bargaining table? In many areas of life, social metrics have been developed specifically to acknowledge that value exchange need not be limited to financial consideration. In Australia, measurements of social value have already been used in different areas of public life. The state government of New South Wales created the first 'social impact bond' (Ahuri, 2020) whereby investors were encouraged to buy bonds that would support the development of new programs that reduce recidivism. The social value of this drop in repeat jailing was then calculated as a (dollar-proxy) cost benefit to the government and paid as a return to investors. Triple bottom-line accounting has also been used to manage the crucial issue of distributing highly valuable water allocation across the three competing areas of farming, environmental and cultural/social needs – albeit not without difficulties and controversy (Simons, 2020, p. 57).

The underlying assumption here is that high-quality journalism is more socially useful than poor-quality journalism. This is borne out in the literature. An extensive review carried out as part of the Inquiry found that broader social functions is one of three key categories through which quality news is identified. Table 11.1 presents what the Centre for Media Transition identified (in 2018) as the most useful quality indicators discussed in the academic literature. It attempts to distill the most effective quality criteria into a manageable and organized list with content attributes sub-classified into:

- Core standards of practice
- Core professional practice indicators
- Broader social functions.

The individual indicators should not be considered to necessarily carry equal weight; the table is a guide to factors that can be taken into account. This is

180 Chrisanthi Giotis, Sacha Molitorisz and Derek Wilding

TABLE 11.1 Quality indicators – content attributes table

Indicator	What it indicates	Indicator	What it indicates
A. Core Standards of Practice		**B. Broader Social Functions**	
Accuracy	Content is factual, verified and not misleading; opinion is based on accurate information and does not omit facts; material presented in the body corresponds with the headline.	Power watchdog	Scrutinizes the activities and conduct of powerful interests so they can be held democratically and socially accountable.
Clarity	Easy to understand; distinguishes fact from opinion.	Public sphere	Facilitates deliberative, rational and representative public discourse
Fairness	Material is fairly presented; persons or groups unfavourably portrayed given right of reply.	Critical Information Needs (CINs)	Gives details of emergencies, risks, health, welfare, education, transportation, economic opportunities, environment, civic information and political information.
Privacy and protection from harm	Respects privacy; avoids causing substantial offence, distress, or risk to health or safety (unless it is in the public interest).	Geographic relevance	Provides original local news voice for local communities; reports on local institutions, decision-making processes and events.
Balance	Presentation of contrasting information and viewpoints from different sources.	Usefulness	Provides citizens with information they can use to make effective decisions that benefit their personal and civic lives.
Integrity and transparency	Avoids or discloses potential conflicts of interest; content has not been produced via unethical or deceptive means.	Diversity (social)	Positive coverage of minority groups; variety of content appeals to a range of social groups; multicultural references.

How Australia's competition regulator supports news, not quality **181**

TABLE 11.1 (Cont.)

Indicator	What it indicates	Indicator	What it indicates
C. Core Professional Practice Indicators			
Immediacy	Publication and updating of breaking news as soon as practicable (after fact-checking) for each given format.	Analysis	Rational, knowledgeable and insightful interpretation of events and issues that helps people make sense of their world.
Authority	Stories use the expertise of authoritative and reliable sources; corporate or partisan sources are clearly identified.	Originality	Content is produced in-house through original research, interviews, verification of information, self-taken photos.
Depth and breadth of coverage	Explaining background context, causes and consequences involved; range of content from range of genres.	Creativity	Written and illustrated with creative flair; innovative use of technology; evinces multimedia richness (websites).
Ethical conduct in news gathering	Uses fair, honest, responsible means to gather material.	Presentation	Uses a gratifying narrative and layered information; format is captivating, aesthetically pleasing, well-illustrated, technically and textually error-free, and easy to navigate (e.g., websites).

Source: adapted from Wilding et. al., 2018, p. 86.

because value to society is created through quality news which undertakes watchdog functions, services critical information needs, is geographically relevant, and represents social diversity.

There is of course a danger in trying to reduce conceptual complexities to quantifiable variables (O'Donnell, 2009); nevertheless, this table of quality indicators helps to build a picture of overall quality factors. We acknowledge, however, that development of a more dynamic matrix to suit the contemporary environment requires separate research. For example, it is worth noting that impartiality is labelled in the table as a *professional* indicator of quality; however, in the current politically polarized media discourse, it is instead being discussed by audiences as socially useful. A 2018 survey found that for 40 per cent of adult Australians, the second most mentioned reason for avoiding news was 'I feel that news content is biased towards a particular ideology' (Roy Morgan Research, 2018, p. 21). Internationally, while the Reuters Institute noted some variation in its recent examination of impartiality, it found that across the four markets of the US, the UK, Brazil and Germany, there was 72 per cent support for the proposition that, when reporting social and political issues, news outlets should give equal time to all sides (Newman et al., 2021, p. 40).

The key point in introducing Table 11.1 is to highlight that categories of news social utility exist and could be turned into metrics of quality. Metrics, relying on professional and public participation, have already been developed to measure quality in cultural products, with UK government funding tied to this demonstration of quality. These metrics include social utility aspects such as local impact and relevance, for example, the Arts Council England (n.d.). Of course, this process is not without its critics (Phiddian et al., 2017) and many obstacles would arise in translating the process to news.

First, Google and Facebook would need to recognize that having a greater quantity and variety of quality, socially useful information in their ecosystems is more valuable for the platforms than one populated by partisan poor-quality information. Here, the case may be made by the platforms themselves. Stray (2020) points to the 'well-being' metrics that both Facebook and YouTube have incorporated into their algorithmic decision making. Of particular interest is the way YouTube incorporated changes to make tabloid content less readily accessible to 'improve the quality of the product and the effects on users' (Stray, 2020, p. 450). These initially had a negative impact on time spent on site; but, within three months, user watch time had not only recovered but increased. The same people spent more time on quality videos once tabloid products were less prominent in their feeds.

The next obstacle would be to put dollar proxies on the social utility of different types of news items. This means that, to be eligible for a bargaining credit of a certain amount under social accounting mechanisms, it must be demonstrated that the news item is socially useful and then shown that it is more socially useful than it would have otherwise been because it is of high quality. Setting the value of this bargaining credit is no easy proposition. Nor is it likely to be universally welcomed. In a 2015 article surveying the field of social metrics in journalism, Anya Schiffrin and Ethan Zuckerman wrote: 'The task of "proving impact" doesn't come naturally to most journalists. They reject a utilitarian view of their worth, preferring to believe that news is a public good that merits support for its own sake' (Schiffrin & Zuckerman, 2015, p. 48). Yet with advertising and subscription dollars falling and more news organizations turning to philanthropic support, various tools to measure impact have had to be developed (Giller & Wroth, 2015). Some of these might prove useful to adapt for bargaining purposes. However, to be clear, the metrics needed for Australia's Code (or overseas versions thereof) are very different than those developed for non-profit foundations. The task is

How Australia's competition regulator supports news, not quality   **183**

to prove value to an information economy. The metric is not about social justice effects, but rather the output of quality news with the value of that quality tied to its social utility.

It is also worth highlighting that while geographic relevance is an aspect of quality news understood to provide social utility, this has been disadvantaged by the Code's emphasis on bargaining. An A\$150,000 revenue threshold is needed for news media businesses to be covered by the legislation. The logic seems to be that news media businesses need to be of a sufficient size for digital platforms to gain some commercial benefit from their presence – which may be true. Yet it is also true that the size of a business is not necessarily a proxy for social utility, and size is a particularly vexed question for local news organizations disadvantaged in the online environment (Hindman, 2018).

Conclusion

The Code was never intended to be a silver bullet for the ills troubling news media businesses. Much less was it intended to single-handedly rescue public interest journalism. The Code had a specific goal: to redress an unfair value exchange between news media businesses and digital platforms. In the success of some 'side deals' struck to avoid the Code's application, arguably that goal has been achieved. Furthermore, the Code as legislated has a clear focus on protecting public interest journalism in its definition of 'core news'. The issue is that quality was handballed from one regulator to another (ACCC to ACMA) and, in the process, slipped into a regulatory crevice. It remains a missed opportunity, meaning that further policy measures are needed to shore up both public interest journalism and quality journalism.

Stronger arguments must be made for the value of an information ecosystem populated by diverse, quality news offerings. Social accounting may help, but there is much to work out in terms of creating these metrics. Further options might include: media business tax offsets for the costs incurred in the production of quality, public interest journalism; making subscriptions for certain types of news tax deductible for consumers; increasing funding for public broadcasters; and channeling money directly into public interest journalism and quality journalism (Lee & Molitorisz, 2021).

In giving an overall assessment of the Australian Code, we think a defining feature – and inherent limitation – is that despite its genesis in a far-ranging Inquiry that commenced in late 2017 and an implementation process that started in late 2019, the Code suffers from the decision to advance to the question of *how much digital platforms should pay news organizations* without having first decided *how to calculate the value of the benefit.* This is one reason why quality receives such scant attention. But in our view there is another, perhaps more funda-mental, defining feature and inherent limitation, and one that may be of interest to other jurisdictions: the decision to use competition law – rather than media regulation – to support journalism. The genesis and location of the scheme within competition law defines the overall approach and objectives of this attempt to regulate bargaining. And yet, if the encouragement of quality news is also one of our goals (as it should be), then a competition regulator will necessarily need to approach the task in a roundabout manner. For holistic and lasting reform, it may be unreasonable to expect a competition regulator to judge the difference between quality news and non-quality news, and to take social utility into account. It is not unreasonable, however, to expect it to guard against arrangements that *undermine* the quality of news.

References

ACCC (2018, August). Summary of digital platforms inquiry journalists forum. www.accc. gov.au/system/files/DPI%20-%20Journalists%20forum%20summary%20-%2020%20 August%202018_0.pdf

ACCC (2019). Digital platforms inquiry: Final report. www.accc.gov.au/publications/digi tal-platforms-inquiry-final-report

ACCC (2020a). ACCC mandatory news media bargaining code – concepts paper. www. accc.gov.au/system/files/ACCC%20-%20Mandatory%20news%20media%20bargain ing%20code%20-%20concepts%20paper%20-%2019%20May%202020.pdf

ACCC (2020b). Treasury laws amendment (news media and digital platforms mandatory bargaining code, Bill 2020 – exposure draft explanatory materials. www.accc.gov.au/sys tem/files/Exposure%20Draft%20EM%20-%20NEWS%20MEDIA%20AND%20DIGI TAL%20PLATFORMS%20MANDATORY%20BARGAINING%20CODE%20B ILL%202020.pdf

ACMA (2020a). Misinformation and news quality on digital platforms in Australia: A pos- ition paper to guide code development. www.acma.gov.au/australian-voluntary-codes- practice-online-disinformation

ACMA(2020b). News in australia: Diversity and localism – news measurement frame- work. www.acma.gov.au/publications/2020-12/report/news-australia-diversity-and- localism

ACMA (2022). Register of eligible news businesses. www.acma.gov.au/register-eligible- news-businesses

Ahuri (2020, January 21). What are social impact bonds and how do they work? www. ahuri.edu.au/research/ahuri-briefs/what-are-social-impact-bonds

Arts Council England (n.d.). Quality metrics pilot. www.artscouncil.org.uk/quality-metr ics/quality-metrics#section-6

Brevini, B., & Ward, M. (2021) Who controls our media? Exposing the impact of media concentration on our democracy. GetUp. www.getup.org.au/media/releases/post/ new-getup-report-finds-australian-media-concentration-at-crisis-point

Brown, C., & Levin, J. (2020, June 30). Prioritizing original news reporting on Facebook. https://about.fb.com/news/2020/06/prioritizing-original-news-reporting-on- facebook/

Burrowes, T. (2021a, September 4). Orphans and elephants: What earnings month told us about the coming media ownership dance. *Unmade Blog.* www.unmade.media/p/orph ans-and-elephants-what-earnings

Burrowes, T. (2021b, September 23), Who gets to decide which media companies are deserving: Facebook or the ACMA?, *Unmade Blog*. www.unmade.media/p/should-facebook-or-the-acma-decide

Butler, B. (2021, December 19). "Look at that penalty": After taking on Google and Facebook, Rod Sims departs ACCC with a warning. *The Guardian Australia*, www.theguardian.com/australia-news/2021/dec/19/look-at-that-penalty-after-taking-on-google-and-facebook-rod-sims-departs-accc-with-a-warning

Cheik-Hussein, M. (2020, June 1). Google says it makes only $10 million in ad revenue from news in Australia, *AdNews* www.adnews.com.au/news/google-says-it-makes-only-10-million-in-ad-revenue-from-news-in-australia.

DFAT (2020). About Australia. www.dfat.gov.au/about-australia/Pages/about-australia

Doyle, G., (2013). *Understanding media economics* (2nd ed.). Sage.

Dwyer, T., Wilding, D., & Koskie, T. (2021). Australia: Media concentration and deteriorating conditions for investigative journalism', in J. Trappel & T. Tomaz (Eds.), *The media for democracy monitor 2021: How leading news media survive digital transformation* (Vol. 1) (pp. 59–94). Nordicom.

Facebook (2020a, September). Facebook's response to Australia's proposed news media and digital platforms mandatory bargaining code. https://about.fb.com/wp-content/uploads/2020/08/Facebooks-response-to-Australias-proposed-News-Media-and-Digital-Platforms-Mandatory-Bargaining-Code.pdf

Facebook (2020b). Response to the Australian mandatory news media bargaining code concepts paper. www.accc.gov.au/system/files/Facebook.pdf

Flew, T., & Wilding, D. (2020). The turn to regulation in digital communication: The ACCC's digital platforms inquiry and Australian media policy. *Media, Culture & Society*, *43*(1), 48–65.

Giller, C., & Wroth, K. (2015). Can we measure media impact? Reading between the lines. *Stanford Social Innovation Review, Fall*, 52–55.

Gingras, R. (2019, September 12). Elevating original reporting in Search. www.blog.google/products/search/original-reporting/

Google (2020, August 24). 13 things you need to know about the News Media Bargaining Code. https://australia.googleblog.com/2020/08/13-things-you-need-to-know-about-news.html

Hindman, M. (2018). *The internet trap: How the digital economy builds monopolies and undermines democracy*. Princeton University Press.

Leaver, T. (2021). Going dark: How google and facebook fought the australian news media and digital platforms mandatory bargaining code. *M/C Journal*, *24*(2). https://doi.org/10.5204/mcj.2774

Lee, K., & Molitorisz, S. (2021). The australian news media bargaining code: Lessons for the UK, EU and beyond. *Journal of Media Law*, *13*(1), 36–53.

Lee, K., & Wilding, D. (2022). The case for reviewing broadcasting co-regulation. *Media International Australia*, *182*(1), 67–80.

Mason, M. (2020, May 14). Tech giants must pay much more than $600m for news: News Corp. *Australian Financial Review*. www.afr.com/companies/media-and-marketing/news-corp-boss-says-600m-from-tech-giants-not-enough-20200514-p54t45

Media Watch (2018, March 28). Daily Mail's African gang obsession. www.abc.net.au/mediawatch/episodes/daily-mails-african-gang-obsession/9972312

Newman, N., with Fletcher, F., Schulz, A., Andı, S., Robertson, C. T., & Nielsen, R. K. (2021). Reuters Institute Digital News Report 2021. https://reutersinstitute.politics.ox.ac.uk/digital-news-report/2021

O'Donnell, P. (2009). That's Gold! Thinking about excellence in Australian journalism. *Australian Journalism Review, 31*(2), 47–60.

Papandrea, F., & Tiffen, R. (2016). Media ownership and concentration in Australia. In E. Noam (Ed.), *Who owns the world's media: Media concentration and ownership around the world* (pp. 703–734). Oxford University Press.

Phiddian, R., Meyrick, J., Barnett, T., & Maltby, R. (2017). Counting culture to death: An Australian perspective on culture counts and quality metrics. *Cultural Trends, 26,* 174–80.

PIJI (Public Interest Journalism Initiative) (2021). The Australian newsroom mapping project. https://anmp.piji.com.au/

Podger, A. (2019). Fake news: Could self-regulation of media help to protect the public? The experience of the Australian Press Council. *Public Integrity, 21*(1), 1–5, https://doi.org/10.1080/10999922.2018.1549341

Roy Morgan Research Research (2018). Consumer use of news: Final report prepared for ACCC. www.accc.gov.au/system/files/ACCC%20consumer%20survey%20-%20Consumer%20use%20of%20news%2C%20Roy%20Morgan%20Research.pdf

Schiffrin, A., & Zuckerman, E. (2015). Can we measure media impact? Surveying the field. *Stanford Social Innovation Review, Fall,* 47–51.

Simons, M. (2020, March). Cry me a river: The tragedy of the Murray-Darling Basin. *Quarterly Essay.* www.quarterlyessay.com.au/essay/2020/03/cry-me-a-river

Sims, R. (2019, July 26). Press conference. www.accc.gov.au/about-us/tools-resources/social-media/transcripts/accc-digital-platforms-inquiry

Stray, J. (2020). Aligning AI optimization to community well-being. *International Journal of Community Well-Being, 3,* 443–463.

Wilding, D., (2021). Regulating news and disinformation on digital platforms: Self-regulation or prevarication? *Journal of Telecommunications and the Digital Economy, 9*(2), 11–46. https://doi.org/10.18080/jtde.v9n2.415

Wilding, D., Giotis, C., & Koskie, T. (2020). News in Australia: Diversity and localism – Review of literature and research. ACMA. www.acma.gov.au/publications/2020-12/report/news-australia-diversity-and-localism

Wilding, D., Fray, P., Molitorisz, S., & McKewon, E. (2018). *The impact of digital platforms on news and journalistic content,* University of Technology Sydney, NSW. www.accc.gov.au/system/files/ACCC%20commissioned%20report%20-%20The%20impact%20of%20digital%20platforms%20on%20news%20and%20journalistic%20content%2C%20Centre%20for%20Media%20Transition%20%282%29.pdf

12

GOVERNMENT INTERVENTIONS INTO NEWS QUALITY

Philip M. Napoli and Asa Royal

Introduction

A fundamental motivation for this volume is the fact that while news quality is an inherently complex and challenging concept to define and measure, it is, nonetheless, something for news organizations to strive for, news consumers to demand, media researchers to measure, and—as this chapter explores—perhaps even something for media policymakers to pursue. If a healthy news and information ecosystem is something that we consider within the purview of policymakers' concerns, then news quality is a concept that may then become a central component of media policymaking (see, e.g., Lyubareva & Rochelandet, 2021). Of course, there is also a compelling argument to be made that such concerns should be outside the purview of policymakers, given the valid concerns about press freedom that surround any government interventions into the operation of the press. To give policymakers influence over as fundamental an element of news as *quality* may be a recipe for putting a free press at risk.

However, in the current environment, in which economic, structural, and technological changes have combined to undermine the production, distribution, and consumption of quality journalism to a degree that may undermine the very functioning of the democratic process (Napoli, 2019), traditional positions regarding the need for the absolute and complete separation of press and government increasingly have the appearance of an ostrich burying its head in the sand. The preservation of the institution of journalism is a necessary and unavoidable component of the contemporary media policy agenda in many countries that operate under the precept that a healthy press is essential for a well-functioning democracy (Napoli, 2020; Napoli & Stonbely, 2018). Whether the preservation

DOI: 10.4324/9781003257998-16

and promotion of quality journalism should be a focal point for such efforts is, however, a difficult question.

These tensions related to the pursuit of news quality as a policy goal are the focus of this chapter, with particular attention to recent policy initiatives that have been motivated by the impact that technological changes have had upon the economics of the journalism industry and by the rise of disinformation. The rise of large digital platforms plays a prominent role in both of these phenomena (Napoli, 2019).

Policymakers in many countries have begun to engage with the question of whether it is necessary for governments to intervene in the relationships between large digital platforms, the news media, and news consumers (Royal & Napoli, 2022). This imperative has become more pronounced as platforms have become an increasingly prominent gateway to news, and have employed various mechanisms to curate algorithmically the flow of news in users' news feeds (Napoli, 2019).

As definitionally complex and as politically charged as the notion of news quality may be, it has, nonetheless, played a prominent role in certain policy deliberations that have focused on this increasingly urgent issue, given how these new journalism intermediaries may be affecting the production, distribution, and consumption of quality news. Countries are at different stages in terms of determining what, if any, policy interventions may be necessary on behalf of protecting and promoting quality journalism in these platform ecosystems that have been shown, in many instances, to undermine, rather than enhance, exposure to quality news (Napoli, 2019).

Through an analysis of policy initiatives in three English-language contexts (the U.S., the U.K., and Australia), this chapter explores how notions of news quality factor into contemporary media policy. This chapter pays particular attention to the political dynamics surrounding news quality as a policy goal, which are often intertwined with conflicting interpretations of press freedom and the role of government in the news ecosystem. This analysis will also touch upon basic practicalities, such as definitional issues and measurement challenges. As this chapter will illustrate, for both political and practical reasons, news quality has tended to get pushed to the margins of recent media policy initiatives.

The first section of this chapter explores news quality as a goal of government intervention in these three national contexts. This section considers how the politics of news quality and the definitional and empirical challenges surrounding the concept of news quality intertwine to (for the most part) discourage the articulation and pursuit of news quality as an explicit policy goal. Instead, news quality seems to morph over the time span of particular policy initiatives into more general terms such as public interest journalism or community information needs; or to be broken down and represented in terms of one or two of its component parts, such as accuracy or diversity. This section draws upon relevant policy documents as well as personal experience conducting research in connection with a government proceeding motivated, in part, by concerns about quality journalism.

Government interventions into news quality **189**

The second section discusses the broader ramifications of the patterns identified in the previous section for the future of quality journalism. In addressing this issue, this section also addresses the related question of whether the various conceptual proxies that are adopted as replacements for the notion of news quality are fundamentally less problematic or more pragmatic substitutes. These questions are considered in light of recent examples from contexts such as Switzerland and the Council of Europe, in which an explicit focus on news quality is maintained.

The concluding section summarizes the chapter's key findings, considers them in relation to the distinctive characteristics of different national contexts, and offers some very preliminary thoughts about possible paths forward.

The politics and practicalities of news quality

In today's political environment, in which political extremism and partisanship have taken root in many countries' media policy spheres to an extent that we haven't seen in the modern journalistic era (Napoli & Dwyer, 2018), interpretations of the notion of quality in journalism become more politically charged. This situation heightens the imperative for policymakers and policy researchers to approach the concept of quality in journalism through (theoretically) less politically charged terminology and framing.

Critical information needs and news quality: The U.S. case

This situation is well-exemplified by efforts initiated roughly a decade ago by the U.S. Federal Communications Commission (FCC) to gain a deeper understanding of how well local news sources were meeting communities' critical information needs, in the face of dramatic technological and economic change (Waldman & Working Group on the Information Needs of Communities, 2011). This high-profile proceeding, ambitiously dubbed the "Future of Media" proceeding, resulted in a massive, widely discussed report.

This proceeding became, in many ways, a case study in the politicization of media policymaking—and of media policy research in particular (Friedland, 2014; Napoli & Friedland, 2016). In this case, as much as the notion of critical information needs became the driving conceptual force behind the work, it is important to note the extent to which the notion of news quality undergirded this proceeding at its outset. In its report, the Commission notes that "it is extremely difficult—constitutionally and practically—to assess quality" (Waldman & Working Group on the Information Needs of Communities, 2011, p. 312) Nonetheless, the term *quality* was used in the report in reference to news *nearly 100 times*, without any explicit definition ever being offered.

That being said, in a few instances, the term was used in conjunction with specific qualitative dimensions of news, such as financial investment, numbers of reporters, the presence of investigative journalism, and the degree of reliance on sponsored content (Waldman & Working Group on the Information Needs of Communities, 2011). In the overwhelming majority of instances, however, the report referenced the notion of news quality without any explicit articulation of what the term means—particularly for the agency itself—as if no definitional foundation were necessary.

The end result is a somewhat schizophrenic impression, in which the FCC simultaneously expresses its hesitancy to wade into the waters of assessing news quality (for both constitutional and practical reasons), while at the same time repeatedly referencing news quality in a way that suggests that there is a mutually agreed-upon understanding of how news quality is defined and assessed. The takeaway from this proceeding, then, is that, within the policymaking context, the notion of news quality can, to some extent, serve as an abstract point of discussion. However, in the transition to the necessarily more concrete phases of policy research and, subsequently, policymaking, such ambiguity is problematic, with the path toward greater specificity being one in which the notion of news quality is replaced by related, but less loaded, proxies.

We see this in the next stages of the proceeding, which involved a plan by the FCC to commission multi-method studies in six media markets in the U.S. These studies were intended to help the FCC develop a clearer understanding of how local news outlets in those communities assessed and met their communities' critical information needs. The meeting of critical information needs became the dominant analytical focus, with the notion of quality so prominent in the Future of Media report largely falling by the wayside.

Specifically, the FCC laid out a plan for research that would examine six U.S. media markets via two components: (1) a media market census, and (2) a community ecology study. The media market census would include a content analysis of broadcast, newspaper, and online content to determine the extent to which this content was addressing *critical information needs* (for a more extensive discussion, see Napoli & Friedland, 2016). This notion of identifying the extent to which local news outlets meet a community's information needs can be seen as at least congruent—if not synonymous—with the notion of news quality. Utilizing the critical information needs terminology, however, allowed the Commission to sidestep the more politically charged, and arguably more subjective notion of quality. The FCC's research was also to include in-depth interviews with local media providers. The community ecology study would include general population surveys directed at measuring communities' actual and perceived critical information needs, as well as in-depth interviews with community members (Social Solutions International, 2013).

This proposed research produced a firestorm of controversy, which was touched off when Republican FCC Commissioner Ajit Pai (2014) published an editorial in the *Wall Street Journal* chastising the FCC for an initiative to "thrust the federal government into newsrooms across the country ... to grill reporters, editors, and station owners about how they decide which stories to run." Congressional hearings ensued, as well as threatened legislation to kill the research. Industry groups expressed opposition as well (see Napoli & Friedland, 2016). As Pai's (2014) statement illustrates, the focal point of critiques was the component of the study involving interviews with outlet owners, journalists, and editors about their editorial decision making, under the notion that such research represented an overt intrusion by the federal government into the operation of journalism, and thus a threatened intrusion on First Amendment freedoms. The newsroom interviews element of the study was ultimately dropped in response to these objections (Federal Communications Commission, 2014a). However, criticism and pressure continued to mount until the FCC ultimately canceled the entire study (Federal Communications Commission, 2014b).

Thus, as this case study illustrates, even the discursive shift to the notion of community information needs was ineffective at blunting the intense politicization and polarization that characterizes contemporary media policymaking and policy research (see, e.g., Napoli, 2021; Napoli & Dwyer, 2018).

Indeed, in subsequent work in which the first author was involved, foundations sought to pick up the research torch that the FCC had dropped, under the presumption that foundations were better insulated from political pressures. Our research team developed a methodological approach for assessing what we primarily defined as the "robustness" of local news (Napoli et al., 2017), as part of an ongoing research initiative called the News Measures Research Project. The News Measures Research Project's robustness measures included the extent to which a local news outlet's news stories were original, local, and addressed critical information needs (Napoli et al., 2017).

One could certainly argue that these criteria represent a meaningful set of indicators for news quality. Whether a news story reflects original reporting (as opposed to repurposing the work of other outlets) would seem to be a reasonable indicator of quality, given the extent to which it reflects the magnitude of financial investment that an outlet is making towards news production (see, e.g., Lyubareva & Rochelandet, 2021). And within the context of the study of local news sources, whether a news story is indeed about the local community also would seem to be a reasonable quality indicator, given the extent to which it reflects how well an outlet is covering the community it serves. And finally, the extent to which a story addresses community information needs was, ultimately, an effort to reflect the dimension of news quality that remained in the FCC's work as it evolved over time; with the notion of community information needs being defined in terms of a set of topic areas that, in a prior review of the relevant literature that we had conducted for the FCC, we had determined were closely tied to the effective functioning of the democratic process at the local level (Friedland et al., 2012).

Nonetheless, cognizant as our research team was of the complexity and subjectivity inherent in the notion of quality, and the relatively simple and limited

192 Philip M. Napoli and Asa Royal

indicators we were bringing to bear in our empirical approach, we collectively concluded that the foregrounding of the *quality* terminology made our work somewhat more vulnerable to critique than the *robustness* terminology. Consequently, we self-consciously placed the term *quality* in quotation marks in those rare instances in which we did employ it in reference to our findings (Mahone et al., 2018; Napoli et al., 2017, 2018), as a means of indicating the extent to which we recognized the potential contentiousness of using our metrics and findings in relation to the notion of news quality. At the same time, however, we did acknowledge that our findings could be interpreted as having a bearing on our understanding of how the quality of local journalism varied across different types of communities. In this way, we essentially replicated the FCC's hesitancy to engage directly with the notion of news quality.

It is perhaps worth noting that, as of this writing, the U.S. Government Accountability Office (GAO) is in the early stages of preparing a report to Congress on the state of local journalism, in an effort to inform ongoing deliberations as to whether some form of government intervention is necessary or appropriate. The GAO is utilizing our research on measuring the robustness of local journalism, and has interviewed members of our research team. It remains to be seen, however, if/how the GAO frames or interprets the findings of this body of work in relation to any notions of news quality. It seems reasonable to expect that the GAO will maintain the arms-length distance that has largely characterized U.S. policymakers' relationship to the notion of quality in news.

Public interest journalism and news quality: The U.K. case

The U.K.'s *Cairncross Review on A Sustainable Future for Journalism* (Cairncross, 2019), commissioned by the Secretary of State for Digital, Culture, Media, and Sport, was similar to the FCC's Future of Media proceeding in terms of the breadth of its scope. However, unlike the FCC's proceeding, the Cairncross Review includes an effort to define high-quality journalism. As the report notes in its first chapter, there are "widely differing and conflicting suggestions for how that term should be defined" (Cairncross, 2019, p. 16).

Elements that the report associates with high-quality journalism include:

- Professionally trained journalists
- Audience attention
- Consumer willingness to pay.

The report concludes its definitional section as follows:

> Ultimately, "high-quality journalism" is a subjective concept that depends neither solely on the audience nor the news provider. It must be truthful

Government interventions into news quality **193**

and comprehensible and should ideally – but not necessarily – be edited. You know it when you see it; but this is not a definition that justifies direct public support.

(Cairncross, 2019, p. 16)

This is clearly a fairly unsatisfactory endpoint to the question of how policymakers should operationalize the notion of quality in journalism. The Cairncross definition borrows from U.S. Supreme Court Justice Potter Stewart's famous characterization of pornography as something that can't be precisely defined but "I know it when I see it" (Lattman, 2007). And so, in a transition that in some ways reflects the transition to the notion of serving critical information needs that characterized the FCC's work, the Cairncross Review report pivots from high-quality journalism to the notion of "public interest journalism," noting that "'High-quality journalism' is desirable, but that alone does not justify specific government intervention to ensure that it survives, or is available to the right people … What needs support … is not 'high-quality journalism' but 'public-interest news and information'" (Cairncross, 2019, p. 16). Public interest news is, in turn, defined primarily in terms of investigative and campaign reporting, and in terms of local governmental reporting (Cairncross, 2019).

It is interesting to note how, in the U.K., the term *public interest* has become narrowly and precisely associated with some very specific types of journalism. In other national contexts (for instance, the U.S.), the public interest terminology has been a focal point for debate and competing interpretations. On the one hand, in the U.S., we have had a long history of public interest obligations imposed on broadcasters, that in the past included requirements to provide minimum amounts of news programing (though these obligations did not specify the nature of the news programing that would fulfill these obligations). On the other hand, we have also had moments in the U.S.'s media regulatory history in which the notion of the public interest was defined primarily in terms of whatever interested the public (Napoli, 2001).

And yet, despite the fact that the report's expressed focal point shifts from high-quality journalism to public interest news and information, references to *quality journalism* subsequently appear over 150 times in the remainder of the report, while the term *public-interest news* appears 129 times throughout the report (Cairncross, 2019). It would seem, then, that the report is not quite as able to transition away from the notion of quality journalism to the notion of public interest news as the focal point for analysis and subsequent policy interventions as the report itself advises.

This is well-reflected in how the Cairncross Review (Cairncross, 2019) addresses the issue of possible platform regulations directed at protecting and promoting quality news. One of the report's recommendations is a "News Quality Obligation," which involves imposing regulatory supervision over digital platforms' efforts to help users identify the reliability and trustworthiness of news sources. The report considers, but ultimately does not advocate, that platforms be required to prioritize high-quality news in users' news feeds. The hesitancy to recommend such a step is premised upon the assessment that it "would be difficult, given how hard it is to define high-quality news" (Cairncross, 2019, p. 94). Instead, the report recommends that "government should place an obligation on the larger online platforms to improve how their users understand the origin of an article of news and the trustworthiness of its source, thereby helping readers identify what 'good' or 'quality' news looks like" (Cairncross, 2019, p. 95). The report does not, however, specify how the platforms should go about this task. Essentially, then, while the report embraces an obligation that platforms help users identify quality news, it does so in a way that defers to the platforms as to how to signify quality, rather than have the government take a pro-active definitional role. And importantly, the report recommends that the platforms' efforts focus on providing users with more information to facilitate their own autonomy in making determinations about news quality, essentially adopting an audience-centric approach to news quality that is a well-established approach within the news quality literature (see, e.g., Bachmann et al., 2021; Lyubareva & Rochelandet, 2021). This is very different from the platforms making decisions about the availability or reach of content posted on their platforms based on their own assessments of the content's quality.

And so, once again, we see a tendency amongst policymakers to shying away from—rather than tackling head-on—news quality as a policy principle to be directly pursued. The takeaway here seems similar to what we observed in the FCC's Future of Media proceeding, in which quality journalism truly appears to be the policy goal being pursued, but yet is—at least to some extent—subordinated in favor of a more concrete, less subjective, or perhaps less politically charged term.

Public interest journalism and news quality: The Australia case

The Australian government has, in many ways, taken precedent-setting actions to support journalism through its imposition of a mandatory bargaining code that requires digital platforms such as Google and Facebook to negotiate compensation terms with Australian news outlets (Royal & Napoli, 2022). This initiative, and the role that the notion of news quality plays (or, more specifically, does not play) is the focal point of the next chapter in this volume. We touch upon the Australian case here as further evidence of the pattern described in the U.S. and U.K. cases outlined above.

In Australia, as has been the case in the U.K., we have seen the notion of news quality shift from the foreground to the background of the policymaking process in a similar manner. As was the case in the U.K., the notion of quality journalism has, to some extent, been displaced by the notion of public interest journalism. As Giotis, Molitorisz, and Wilding note in their chapter in this volume, the objectives of the proceeding initiated by Australia's Competition and Consumer Commission (ACCC) to compel digital platforms to provide compensation to news outlets seem to have shifted somewhat as the policymaking process progressed, replicating the pattern we saw in the U.K., in which the notion of quality journalism has been replaced with the broader notion of public interest journalism. As Giotis and colleagues note, this was a surprising pivot on the part of the ACCC, given that one of the expressed motivations of the proceeding in the first place was to address the potential of digital platforms to erode news organizations' capacity to produce quality journalism.

In landing on public interest journalism as the primary point of focus for this policy intervention, the ACCC did provide an explication of the points of distinction that it was employing to differentiate between quality journalism and public interest journalism. According to the ACCC:

> It is important to distinguish "high quality journalism" from "public interest journalism" ... journalism may be produced with the purpose of examining matters of public significance, meeting the definition of "public interest journalism," without meeting minimum quality standards—for example by failing to be accurate or failing to clearly distinguish reporting from the presentation of opinion.
>
> (Australian Competition & Consumer Commission, 2019, p. 287)

The definitional difference here is obviously substantial, as the ACCC defines public interest journalism purely in terms of its subject matter and not at all in terms of its qualitative attributes. As the ACCC explicitly acknowledges, public interest journalism can potentially be devoid of vital attributes for effective self-governance, such as accuracy or clear demarcations between fact and opinion—attributes that seem fundamental to any notion of quality in journalism. This shift in definitional priorities, which would seem to lead the ACCC astray from one of the motivating factors for the intervention, leads Giotis and colleagues to pointedly ask: "Can there be public interest journalism without quality?" From the ACCC's standpoint, the answer would seem to be "yes". Such a position opens up a separate debate (beyond the scope of this chapter) as to how the notion of public interest journalism should be defined from a policymaking standpoint.

Ultimately, as Giotis and colleagues note, "quality was handballed from one regulator to another," as the concept featured prominently in the initial position paper of Australia's Communications and Media Authority (2020), which was pursuing the less intrusive (from a regulatory standpoint) task of developing a voluntary code of conduct for digital platforms in relation to the policing of disinformation and "credibility signaling for news content" (Digital Industry Group Inc., 2021, p. 2). As was the case in the FCC's Future of Media report and the U.K.'s Cairncross report, the Australian Communications and Media Authority (ACMA)

196 Philip M. Napoli and Asa Royal

was hesitant to take an explicit definitional stand in relation to the notion of news quality. As the ACMA noted:

> Even within the parameters of professional news, the concept of news quality can be subjective, with consumers differing significantly in their preferences for, and judgements on the quality of, news sources. Given these differences, it is challenging to develop an agreed set of criteria or a single definition as the basis for an objective measure of news quality.
>
> (Australian Communications and Media Authority, 2020, p. 9)

Nonetheless, the ACMA did offer a general definition of quality news. According to the ACMA, quality news and information is defined as "news and information that is accurate, reliable and timely, providing people with the knowledge they need to make informed choices and to participate in public life" (Australian Communications and Media Authority, 2020, p. 9).

However, despite the fact that the ACMA did venture forth with a concrete definition of quality news, and despite the fact that references to quality news and information appeared over 60 times in the ACMA's position paper, the term *quality* appears only once in the Code of Practice that was ultimately produced—and that one occurrence is in reference to the title of the position paper that served as the starting point for the development of the Code (Digital Industry Group Inc., 2021). The closest that the Code comes to engaging with the issue of news quality head-on is in "Objective 4: Empower Consumers to Make Better Informed Choices of Digital Content" (Digital Industry Group Inc., 2021). Sample measures that the Code identifies as ways that digital platforms could pursue this objective include: "the use of technological means to prioritise or rank Digital Content to enable users to easily find diverse perspectives on matters of public interest", and the "provision or use of technologies which signal the credibility of news sources, or which assist digital platforms or their users to check the authenticity or accuracy of online news content, or to identify its provenance or source" (Digital Industry Group Inc., 2021, pp. 13–14).

In these suggested practices, we see a few concepts that can be understood as individual components of the broader notion of news quality, such as diversity— a concept that has become less tied to notions of news quality as the available sources and content in the news ecosystem have expanded dramatically (Lyubareva & Rochelandet, 2021)—and accuracy. However, the almost complete absence of the notion of quality in the ACMA's Code of Practice has the unfortunate effect of decoupling the disinformation problem from the broader concern about news quality. And so once again, it would seem that the more holistic and comprehensive notion of news quality has moved from the center to the periphery of a media policy initiative as it has progressed over time, with but a select few elements of this multi-faceted concept receiving explicit articulation, and the broader concept as a whole falling by the wayside of the policy discourse as it progresses.

Discussion

As this examination of recent policy initiatives that have been motivated by concerns about the production, distribution, and consumption of quality journalism in the U.S., U.K., and Australian contexts has indicated, the patterns in how policymakers have approached the notion of quality in journalism are quite consistent. In particular, we have seen policymakers be very explicit upfront about sustaining and supporting quality journalism as a policy priority, while acknowledging the complexity and subjectivity inherent in translating a multi-faceted concept such as journalistic quality into concrete policy interventions or performance metrics. Consequently, as these policy initiatives have progressed, the notion of journalistic quality has tended to shift from the center to the periphery, or to at least be replaced, to some extent, by what are presumably seen as more pragmatic semi-proxies, such as journalism that addresses community information needs, "public interest" journalism, or journalism that is credible or diverse.

A key question that needs to be addressed is: what are the ramifications of this tendency? That the governments' studies have been hesitant to impose heavy-handed, top-down obligations and criteria related to the notion of quality in journalism is, in many ways, commendable, given legitimate concerns about how such mechanisms could be corrupted to dramatically shift the balance of power between the press (and thus the public) and the government. From this standpoint, the offloading of quality determinations to platforms, and—to a larger degree—their users, via mechanisms for better-informed consumption, that we see in the U.K. and Australian contexts, seems prudent. But are such approaches a case of too little too late given: a) how the news and information ecosystem has evolved over the past decade; b) the content curation/moderation track records that digital platforms have demonstrated to this point, and c) how political dynamics have devolved in so many countries? What may be the most politically viable approach may have very little practical effect. Ultimately, as notions of misinformation and disinformation become more tightly and visibly intertwined with notions of news quality (see, e.g., Digital Industry Group Inc., 2021), the imperatives for policies that support quality journalism grow, as do the political challenges borne of diminished consensus regarding agreed-upon facts that tend to break along party fault lines.

Another key question that arises from this pattern is: are these other concepts that are being emphasized instead of quality necessarily inherently less problematic, either from political, legal, or empirical standpoints, than the concept they are being employed to replace? Policymakers in a wide range of national contexts have long histories of implementing polices directed at similarly complex, subjective, and (in some cases) politically charged concepts such as diversity, pluralism, localism, and objectivity (Karppinen, 2013; Napoli, 2001). Are quality-focused initiatives fundamentally more intrusive into press freedom than polices that have

198 Philip M. Napoli and Asa Royal

been put in place in pursuit of these other goals? Perhaps, but this is a question that has yet to receive the full interrogation that it deserves.

But in this regard, perhaps research can help to thread this needle. The body of conceptual and empirical literature that has developed to enhance our understanding of what the notion of quality in journalism should mean, and how it can be put into practice as performance metric and, potentially, as regulatory requirement is, at this point, quite substantial (Bachmann et al., 2021; Beckett, 2018; McQuail, 1992; Stvilia, 2021), with this volume representing the most recent contribution. This work can be a valuable resource to policymakers; and it is safe to say that up to this point it has been under-utilized in policymaking contexts.

In closing this discussion, it is important to note that in some national contexts, such as Switzerland, the comprehensive and systematic analysis of news quality is an institutionalized component of their system of media governance (see, e.g., Bachmann et al., 2021; Udris et al., 2020; University of Zurich, 2021). Also, at the multi-national level, the Council of Europe has issued an extensive set of guidelines for policymakers, news organizations, and digital platforms "designed to stimulate and reinforce independent, accurate and reliable quality journalism" (Committee of Experts on Quality Journalism in the Digital Age, 2019, p. 7). These examples represent cases of the notion of quality in journalism being tackled more directly and comprehensively, rather than obliquely, by policy researchers and policymakers, in contrast to the pattern in the three English-language national contexts studied here.

Conclusion

There is, of course, no one-size-fits-all approach to how policymakers should approach the challenges confronting the production, distribution, and consumption of quality news and information, given the ways that the political, technological, and legal contexts can very across countries. And certainly—and perhaps most importantly—the degree to which we should be wary of more overt governmental interventions in pursuit of news quality also varies in accordance with the political dynamics in different countries.

This chapter has illustrated a particular tendency—at least within the three English-language countries studied—amongst policymakers to shy away from directly engaging with the issue of news quality; even when concerns about news quality represent an explicitly articulated area of policy concern. In these contexts, and in light of the challenges facing the news and information ecosystems in these countries, it may be preferable for policymakers to continue on the path of directly engaging with the news quality issue, rather than shuffling it to the margins, and to focus on doing so in a way that draws upon the substantial empirical and conceptual work around news quality for guidance, and that considers institutional arrangements that insulate decisions regarding how news quality is defined and measured from direct government input—perhaps through empowering organizations such as fact-checkers, news industry associations, or through the creation of a new multi-stakeholder body that could be granted governance authority (see, e.g., Napoli & Napoli, 2019; Wheeler et al., 2020). Given the perilous state of journalism in so many countries—and thus, by association, the more perilous state of democracy—the time would seem to be right for policymakers to press forward rather than pull back.

References

Australian Communications and Media Authority (2020). Misinformation and news quality on digital platforms in australia: A position paper to guide code development. www.acma.gov.au/sites/default/files/2020-06/Misinformation%20and%20news%20quality%20position%20paper.pdf

Australian Competition & Consumer Commission (2019). Digital platforms inquiry: Final report. Australian competition & consumer commission.

Bachmann, P., Eisenegger, M., & Ingenhoff, D. (2021). Defining and measuring news media quality: Comparing the content perspective and the audience perspective. *The International Journal of Press/Politics*, 27(1), 9–37. https://doi.org/10.1177/194016122 1999666

Beckett, C. (2018, June 5). What is quality journalism? The most important question for news organisations today, but do we know what it means? *Polis*. https://blogs.lse.ac.uk/polis/2018/06/05/what-is-quality-journalism-the-most-important-question-for-news-organisations-today-but-do-we-know-what-it-means/

Cairncross, F. (2019). The Cairncross Review: A sustainable future for journalism, www.gov.uk/government/publications/the-cairncross-review-a-sustainable-future-for-jou rnalism

Committee of Experts on Quality Journalism in the Digital Age (2019). Draft recommendation of the Committee of Ministers to Member States on promoting a favorable environment for quality journalism in the digital age. Council of Europe. https://rm.coe.int/msi-joq-2018-rev7-e-draft-recommendation-on-quality-journalism-fina lis/168098ab76

Digital Industry Group Inc. (2021, October). Australian code of practice on disinformation and misinformation. https://digi.org.au/wp-content/uploads/2021/10/Australian-Code-of-Practice-on-Disinformation-and-Misinformation-FINAL-WORD-UPDA TED-OCTOBER-11-2021.pdf

Federal Communications Commission (2014a, February 21). Setting the record straight about the draft study. https://transition.fcc.gov/Daily_Releases/Daily_Business/2014/db0221/DOC-325722A1.pdf

Federal Communications Commission (2014b, February 28). Statement on critical information needs study. www.fcc.gov/document/statement-critical-informat ion-needs-study

Friedland, L. (2014, February 28). The real story behind the FCC's study of newsrooms. *Washington Post*. www.washingtonpost.com/news/monkey-cage/wp/2014/02/28/the-real-story-behind-the-fccs-study-of-newsrooms/

Friedland, L., Napoli, P. M., Ognayanova, K., Weil, C., & Wilson, E. J. (2012). Review of the literature regarding critical information needs of the American public. Federal Communications Commission. https://transition.fcc.gov/bureaus/ocbo/Final_Litera ture_Review.pdf

Karppinen, K. (2013). *Rethinking media pluralism*. Fordham University Press.

Lattman, P. (2007, September 27). The origins of Justice Stewart's "I know it when I see it." *Wall Street Journal*. www.wsj.com/articles/BL-LB-4558

Lyubareva, I., & Rochelandet, F. (2021). From news diversity to news quality: New media regulation theoretical issues. In S. A. Matei, F. Rebillard, & F. Rochelandet (Eds.), *Digital and social media regulation: A comparative perspective of the US and Europe* (pp. 117–141). Springer International Publishing. https://doi.org/10.1007/978-3-030-66759-7_6

Mahone, J., Wang, Q., Napoli, P. M., Weber, M., & Mccollough, K. (2018). Who's producing local journalism? Assessing journalistic output across different outlet types (News Measures Research Project white paper). DeWitt Wallace Center for Media & Democracy, Duke University. https://dewitt.sanford.duke.edu/wp-content/uploads/sites/9/2019/08/Whos-Producing-Local-Journalism_FINAL.pdf

McQuail, D. (1992). *Media performance: Mass communication and the public interest*. Sage.

Napoli, P. M. (2001). *Foundations of communications policy: Principles and process in the regulation of electronic media*. Hampton Press.

Napoli, P. M. (2019). *Social media and the public interest: Media regulation in the disinformation age*. Columbia University Press.

Napoli, P. M. (2020). Connecting journalism and public policy: New concerns and continuing challenges. *Digital Journalism, 8*(6), 691–703. https://doi.org/10.1080/21670811.2020.1775104

Napoli, P. M. (2021). The symbolic uses of platforms: The politics of platform governance in the United States. *Journal of Digital Media & Policy, 12*(2), 215–230. https://doi.org/10.1386/jdmp_00060_1

Napoli, P. M., & Dwyer, D. (2018). U.S. media policy in a time of political polarization and technological evolution. *Publizistik, 63*(4), 583–601.

Napoli, P. M., & Friedland, L. (2016). U.S. communications policy research and the integration of the administrative and critical communication research traditions. *Journal of Information Policy, 6*, 41–65. https://doi.org/10.5325/jinfopoli.6.2016.0041

Napoli, P. M., & Napoli, A. B. (2019). What social media platforms can learn from audience measurement: Lessons in the self-regulation of "black boxes." *First Monday, 24*(12). https://doi.org/10.5210/fm.v24i12.10124

Napoli, P. M., & Stonbely, S. (2018). Policy issues surrounding journalism. In *Oxford research encyclopedia of communication*. Oxford University Press. www.academia.edu/36582099/Oxford_Research_Encyclopedia_of_Communication_Policy_Issues_Surrounding_Journalism

Napoli, P. M., Stonbely, S., McCollough, K., & Renninger, B. (2017). Local journalism and the information needs of local communities: Toward a scalable assessment approach. *Journalism Practice, 11*(4), 373–395. https://doi.org/10.1080/17512786.2016.1146625

Napoli, P. M., Weber, M., Mccollough, K., & Wang, Q. (2018). Assessing local journalism: News deserts, journalism divides, and the determinants of the robustness of local news (News Measures Research Project white paper). DeWitt Wallace Center for Media & Democracy, Duke University.

Pai, A. (2014, February 10). The FCC wades into the newsroom. *Wall Street Journal*. www.wsj.com/articles/SB10001424052702304680904579366903828260732

Royal, A., & Napoli, P. M. (2022). Platforms and the press. In T. Flew & F. R. Martin (Eds.), *Digital platform regulation: Beyond transparency and openness*. Palgrave Macmillan.

Social Solutions International (2013). Research design for the multi-market study of critical information needs. https://transition.fcc.gov/bureaus/ocbo/FCC_Final_Research_Design_6_markets.pdf

Stvilia, B. (2021). An integrated framework for online news quality assurance. *First Monday*, *26*(7). https://doi.org/10.5210/fm.v26i7.11062

Udris, L., Eisenegger, M., Vogler, D., Schneider, J., & Häuptli, A. (2020). Mapping and explaining media quality: Insights from Switzerland's multilingual media system. *Media and Communication*, *8*(3), 258–269. https://doi.org/10.17645/mac.v8i3.3140

University of Zurich (2021). *Jahrbuch Qualität der Medien 2021*. Schwabe Verlag. www.foeg. uzh.ch/dam/jcr:80fd64b0-c078-4ba7-8bba-e2c79bf1a654/2021_Gesamtausgabe.pdf

Waldman, S., & Working Group on the Information Needs of Communities (2011). *The information needs of communities: The changing media landscape in a broadband age*. Federal Communications Commission.

Wheeler, T., Verveer, P., & Kimmelman, G. (2020). New digital realities; new oversight solutions: A case for a digital platform agency and new approach to regulatory oversight. Shorenstein Center on the Press, Politics, and Public Policy. https://shorensteincenter. org/new-digital-realities-tom-wheeler-phil-verveer-gene-kimmelman/

13
CONCLUSION

Regina G. Lawrence and Philip M. Napoli

As we put the finishing touches on this collection, and prepare to send it off to the publisher (May, 2022), we find ourselves persistently confronted by compelling case studies that highlight the importance of quality news for a well-functioning democracy, and that also illustrate the perhaps unprecedented challenges that quality news faces in terms of sustainability, visibility, and impact in a crowded, complex, and economically challenging news and information ecosystem.

As is the case now with virtually every national or global event, the war in the Ukraine has raised fresh concerns about how propaganda and disinformation can be integrated into content that can look—at least superficially—like legitimate news (Collins, 2022; Scott, 2022). As a result, Ukrainians with friends and relatives in Russia are literally dumfounded by how egregiously misinformed these friends and relatives can be about the realities of how and why the war has taken place, and how it has progressed (Hopkins, 2022). The deluge of falsehoods emanating from Russian news outlets has compelled many digital platforms (and even some traditional media distributors such as cable and satellite systems) to take actions such as removing Russian state-run media outlets from their systems (Culliford, 2022; Lomas, 2022; Nickinson, 2022).

As part of its Ukrainian disinformation campaign, the Russian government has pushed the envelope a bit further, developing and deploying bogus fact-checking organizations that generate false fact checks to support the government's propaganda messaging (Moshirina, 2022). And so begins the process of subverting one of the lynchpin institutions intended to help news consumers to navigate an increasingly fraught media environment and to effectively distinguish high-quality news and information from low-quality news and information.

The continued prominence of right-wing extremism in the U.S., the continuing congressional investigation of the events surrounding the U.S. Capitol

DOI: 10.4324/9781003257998-17

attack on January 6th, 2020, and the 2022 mid-term elections have all contributed to an ongoing conversation within the journalism community as to how the practice of journalism should evolve in a political environment in which democracy appears to be under threat from within (Rubin, 2022; Sargent, 2022; Sullivan, 2022). Implicit in these journalistic self-evaluations is the question of whether traditional journalistic dimensions of "quality" (e.g., balance, reliance upon official sources) remain relevant in today's political landscape. That is, are there ways in which the norms for producing quality journalism can be exploited and subverted by political actors with anti-democratic intentions? For example, while "balanced" reporting can be a hallmark of quality news, distinguishing it from mere opinion, the admonition to report "both sides" of a conflict would become problematic if one side were trading primarily in falsehoods. These re-evaluations of the political implications of established journalistic norms serve as a powerful reminder that notions of news quality cannot be treated as static and should also be approached as, to some degree, context dependent.

To draw upon one more U.S. example, we are currently witnessing a process in which traditional local news organizations are being slowly replaced by outlets that differ from their predecessors across important vectors. In some cases, these emergent local news sources are (unlike their predecessors) non-profits, many devoted to independent investigative reporting (Izadi, 2021). In other cases, they are part of large networks of purportedly local news sites that are centrally run by organizations with strong connections to political activism, often including algorithmically generated content (Bengani, 2021). The U.S. Federal Elections Commission fielded complaints asserting that these news networks should be classified as political committees rather than news organizations (and should thus be regulated as such) (Markay, 2022). Research is beginning to explore the output of these emergent news outlets (see, e.g., Bengani, 2019, 2020), and has, in some cases, raised questions about whether these new news sources exhibit sufficient commitment to basic dimensions of news quality such as timeliness and originality, and whether they indeed may behave in ways that reflect political strategy more than journalistic norms (Royal & Napoli, 2023).

All of these examples highlight the need for continued research attention to the dynamics surrounding the production, distribution, and consumption of quality news. On this front, the chapters in this volume have highlighted both the importance and the challenges of making the notion of quality news something tangible and concrete, and not letting it remain something amorphous that can be dismissed out of hand as inherently resistant to precise definition or measurement.

Yes, quality is, to some degree, an inherently subjective concept. However, as many of the chapters in this volume have shown us, it is in fact possible to construct meaningful and defensible definitions and measures of news quality that can be put into practice in a variety of contexts—including within the context of the operation and governance of the digital platforms that have become such central components of the contemporary news and information ecosystem. At a time when we are legitimately concerned about whether journalism is doing enough to protect and serve an increasingly fragile democracy (see above), it is not a time for researchers—or, for that matter, policymakers, platforms, news organizations, or public interest advocates—to shy away from taking explicit stands on what does—and what does not—meet the threshold of quality news.

Which brings us to the question of what can—or should—be done with the type of research presented in this volume? That is, how can the processes of defining and measuring news quality, and exploring the factors that impact its production, dissemination, and consumption, move beyond the academic arena and inform the wide range of institutions and practices that contribute directly to an informed citizenry?

First, as a number of chapters in this volume have illustrated, some key stakeholders, such as digital platforms and policymakers, have been hesitant to directly engage with the notion of news quality. Obviously to do so invites critique, especially from those outlets whose content is deemed to fall short in relation to basic quality thresholds. And, unfortunately, the patterns likely to be exhibited here will, to some degree, fall along existing partisan divisions, thereby making the issue of news quality as ripe and vulnerable to politicization as so many other policy issues—both within and beyond the media context (see, e.g., Napoli, 2021).

Platforms, in particular, need to embrace their role as arbiters of quality news. Some recent circumstances, such as the January 6th insurrection, the coronavirus pandemic, and the war in the Ukraine, have compelled more aggressive action on the part of the platforms than we have seen in years past (Douek, 2020). Yet there is still plenty to be concerned about in terms of how well the platforms can be expected to perform as arbiters of quality news. Their track records up to this point do not inspire confidence. Further, at the time of this writing, Elon Musk, the world's richest man, is in an on-again, off-again flirtation with buying Twitter, one of the most politically significant (though not one of the most widely used) social media platforms (Kleinman, 2022). The prospect of Musk's purchase of Twitter raises a host of concerns that are representative of the troubling gatekeeping power that a relatively small number of digital platforms (controlled by a select few very rich, white, men) have attained in the news and information ecosystem (Neate, 2022; Olson, 2022). (These concerns were all legitimated as this manuscript went to press.)

This is where, hopefully, the development and implementation of a more comprehensive regulatory framework can come into play. Policymakers can be doing more to support and encourage the relative prominence of quality news and information on digital platforms. The U.S. has been notoriously slow-moving on this front, particularly in relation to our European counterparts (see, e.g., Napoli, 2021). Globally, countries including Canada, Australia, India, Germany, and the U.K. are in more advanced stages in terms of applying basic regulatory obligations to digital platforms' content curation and moderation practices (Mackrael & Hoyle, 2022).

However, recent developments in the U.S. may offer some promise. Michael Bennett, the Democratic senator from Colorado, introduced the Digital Platform Commission Act (2022). This Act proposes the creation of a new regulatory agency devoted explicitly to the oversight of digital platforms. Perhaps most important, this proposed legislation includes the imposition of a *public interest* regulatory framework upon these platforms, which echoes the public interest regulatory framework that has long applied to broadcasters. Essentially, then, these digital platforms would operate more like *public trustees* (as broadcasters have), which is a much-needed evolution in how we approach the institutional role and function of these platforms in the news and information ecosystem (see, e.g., Napoli & Graf, 2022). Under such a framework, one could imagine, for example, affirmative obligations for these platforms' algorithmic systems to better prioritize the surfacing of quality news and information, rather than (under the current norms) news and information that generates the highest levels of user engagement. Of course, as some of the chapters in this volume make clear, effectively taking actions such as these is no easy task (see, e.g, Stray), and the devil is certainly in the details. But this is nonetheless an area in which research of the type collected in this volume could make meaningful contributions.

Such enhanced commitments to quality news by policymakers need not be confined to the digital platform context. The economic crisis confronting journalism (particularly at the local level) has, at last, begun to inspire concrete policy proposals, ranging from the Australian legislation directed at compelling platforms to provide financial compensation to news organizations (see Giotis et al.'s chapter), to as-yet unsuccessful legislative proposals in the U.S. like the Local Journalism Sustainability Act (2021), which seeks to provide tax credits that would empower individual news consumers to direct financial support to the local news outlets of their choice. Though there is certainly room for legislation in this vein to be more committed to the support of quality news, it is heartening that this proposed legislation specifies that eligibility to receive such public support depends, in part, on news outlets meeting some basic quality indicators, such as producing primarily original content derived from primary sources; though there is certainly room for legislation in this vein to be a bit more committed to the support of quality news.

In the end, the research collected in this volume has, we hope, made the concept of news quality more tangible, and in so doing has also hopefully made it more actionable. Our hope is that researchers build upon and extend the work collected here, but also that platforms, news organizations, policymakers, and NGOs draw upon the findings and conclusions of this work to inform their own redoubled efforts to ensure that the contemporary news and information ecosystem is one in which quality news is sustainable, discoverable, and impactful. A well-functioning democracy requires no less.

References

Bengani, P. (2019, December 18). Hundreds of 'pink slime' local news outlets are distributing algorithmic stories and conservative talking points. *Columbia Journalism Review.* www.cjr.org/tow_center_reports/hundreds-of-pink-slime-local-news-outlets-are-distributing-algorithmic-stories-conservative-talking-points.php/

Bengani, P. (2020, August 4). As election looms, a network of mysterious 'pink slime' local news outlets nearly triples in size. *Columbia Journalism Review.* www.cjr.org/analysis/as-election-looms-a-network-of-mysterious-pink-slime-local-news-outlets-nearly-triples-in-size.php

Bengani, P. (2021, October 4). Advocacy groups and Metric Media collaborate on local 'community news.' *Columbia Journalism Review.* www.cjr.org/tow_center_reports/community-newsmaker-metric-media-local-news.php/

Collins, M. (2022, May 8). Russia's 'firehose of falsehood' in Ukraine marks latest use of propaganda to try to justify war. *USA Today.* www.usatoday.com/story/news/politics/2022/05/08/russia-unleashes-firehose-falsehood-justify-war-ukraine/7317819001/

Culliford, E. (2022, February 28). Facebook owner Meta will block access to Russia's RT, Sputnik in EU. *Reuters.* www.reuters.com/business/media-telecom/facebook-owner-meta-will-block-access-russias-rt-sputnik-eu-2022-02-28/

Digital Platform Commission Act of 2022, 117th Congress, 2nd Session (2022). www.bennet.senate.gov/public/_cache/files/9/c/9cdacd51-41dd-470f-89d7-4cfa6a700cb8/DC68CD6481E262D668211395ABEA0EE2.05.09.21---bennet-digital-platform-commission-act---final-text.pdf

Douek, E. (2020, December 28). The year that changed the Internet. *The Atlantic.* www.theatlantic.com/ideas/archive/2020/12/how-2020-forced-facebook-and-twitter-step/617493/

Hopkins, V. (2022, March 6). Ukrainians find that relatives in Russia don't believe it's a war. *New York Times.* www.nytimes.com/2022/03/06/world/europe/ukraine-russia-families.html

Izadi, E. (2021, December 6). The troubling new void in local journalism—and the nonprofits trying to fill it. *Washington Post.* www.washingtonpost.com/media/2021/12/06/media-states-newsroom-government/

Kleinman, Z. (2022, May 13). Elon Musk puts Twitter deal on hold over fake account details. *BBC News.* www.bbc.com/news/business-61433724

Local Journalism Sustainability Act of 2021 H.R.3940—117th Congress. 1st Session (2021/2022). (2021, June 16). [Legislation]. www.congress.gov/bill/117th-congress/house-bill/3940/text

Lomas, N. (2022, March 11). YouTube is now blocking Russia state-affiliated media globally. *TechCrunch.* https://social.techcrunch.com/2022/03/11/youtube-is-now-blocking-russia-state-affiliated-media-globally/

Mackrael, K., & Hoyle, R. (2022, May 11). Social media regulations expand globally as Elon Musk plans Twitter takeover. *Wall Street Journal.* www.wsj.com/articles/social-media-regulations-expand-globally-as-elon-musk-plans-twitter-takeover-11652285375

Markay, L. (2022, April 29). The Federal Election Commission tosses challenge to progressive news network Courier. *Axios.* www.axios.com/fec-progressive-news-network-4f4f8da6-095b-490c-8109-6e8ffc1a556e.html

Moshirina, A. (2022, March 31). Russia's diabolical new approach to spreading misinformation. *Slate.* https://slate.com/technology/2022/03/russia-false-flag-fact-checking-propaganda.html

Napoli, P. M. (2021). The symbolic uses of platforms: The politics of platform governance in the United States. *Journal of Digital Media & Policy, 12*(2), 215–230. https://doi.org/10.1386/jdmp_00060_1

Napoli, P. M., & Graf, F. (2022). Social media platforms as public trustees: An approach to the disinformation problem. In T. Pihlajarinne & A. Alen-Savikko (Eds.), *Artificial intelligence and the media* (pp. 93–122). Edward Elgar.

Neate, R. (2022, May 3). 'Extra level of power': Billionaires who have bought up the media. *The Guardian.* www.theguardian.com/news/2022/may/03/billionaires-extra-power-media-ownership-elon-musk

Nickinson, P. (2022, March 4). Dish and Sling TV also drop Russia Today channel. *Digital Trends.* www.digitaltrends.com/movies/sling-tv-dish-rt-america/

Olson, P. (2022, March 28). Musk and other tech billionaires are out of control. *Washington Post.* www.washingtonpost.com/business/musk-and-other-tech-billionaires-are-out-of-control/2022/04/28/8d8114c8-c6eb-11ec-8cff-33b059f4c1b7_story.html

Royal, A., & Napoli, P. M. (2023, in press). Local journalism's possible future: Metric Media and its approach to community information needs. *Journal of Creative Industries and Cultural Studies.*

Rubin, J. (2022, April 19). The media still haven't learned how to cover the GOP threat to democracy. *Washington Post.* www.washingtonpost.com/opinions/2022/04/19/media-still-dont-know-how-to-cover-republicans-gop-democracy/

Sargent, G. (2022, January 6). How the both-sides media would cover a successful Trump coup. *Washington Post.* www.washingtonpost.com/opinions/2022/01/06/trump-coup-both-sides-media/

Scott, M. (2022, March 10). As war in Ukraine evolves, so do disinformation tactics. *Politico.* www.politico.eu/article/ukraine-russia-disinformation-propaganda/

Sullivan, M. (2022, May 16). Democracy is at stake in the midterms. The media must convey that. *Washington Post.* www.washingtonpost.com/media/2022/05/15/democracy-midterms-vote-integrity-media-coverage/

INDEX

Note: References to figures appear in *italic type*; those in **bold type** refer to tables.

accuracy 8, 17, 35, 42, 86–87, 100, 118, 121, 151, 160, **180–181**, 188, 195–196
affective polarization 18, 23, 161
AI systems 131, 151; interactive feedback methods of 159; and metrics 156; principles documents of 154; *see also* algorithms
algorithmic curation 135
algorithmic filtering 15, 16, 20, 99
algorithmic gatekeeping 120, 135; and human editors 141; in news production processes 139–140; and quality content 140–142; stages of 140; theory 137–138
algorithmic selection: limitations 135; by users 119
algorithms 6, 41, 117, 146–147, 151–152, 176, 177, 203; of Amazon 39; and audience metrics 38; blackbox-like 38; civic role of 42; and data set 158; design orientation towards 152–154; diversification 155; and feedback method 159; and journalism 134, 136–137; and local news flows 106, 110; manipulation of metrics through 34; meta-data-based recommendation 122; and metrics 156, 157; news selection ways 122; personalization 117–118, 135, 136, 145; and platform curation 99, 106–110; proprietary 7; public

interest-minded 42; recommendations/recommenders 6, 7, 33, 118–119, 121, 136, 142–145; role in news distribution and production 135–136; tweaking by Facebook 21, 38; Twitter's timeline algorithm 98, 99, 104, 106, 110; values-driven 151, 153, 161; *see also* "blossom" algorithm *(Times)*
Amazon 39
Associated Press (AP): and online incivility 68, 70, 73; and perception of news quality 74, 77, 81
Associated Press (AP), website versus Twitter account: assessment of news-ness in 51, 54, 56, 57–60; attention and news cue 52; comments, audience evaluations of 51; headline and byline 51–54, 58–61; story element 54; *see also* news-ness
attention 23–24, 33, 39, 146, 192; allocation 22; constraint on 8, 9, 19; and exposure 19; importance of 20; and incivility 68; market 41, 42, 43; metrics for 21; and news cue 52; and news source quality 37; and obtrusive issues 71, 80; and recommendation algorithms 38; scarcity 20
attitude-consistent conclusions 17
audience metrics 33, 38, 41
audience/user preferences 22, 34, 118, 121–122, 126, 127, 146, 196

Index 209

Australia: broader social functions, as quality indicator 179, **180**; Centre for Media Transition 179; Commercial Television Industry Code of Practice 175; core news in 175–177, 183; core professional practice indicators 179, **181**; core standards of practice 179, **180**; critical information needs 181; disinformation in 174, 177, 178; Facebook in 170–173, 177, 178–179, 182; Google in 170, 171, 172–173, 177, 182; media standards in 177–179; News Media Bargaining Code 169–170; news media businesses and digital platforms in 172–173; news quality indicators in 179, **180–181**; news values in 170–171, 179, 181, 183; political polarization in 181; public interest journalism in 170–172, 174–177, 183, 194–196; quality journalism in 169–170; social accounting in 179–183; social diversity in 170, 181; Treasury Laws Amendment (News Media and Digital Platforms Mandatory Bargaining Code) Act 2021 173, 175

Australian Code of Practice 174, 175, 196

Australian Communications and Media Authority (ACMA) 171, 195; notion of news quality 195–196; regulatory roles of 175, 177

Australian Competition and Consumer Commission (ACCC) 169–170; Concepts Paper 178–179; Final Report of Inquiry and quality journalism 171–172, 174–175, 177; media standards incorporation, problems with 178; on news business 172, 173, 176, 195; on news quality 174–175, 177; on public interest journalism 171–172, 174, 176, 195; role of 171

authority 147, **181**

automated journalism 117, 136, 147, 152; *see also* algorithms

autonomy 137, 151, 194

balance 86, 139, **180**, 197, 203

Barbara, P. 87

Barkan, R. 101, 103

Bennett, M. 205

Bennett, W. L. 4

"blossom" algorithm *(Times)* 98, 101, 103–104; in editorial curation 106;

@nytimes Twitter account, impact on 98, 110; and social media 101, 103

Bodo, B. 135

Brazil, presidential election of 4

broader social functions, as news quality indicator 179, **180**

Bucher, T. 119

Cairncross Review on A Sustainable Future for Journalism 192–193, 195

Carlson, M. 136, 137, 147

change-score approach 75, 76, 77, 79

choice gap 100

Chung, D. S. 123

Chung, M. 40

civil comments 67, 73, 80, 81

clarity 155, **180**

Clerwall, C. 136

clickbait 39, 40, 141, 142, 143, 153, 158

click-to-share ratio 158

cognitive biases 13, 14, 17, 18, 19, 21, 22, 23, 24

collaborative recommender systems 122

comments: AP news, and online incivility 68, 70, 73, 74, 77, 81; audience evaluations 51, 68, 69; authenticity and sentiment of 69; change-score approach 75, 76, 77, 79; civil 67, 73, 80, 81; diversity 68, 69; heuristic cues 69–70, 77, 80; human-selection cues 67; multilevel modelling 75–77, **76**; obtrusive issues 67, 71–72, 73, 77–78, 80, 81; social endorsement cues 67; uncivil 67–68, 69, 72, 77, 80–81; unobtrusive issues 67, 71–72, 73, 77, 80, 81; *see also* incivility; perceptions, of news quality

completeness 86

comprehensiveness 35, 151, 179, 196

Conlin, L. 69

content diversity 154

content-level analysis 100

content offerings 13, 15

control versus feeling of being in control 128

convenience 86

core news 175–177, 183

core professional practice indicators 179, **181**

core standards of practice 179, **180**

Council of Europe, quality journalism in 198

coverage depth and breadth 22, 143, **181**

covered news 175, 176, 177

210 Index

COVID disinformation 4–5
creativity **181**
credibility rating data sets 158
critical information needs 58, **180**, 181, 189–192, 193
crowdsourcing/crowdsourced data collection 6, 153, 158, 160
curated flows model 98–99, 101–102, *102*
customization 121, 123–129

Dalen, A.V. 138
Day, A. G. 101
deliberations 69, 151, 154, 192
democracy, threats to 14–22
DeVito, M. A. 153
Diakopoulos, N. 135, 137, 152
digital advertising market 39, 88, 110
digital media environment: challenges of 13–14; characteristics of 15
Digital Platform Commission Act 205
digital platforms: curation 99, 106–110; definition for 6–7; Lucid Theorem platform 53–54; and news consumption 51; and news-ness 50–51, 53; platform-specific cues 52–53; and quality information 5–6; *see also* social media platforms
Digital Platforms Inquiry 169, 171
Digital Services Act 117
digital trace data 85, 87, 88, 92
disinformation 35, 145–146, 188, 197, 202; about COVID-19 pandemic 4–5; in Australia 174, 177, 178, 195, 196; on elections 6; exposure to 18; order of 4; spreader of 3, 4
disseminators 139, 142, 146
diversification algorithms 155
diversity 35, 101, 118, 155, **180**, 197; exposure 16; as quality indicator 68, 69, 100; in recommender design 154–155; and recommender system 135–136, 145, 155, 156; social 170, 181; of social media users 42–43, 49; of source 157–158; value of 153, 154–155
Druckman, H. N. 18
Dunaway, J. 9
Dvir-Gvirsman, S. 52
dwell time 20, 158

earning potential, content with 22
echo chambers 15, 17, 87, 135, 145
editorial curation 97, 98, 101, 103, 106, 108, 113, 135, 144
editorial values, for news recommenders 102–103, 151–155; AI systems 151, 154, 156, 159; content diversity 154; cosine similarity analysis 155; crowdsourcing/crowdsourced data collection 153, 158, 160; and data sets 158–159; and diversity 153, 154–155, 156, 157–158; evaluations protocols of 160–161; feedback methods for 159–160; ideological segregation 156; IEEE standards 154, 161; journalist-technologist collaboration 152, 156, 159; and metrics 156–158; multi-stakeholder recommendation 153, 159; participatory design 152–153; and polarization 161; *see also* algorithms; recommender systems
egocentric publics 99
elections, digital interference in 3–4, 6, 41, 72, 99–100, 203
engagement 21, 92, 106, 142, 147, 205; cross-ideological 157; high-engagement content 21; levels of 110; metrics of 21, 112–113; in news recommender systems 117–119, 120; social media 34, 37, 38–39
ethics 6, 68, 69, 92, 154, 178, **181**
Eveland Jr., W. P. 50
experience goods, news as 35
explicit personalization *see* customization
explicit satisfaction 127
eye-tracking technology 52

Facebook 43, 135, 158; advertising revenue 39, 88, 110; algorithmification of gatekeeping 138; algorithms tweaks 21, 38; in Australia 170–173, 177, 178–179, 182, 194; and COVID-19 misinformation 5; and election misinformation 3–4; misinformation struggles 21–22; and news cues 52; News Feed 152, 153, 177; on news feed algorithm 38–39; News Tab 173; and polarization 20; referrals 20; regulation of unwanted content 157; sharing of user data 172; as source of news 33; well-being metrics of 182
fact-checking and fact-checkers 35, 37, 38, 44, 145–146, 199, 202
Factcheck.org 35
fairness 154, 158, 159, 170, **180**
false content detection 35
false news in social media, spreading of 7, 36–37

Index

figure-ground hypothesis 70
filter bubbles 15, 87, 117, 118, 135, 145
filtered exposure 16
five-step flow model, of communication 99
Fjeld, J. 154
Flanagin, A. J. 50, 51
Flaxman, S. 87
"Future of Media" proceeding 189

Gallup organization 86, 88
gamification, elements of 125
gaming AI *see* algorithms
Gantz, W. 86
gatekeeping *see* algorithmic gatekeeping; journalistic gatekeepers
Gentzkow, M. 87
genuine journalism 41
geographic relevance 100, 103, 170, **180**, 183
George, L. M. 101
Gieber, W. 137
Gillespie, T. 7
Goel, S. 87
Golan, G. 101
Google 5, 43; advertising revenue 39, 88, 110; algorithmification of gatekeeping 138; in Australia 170, 171, 172–173, 177, 182, 194; News 124, 135, 152, 153, 157; well-being metrics of 182
government interventions: and audience/user preferences 196; Australia *see* Australia; Council of Europe 198; and critical information needs 189–192, 193; fact-checking and fact-checkers 199; news and information ecosystem 187, 196, 197; and News Measures Research Project 191–192; news quality as policy goal 188, 194; politics and practicalities, of news quality 189–199; propaganda messaging 202; and Russia–Ukraine conflict 202, 204; Switzerland 189, 198; United Kingdom 192–194; United States 189–191, 192
Graefe, A. 136
Guess, A. 87, 88
Guo, C. 39
Guzman, A. L. 117

Hallin, D. C. 139
Hansen, C. 135, 139
hate speech 3–4, 157–58, 162
Haugtvedt, C. P. 72

He, C. 121
headline and byline 20, 36, 41, 51–54, 58–61, 141, 146
health misinformation, during COVID-19 pandemic 4–5
Helberger, N. 154, 156
heuristic cues 34, 40, 62, 69–70, 77, 80
high-choice news environment 15, 16, 91
high-quality articles, indicators of 100
high-quality journalism/news 5, 34–35, 100
Hinsley, A. 52
homogeneous social networks 16
human cognition theory 40
human-curated top stories 135
human-selection cues 67
hybrid journalistic-algorithm curation, 103
hyper-partisan news 40

ideological segregation 15, 16, 18, 87, 156
IEEE standards 154, 161
immediacy **181**
implicit personalization (customization) 121–123, 125, 126, 127–129
inaccurate content 16, 18, 22, 24, 51, 170
incivility 68, 69, 81; and attention 68; in comment threads 70; and issue obtrusiveness 71–72; and perceived incivility, proportion of 70, 72, 73, 75; personal-level 69, 73; position effects of 70, 72, 75, 77, 80; primacy effect of 70, 72, 80; public-level 69; recency effect of 71, 72, 80; *see also* comments; uncivil comments
inclusiveness 86, 151
infodemic 4–5
informational cues 20
informational dimensions, of news quality 68
information shortcuts 40
interactive feedback 159, 160
interactive recommender systems *see* recommender systems
internet, impact of 15
interpersonal communication 98
interrupted time series analysis 103
issue obtrusiveness *see* obtrusive issues

Josephi, B. 139
journalism awards 36, 37, 142, 143
Journalism Competition and Preservation Act 10
journalistic algorithms *see* algorithms

212 Index

journalistic gatekeepers 120, 130
journalist-technologist collaboration 152,
  156, 159

Kenski, K. 75
Knight Foundation 86, 88
Krosnick, J. A. 72
Kunaver, M. 155

labels 158; of local news 102–103; verified
  58; warning 38
lede of story 53, 54, 58, 59, 61
Lee, M. K. 159
lemons problem 41, 42–43
Levendusky, M. 18
Lewandowsky, S. 101
Lewin, K. 137
Lewis, S. C. 136, 153, 157
Linden, T. C. 136
linear step flow models, of communication
  99
Livingston, S. 4
local journalism 10, 97, 192
Local Journalism Sustainability Act 205
local news: crisis 97, 110; disappearance,
  consequences of 100; flow, decline in
  104–112; implication of the multi-
  faceted crisis in 112; limitations in
  analysis of 112–113; organizations 87;
  potential interventions 112; production
  in *NYT* 101–106; sources, and
  communities' critical information needs
  189; *see also New York Times*; @nytimes
  Twitter account
local relevance 100, 103, 170, 183
low exposure diversity 16
Lucid Theorem platform 53–54

machine learning (ML) models 35, 153,
  156, 158
Malik, M. M. 103
market: attention 41, 42, 43; -driven
  journalism 34, 41, 42; failure 41;
  structural factors 14; U.S. media market
  190
"marketplace of ideas" metaphor 38
Matthes, K. 86
Matthews, N. 110
meaningful social interactions 21
media attitudes 84–85; credibility
  measurement 85–86; digital trace
  data 85, 87, 88, 92; high-choice
  news environment 91; local news

organizations 87; measurement,
  challenges in 87–88; passive data
  collection 84–85, 87–88; self-reported
  data 84, 85, 87–88, 92; *see also* media
  trust; perceptions, of news quality
media bubbles 87
media choice 13, 15, 17
media environment, structural changes to
  14
media fragmentation 15
media polarization *see* polarization
media selectivity 15, 16, 17, 20, 86
media structures 13–14
media trust: dimensions of 86; indicators
  of 86; measurement of 86; political party
  affiliation 89, 90; and quality, comparison
  between 86–87; and quality rating
  89–90; *see also* media attitudes
medium-based differences 50
Mellado, C. 138, 139
mental processing 40
message repetition concept 70
metrics 156–158; designing 156; and
  diversity 156, 157; problems in 156; role
  in regulation 157; uses of 156–157
Metzger, M. J. 50, 51
Miller, J. M. 72
Milosavljevic, M. 137
Min, S. J. 119
misinformation 23–24, 197; and challenges
  of Opera News Hub participants
  145–146, 147; of elections 3–4, 6, 41, 72,
  99–100, 203; exposure of 14; exposure
  to 13, 16, 18–19; in Facebook 3–4, 5,
  21–22; on health, during COVID-19
  pandemic 4–5; identification of 158;
  and partisans 18; and polarization 17, 19,
  22, 24; in social media 21–22; warning
  labels 38
misperceptions 22; about COVID-19
  4; political 19; and processing-based
  explanations 17; and structural changes
  17
mix of attributes approach 50
Möller, J. 135, 154
Monzer, C. 118
motivated reasoning theories 17–18, 23
Muddiman, A. 69
multilevel modelling 75–77, **76**
multi-stakeholder recommendation 153,
  159, 199
Murdoch, Rupert 171
Musk, E. 204

Mwesige, P. G. 139
Myanmar, and Muslim Rohingya issue 3–4

Napoli, P. 37
narrowcasting 98
Nechushtai, E. 136, 153, 157
negative information, attention to 22
network homophily 16
network step 99
news and information: distribution via mobile devices 5; ecosystem 187, 197, 202, 204–205; exposure to 9; flow of 98–99; public-interest 193; quality, under ACMA 196, 198; sharing through digital platforms 3, 7, 204
news consumption 127, 156; audience metrics 38, 68; function of user agency in 119–121, 129; and incivility 70; platform differences in 51; and recommender systems 118; self-managing element in 120; via social media 33, 38
News Corp 171
news feed 5, 188, 194; algorithms of 38–39, 119; structures 20–21
NewsLens 88–92
news literacy education 62
News Measures Research Project 191–192
news-ness: assessment methods of 53–54, 56–57; assessment of 52–53; conceptual model of 50; definition of 49; elements of people' assessments of 57–61; lede of story 53, 54, 58, 59, 61; measuring 54; mental health issues related to 53, 56–57, 60–61; perceptions of 57–60, 61; and pictures, 54–58; platform effects in 50–51, 53; source cues 49, 54, 58, 59–63; see also Associated Press (AP), website versus Twitter account
news posts 37, 53
NewsQ 36
News Quality Initiative 154, 159
News Quality Obligation 193
news recommender systems see recommender systems
news stories 40, 50–53
New York Times 36, 97; app 152; area of interest covered in 101; curated flows in 101–102; curation, algorithmic platforms 106–110; labelling local news in 102–103; local news at 101, 104, 112, 113; organizational phenomena at 100;

platform effects 50; see also @nytimes Twitter account
Nigeria, algorithmic journalism in see algorithmic gatekeeping; algorithms; Opera News
Nine Entertainment 171
Nolan, H. 37
normative dimensions, of news quality 68
@nytimes Twitter account: curated flows in 101–102; local news flows in 98, 101–102, 104, 106–111; see also New York Times

objectivity 35, 68–69, 87, 156–157, 196–197
obtrusive issues 67, 71–72, 73, 77–78, 80, 81
one-sided news 51
one-step flow model, of communication 98–99
one-time selection procedures 119, 123
OpenAI 159
Opera News 134; Opera News Hub 136, 139, 140, 142–147; Review System 134; see also algorithmic gatekeeping; algorithms
opinion leaders 98, 99
originality 35, 170, 177, **181**, 203

Pai, A. 190
Pariser, E. 117
participatory design 152–153
partisan echo chambers 15
partisan enclaves 15
partisan identity 38
partisan-ideological sorting 18
partisan media 13, 81
Peabody Award 36
peer-to-peer social networks 20
people' assessments of news-ness 57–61
perceptions: about audience attention 21, 22; of algorithmic gatekeeping 139–140; of audience about news 49, 50, 118; of automated and human-written news 136; of credibility 16, 34, 137; of critical information needs 190; of news-ness 57–60, 61; perceived user control 121–123, 125, 127, 128, 129; of users 118, 119, 121
perceptions, of news quality: Associated Press (AP) 74, 77, 81; of conservative consumers 91; limitations of 81; measurement of 74, 87, 91; negative 75; perceived incivility 70,

72, 73, 75; of public 5, 8; in social media 40; and trust 91
personalization algorithm 117–118
personal-level incivility 69, 73
Peterson-Salahuddin, C. 137
Pfeffer, J. 103
Pickard, V. 43
pictures 90, 141; associated with the story 54, 58; and news-ness 58
platforms *see* digital platforms; social media platforms
polarization 15, 87; affective 17, 18, 23, 161; concerns 22–23; and Facebook 20; and misinformation 17, 19, 22, 24; partisan 13, 16; political 100, 161, 181, 191; processing explanation 17, 18; rise of 14–15, 16, 19; and social media 16, 17, 20–21, 87, 99; structural features of 16; and Twitter 87
policy goal , news quality as 188, 194
political party affiliation 53, 89
political trust 90
politics and practicalities, of news quality 189–199
popularity and content quality, relationship between 39–40
Pożrl, T. 155
position effects of online incivility 70, 72, 75, 77, 80
Powell, T. E. 136
preferential attachment 39
presentation **181**
presentation style 19, 35, 86, **180–181**
prevalence metric 157
privacy 154, 170, **180**
Prochazka, F. 68, 69, 74
professional standards test 170, 175, 179
Prolific (online panel) 72
public interest journalism 10, 42, 197; in Australia 170–172, 174–177, 183, 194–196; and quality journalism, difference between 195; regulatory framework 205; in U.K 192–194
public news media, long-term subsidies for 43
public sphere 43, **180**

quality indicators 179, **180–181**
quality ratings 42–43, 75, 89

random news stories 124
Rao, J. 87
Ray, N. 9

readability 68
recommender systems: AI systems 131; algorithms 38, 119, 134, 142–145; audience/user preferences in 118, 121–122, 126, 127; collaborative 122; and customization 121, 123–129; in different fields 118–119; editorial values *see* editorial values, for news recommenders; explicit control 117, 119, 121, 125, 127, 129; function of user agency in 119–121, 129; implicit control 117, 118–119, 121, 127; limitations of 130; and news consumption 127; one-time selection procedures 119, 123; perceived user control 121–123, 125, 127, 128, 129; random news stories 124; self-determined political communication 120–121, 131; self-managing element in 120; similarity-based recommender 122, 124, 126, 127, 128; testing methods for 123–124; topic-based recommender 122, 124, 126; user agency functions in 119–120; users engagement in 117–119, 121–123; and values 122; website usage in 124; *see also* algorithms
Reddit.com 73
relevance 8, 49, 59, 62, 69, 71, 123, 138, 182; geographic 100, 103, 170, **180**, 183; local 100; personal 68, 72, 77
Reuters Institute Digital News Report 2021 171
Reuters Tracer system 159
"rich get richer" phenomenon 39, 40
Roberts, C. 69
role conception versus role performance 138–139
Roper, B. 85–86
Roper question 86
Russia, and news disinformation 202, 204

Salganik, M. J. 39
Saxton, G. D. 39
Scharkow, M. 87
Schiffrin, A. 182
Schmidt, T. R. 86
Scholl, A. 138
Schweiger, W. 68, 74
selective exposure 13, 15, 16, 38, 59, 119
self-determined political communication 120–121, 131
self-reported data 84, 85, 87–88, 92
semi-structured feedback 160
Settle, J. E. 20

Seven West Media 171
Shapiro, J. M. 87
Shin, J. 9
Shoemaker, P. J. 138
similarity-based recommender 122, 124, 126, 127, 128
Snopes 35
social accounting, in Australia 179–183
social endorsement cues 67
social identity theory 17–18
social impact bond 179
social media: algorithms *see* algorithms; audience metrics 33, 38, 41; capital 39; crowd-based quality control measures 42; disinformation 4; ecosystem, current 40–41; engagement 34, 37, 38–39; evaluation of news quality 33–36; fact-checking and fact-checkers 35, 37, 38, 44; icons 54; lemons problem 41, 42–43; market 34, 41, 42, 43; metrics and news quality 33–34; networks 16–17; popularity and content quality, relationship between 39–40; problems in 51; quality journalism in 36–37; *see also* Facebook; Google; Twitter
social media engagement: drivers of 38–39; source quality and 37; *see also* engagement
social media platforms: algorithms *see* algorithms; benefits of 99; negative consequences of 99–100; popularity of news via 33; structural changes in 15–17; structural features of 16
Social Science Research Council 6
societal value, content with 22
source cues 20, 49, 54, 58, 59–63
source diversity 135, 154–155, 157
source-level credibility data 158
standardized metrics 160
story elements 52, 54, 57, 60
Stray, J. 182
structural changes 13–17, 103, 112
structured feedback 159, 160
Sundar, S. S. 52, 121
sustainability, of quality journalism 42–43
Switzerland, quality journalism in 189, 198
system behaviour, impact of structural changes on 103
system-level factors 14–15

Thorson, K. 99
Thurman, N. 135
Times see "blossom" algorithm *(Times)*

time stamp 54, 58
Toff, B. 110
tolerance 16, 151
topic-based recommender 122, 124, 126
transparency 35–36, 86–87, 121, 154, 156, 170, 177, **180**
Trielli, B. 135
triple bottom-line accounting 179
trust in journalists *see* media attitudes; media trust
Trust Project, The 36, 43
Twitter 33, 204; advertising revenue 88; algorithmification of gatekeeping 138; Birdwatch program 42; and elections 3–4; and false news 37; moderation approach 87; source cues 62; timeline algorithm 98, 99, 104; tweets dataset 102; *see also* Associated Press (AP), website versus Twitter account; @ nytimes Twitter account
two-step flow model, of communication 98

Ukraine, disinformation campaign in Russia 202, 204
uncivil comments 67–68, 69, 72, 77, 80–81; *see also* comments; incivility
United Kingdom, public interest journalism in 192–194
United States: community ecology study in 190; Federal Communications Commission (FCC) 189–191; Government Accountability Office (GAO) 192; media markets in 190
unobtrusive issues 67, 71–72, 73, 77, 80, 81
Urban, J. 68, 74
usefulness **180**
user comments *see* comments

values: behavior and written descriptions of 154–155; entertainment values 34, 38; journalistic 36; news values 22, 58, 59, 100, 141, 170–171, 179, 183; and recommender system 122; social value of news 179, 181; value sensitive design 153; *see also* editorial values, for news recommenders; recommender systems
van Dalen, A. 136
van Dyck, J. 7
Vobic, I. 139

Waldfogel, J. 101
Wang, S. 101
Washington Post 37

216 Index

watchdogs 34, 138, 139, 142–143, 146, **180**, 181
Web 2.0 69
Weber, P. 69
Wegener, D. T. 72
Weischenberg, S. 138
well-being metrics 156, 161, 182

Wells, C. 99
White, D. M. 137
Wilding, D. 135, 177
Wolker, A. 136

Ziegler, C.-N. 155
Zuckerman, E. 182